Cultural Influences on Economic Analysis

Also by Rongxing Guo

HANDBOOK OF INTERNATIONAL DISPUTED AREAS
CROSS-BORDER RESOURCE MANAGEMENT
HOW THE CHINESE ECONOMY WORKS
BORDER REGIONAL ECONOMICS
ECONOMIC DEVELOPMENT IN PROVINCIAL BORDER REGIONS OF CHINA (in Chinese)
AN ENGLISH-CHINESE MINING GLOSSARY (co-author)

Cultural Influences on Economic Analysis

Theory and Empirical Evidence

Rongxing Guo

palgrave
macmillan

First published 2006 by
PALGRAVE MACMILLAN
Houndmills, Basingstoke, Hampshire RG21 6XS and
175 Fifth Avenue, New York, N.Y. 10010
Companies and representatives throughout the world

PALGRAVE MACMILLAN is the global academic imprint of the Palgrave Macmillan division of St. Martin's Press, LLC and of Palgrave Macmillan Ltd. Macmillan® is a registered trademark in the United States, United Kingdom and other countries. Palgrave is a registered trademark in the European Union and other countries.

ISBN 13: 978–0–230–01899–0 hardback
ISBN 10: 0–230–01899–8 hardback

This book is printed on paper suitable for recycling and made from fully managed and sustained forest sources.

A catalogue record for this book is available from the British Library.

Library of Congress Cataloging-in-Publication Data

Guo, Rongxing.

Cultural influences on economic analysis : theory and empirical evidence / by Rongxing Guo.
p. cm.
Includes bibliographical references (p.)and index.
ISBN 0–230–01899–8 (cloth)
1. Economics–Sociological aspects. 2. Culture–Economic aspects. I. Title.

HM548.G86 2006
306.3–dc22 2006046323

10 9 8 7 6 5 4 3 2 1
15 14 13 12 11 10 09 08 07 06

Printed and bound in Great Britain by
Antony Rowe Ltd, Chippenham and Eastbourne

This book is dedicated to
the memory of my mother (Hè Yǔhuā, 1927–2005),
who cared for me with all her heart and
is my foremost heuristic teacher
in my life

Contents

List of Figures

List of Tables

List of Boxes

Acknowledgements

This book is the main report of a research project supported by the East Asian Development Network (EADN), as part of a larger grant from the Global Development Network (GDN) under the World Bank Development Grant Facility.

Some parts of the draft were presented at the EADN's Annual Forum held in Hong Kong (2–3 November 2005). The early version of Chapter 5 was presented at UNU-WIDER Jubilee Conference 'WIDER Thinking Ahead: the Future of Development Economics', held in the Marina Congress Centre, Helsinki (17–18 June 2005). The analytical framework used in Chapter 7 was presented at the Fourth Annual Global Development Conference, held in Cairo (19–21 January 2003).

During the project's implementation process, I have benefited from many EADN experts and reviewers. They are (in alphabetical order) Shigeyuki Abe (Doshisha University), Ammar Siamwalla (Thailand Development Research Institute), Chalongphob Sussangkarn (TDRI and EADN Coordinator), Chia Siow Yue (Singapore Institute for International Affairs), Peter Warr (Australian National University), Wing Thye Woo (University of California, Davis), Josef T. Yap (Philippines Institute for Development Studies) and Zhang Yunling (Chinese Academy of Social Sciences).

Steven Pressman (Monmouth University), Eui-Gak Hwang (Korea University), David Lim (Griffith University) as well as an anonymous reviewer have read the draft and provided in-depth comments and constructive suggestions. Hun-Chang Lee (Korea University) helped me correct some errors in Chapter 8. Wang Huayan, Guo Liqing and Xing Youqiang dutifully assisted me in the collection and calculation of the national and cross-national data on the cultural variables.

Many readers and editors at Palgrave Macmillan have also helped me refine the contents. Amanda Hamilton (Senior Commissioning Editor), Katie Button (Assistant Editor for Economics) and Barbara Slater (Editorial Services Consultant) merit particular mention. Without this help, this project could not have been accomplished – at least not in its present form. But all views, drawbacks and errors in this book certainly are mine and are not necessarily those of the supporters and the reviewers.

R.X.G.
Heidelberg, Beijing

Notes from the Author

1. In most cases, data used are as at the end of the twentieth century (or as close as possible).
2. Unless stated otherwise, the monetary values of economic indicators are measured in US dollars.
3. In the cross-section analyses of economies for a specified year or period, due to data unavailability or other reasons, data for years other than the specified year or period (but as close as possible to the specified dates) may sometimes be used for a few of economies.
4. Due to geographical changes of some economies involved in the research, measurement errors may exist for some time-series analyses.
5. Totals in the tables may not add up to 100 per cent due to rounding off.

Introduction

> Development divorced from its human or cultural context is growth without a soul.
>
> (WCCD, 1995)

Since World War II, and especially since the end of the Cold War, a series of global and regional economic issues have puzzled both theorists and practitioners. They include such important questions as: Why have nations with the same or similar natural endowments and political contexts had such different economic performances? Why have trade and economic cooperation been efficient between some nations but more and more difficult between others? These issues are crucial to contemporary policymakers and practitioners, and many nice theories have been constructed in order to assess them. Unfortunately, it is argued that existing theories cannot be used to deal with the above issues satisfactorily. Sometimes they may even yield conflicting information and results. There seem to be two primary causes for this. The first concerns the continuing evolution of the global environment and regional institutions; the second relates to unrealistic assumptions from which some important variables have been excluded or highly simplified.[1]

For a long time culture and economy have been treated as broadly independent areas of research. Furthering the understanding of the determinants of economic activity promised to be one of the major research areas in the postwar era, although past analyses, especially those that are quantitatively based, are mainly focused on economic variables. Since the late twentieth century, however, there have been arguments respecting an increasingly close relationship between economy and culture. With regards to the mechanism of their relationship, one should recognize that economy and culture do not impose upon one another as wholly external forces, but are always intimately associated. Despite the closeness of this association, they have different logics: the one taking account of certain intrinsic or non-instrumental values, the other relating instrumental values to external goals of reproduction. Their interactions are complex as are their effects on economic development and cultural change (Guo, 2003).

It is now increasingly accepted that one of the many reasons underlying the relative lack of success of past economic development efforts is that culture was overlooked in development thinking and practice. This belated resurgence of interest has raised culture to a position of honour in development debates. Even conservative financial planners and technical problem-solvers now recognize that if healthy and sustainable development is to take place culture cannot be ignored. In fact, many social scientists, particularly sociologists, human geographers and political scientists, have been undergoing a 'cultural conversion' in recent decades, evident both in method and content. As a result there has been a long-overdue dialogue with literary studies, and an increased concern with cultural phenomena (see, for example, Cateora and Graham, 1998, pp. 111–50; Kockel, 2002; Harrison, 1993, 2000, 2006; Harrison and Huntington, 2001; Hofstede, 2003 [1980]; and Harris et al., 2004).

Despite the importance of cultural influences on economic performance, mainstream economists have tended to ignore them. Indeed, Ruttan (1991, p. 276) summarizes well the current situation:

> Cultural considerations have been cast into the 'underworld' of developmental thought and practice. It would be hard to find a leading scholar in the field of developmental economics who would commit herself or himself in print to the proposition that in terms of explaining different patterns of political and economic development ... a central variable is culture.[2]

This book examines the influences of various cultural factors on economic activities that could be misinterpreted by existing economic theories. Its most important task is to clarify conditions under which culture may be not a cause of misunderstanding and conflict but a source of creativity and profitability in multicultural cooperation. It will also identify various cultural conditions under which economic policies can (or cannot) be optimally arranged. The theoretical and empirical results in this book are intended to supplement current studies on development economics and international economics, as well as to help policymakers to reappraise the roles of 'cultural factors' in, and to introduce optimal economic and cultural policies into, intercultural economic affairs. This book is divided into nine chapters, as follows.

Chapter 1 introduces the most important cultural elements (ethnicity, language and religion) and their implications for economic analysis. In this book, culture is treated both as a resource for and an obstacle to economic development.

After briefly reviewing the diversities of existing economies, Chapter 2 surveys and assesses various approaches to the conduct of a multidimensional analysis of the world economy. While geographic, political and economic approaches each have their own advantages, the culture area approach is particularly useful for long-term comparative economic analysis.

On the basis of the cross-cultural data and information collected and, where necessary, reconstructed by the author, Chapter 3 presents a cross-cultural comparison of the world economy in terms of macroeconomic indicators and real living standards using the culture areas defined in Chapter 2.

The sources for the cross-cultural economic differences are further examined in Chapter 4, which focuses on six aspects: physical capital, human capital, technological innovation, political and institutional bases, external and boundary conditions and cultural context. The past analyses on the determinants of economic development, especially those that are quantitatively based, are mainly focused on economic variables. But there is no way in which economic activities could be conducted independently of cultural context. The economy is as much a cultural site as any other part of society, such as family, community or school. Culture, however significant it may be as a medium of development, cannot be reduced to a minor position as a mere promoter of or impediment to economic growth.

In existing literature relating to the determinants of economic growth, explanatory variables such as income inequality and cultural diversity have been treated separately. In Chapter 5 we try to discuss their joint effects. Our task is to investigate whether there are any conditions under which income inequality and cultural diversity could encourage (or retard) economic growth. Evidence from a broad panel of nations reveals somewhat ambiguous results in that economic growth is quite independent of the variables of inequality and cultural (linguistic and religious) diversity. But for the post-Cold War era there is also an indication that religious diversity tends to retard growth in high inequality nations and to encourage growth in low inequality places. Besides, there is some evidence that supports the view that inequality tends to encourage growth in low religious diversity nations, but not in high religious diversity places. According to the estimated results, higher religious diversity could become a source of productive factors contributing to economic growth for low inequality nations; but in nations with high degrees of religious diversity, high inequality could seriously affect economic growth. In nations with low degrees of religious diversity, income inequality could generate higher economic growth, since there are very few, if any, intercultural barriers within each religiously homogeneous nation.

Chapter 6 examines – both theoretically and empirically – various aspects of cultural influences on international economic analysis. A review of the past literature indicates that the relationship between cultural links and international trade has been highly simplified. It is generally accepted that, given the markedly differing attitudes and cultural values between different cultural groups, the adoption of common standards is unlikely to prove effective. However 'cultural dissimilarity' may also generate, in addition to the cost of intercultural transactions, some 'economic complementarities' that will have positive influences on international trade. As a result the final output of the cultural influences should be nonlinear, subject to various conditions.

Chapter 7 clarifies various cultural conditions under which international trade may either be encouraged or retarded. A gravity model is built on the basis of the panel data of eight nations (Brazil, China, the Democratic Republic of Congo (Zaire), France, India, Japan, Saudi Arabia and the United States) so as to provide statistical evidence for the cultural influences on international trade during the late twentieth century. In the regressions, if one or more cultural variables were excluded, the estimated results would become less reliable. The estimated results provide evidence to support the view that geographical influence on trade tended to decrease from the 1980s to the 1990s. By way of contrast, the cultural influences on trade tended to increase during the same period. Moreover, the statistical evidence from our modified gravity model shows that cultural dissimilarity tended to retard international trade between low-income countries and to encourage international trade between high-income countries.

Why have some small, culturally different economies managed to form larger economic unions, while other, large, culturally similar economies have not? Why are the culturally heterogeneous entities or unions politically less stable and economically less efficient than the culturally homogeneous ones? To answer these questions, we construct an analytic narrative model for state-building and evolution in the Korean peninsula in Chapter 8. There is an indication that the increasing complexity of managing a large authoritarian area is the major source of administrative inefficiencies when the authoritarian area grows beyond a certain size. On the basis of this model, four propositions relating to the equilibrium location and the optimal size of cultures are proposed, and their political economy implications for the interactions between cultures differing in size are illustrated. As an extension, the case studies of the Association of Southeast Asian Nations (ASEAN), the Chinese area and the European Union (EU) are also briefly addressed.

Since the end of the Cold War era the study of intercultural relations has become one of the most popular topics in the field of global politics and economics. But there have been different views, supporting both intercultural conflict and cooperation. In Chapter 9 various factors that could influence conflicts are examined. Our case studies show that cultural dissimilarity may result in both conflict and cooperation, depending on the various conditions and contexts concerned. Specifically, intercultural co-operation will be very sensitive to the measures of cultural difference in countries where cultural difference leads to serious intranational and international barriers. However cultural dissimilarity has a very small effect on conflict if the diverse groups have learned to live with each other in a politically stable and economically equitable environment.

The cultural data, collected and reconstructed by the author, and used in the quantitative analyses in this book, are arranged in the appendices at the end of the text. This may be useful to readers who intend to re-test the results obtained by the author or to conduct research of their own. A number of boxes are also inserted where appropriate in the text. It is hoped that this will be useful for students and researchers as well as ordinary readers from different academic backgrounds looking to gain more knowledge about the ways in which economy and culture are interrelated.

1
Concepts and Facts

Remember the days of old,
Understand the years of generation after generation.
Ask your father and he will tell you,
Your elders and they will say to you.

(Deuteronomy, 32:7)

1.1 What is culture?

As well as describing the content of libraries, museums, moral and religious codes of conduct, the word 'culture' is commonly used to describe social life. As such, 'culture' is the living sum of symbols, meanings, habits, values, institutions, behaviours and social artifacts which characterize a distinctive and identified human population group. It confers upon individuals identity as members of some visible community and standards for relating to the environment, for identifying fellow members and strangers, and for deciding what is important and what is not important to them (Goulet, 1980, p. 2).

According to *The American Heritage Dictionary of the English Language* (2000, 4th edn, updated in 2003), 'culture' is defined as the following: (a) the totality of socially transmitted behaviour patterns, arts, beliefs, institutions, and all other products of human work and thought; (b) these patterns, traits, and products considered as the expression of a particular period, class, community, or population (such as Edwardian culture, Japanese culture, the culture of poverty); (c) these patterns, traits, and products considered with respect to a particular category, such as a field subject, or mode of expression (such as religious culture in the Middle Ages, musical culture, oral culture); and (d) the predominating attitudes and behaviour that characterize the functioning of a group or organization.

The modern technical definition of culture, as socially patterned human thought and behaviour, was originally proposed by a nineteenth-century British anthropologist, Edward Tylor. In his charter definition of the anthropological concept of culture, for example, Tylor (1871, p. 1) states 'Culture or civilization, taken in its wide ethnographic sense, is that complex whole which includes knowledge, belief, art, morals, law, customs, and any other capabilities and habits acquired by man as a member of society.' This definition is an open-ended list, which has been extended considerably since Tylor first proposed it. Since then some researchers have attempted to create exhaustive universal lists of the content of culture, while others have listed and mapped all the culture traits of particular geographic areas.

The first inventory of cultural categories was undertaken in 1872 by a committee of the British Association for the Advancement of Science. The committee, which was assisted by Tylor, prepared an anthropological field manual that listed 76 cultural topics, in no particular order, including such diverse items as cannibalism and language. The most exhaustive such list is the 'Outline of Cultural Materials', first published in 1938 and still used as a guide for cataloguing great masses of worldwide cultural data for cross-cultural surveys. Like the table of contents of a giant encyclopedia, the outline lists 79 major divisions and 637 subdivisions.[1]

What are the most useful attributes that a technical concept of culture should stress? There has been considerable theoretical debate among anthropologists since Tylor. In 1952, for example, Alfred Kroeber and Clyde Kluckhohn, American anthropologists, published a list of 160 different

Table 1.1 Diverse definitions of culture

Item	Description
Topical	Culture consists of everything on a list of topics, or categories, such as social organization, religion, or economy
Historical	Culture is social heritage, or tradition, that is passed on to future generations
Behavioural	Culture is shared, learned human behaviour, a way of life
Normative	Culture is ideals, values, or rules of living
Functional	Culture is the way humans solve problems of adapting to the environment or living together
Mental	Culture is a complex of ideas, or learned habits, that inhibit impulses and distinguish people from animals
Structural	Culture consists of patterned and interrelated ideas, symbols, or behaviours
Symbolic	Culture is based on arbitrarily assigned meanings that are shared by a society

Source: Bodley (1994).

definitions of culture (Bodley, 1994). Although simplified, their list indicates the diversity of the anthropological concept of culture (see Table 1.1).

Indeed, culture is too complex to define in simple terms and it can seem that each sociologist has a preferred definition. Certain agreed fundamentals, however, appear in this definition by Hoebel (1960, p. 168): 'Culture is the integrated sum total of learned behavioral traits that are shared by members of a society.' Specifically, these fundamentals are:

(i) Culture is a total pattern of behaviour that is consistent and compatible in its components. It is not a collection of random behaviours, but behaviours that are internally related and integrated.
(ii) Culture is learned behaviour. It is not biologically transmitted. It depends on environment, not heredity. Thus, it can be called the man-made part of our environment.
(iii) Culture is behaviour that is shared by a group of people, a society. It can be considered as the distinctive way of life of a people.[2]

1.2 How culture is measured

Although many more complicated compositions for a culture have been suggested, we will only discuss three elements here – ethnicity, language and religion. Of course, our discussion of these cultural elements is not definitive and perhaps would not satisfy anthropologists. Nevertheless, our consideration is due to the concerns that (a) 'ethnicity' provides a genetic basis in which socioeconomic behaviours between groups of people can be easily differentiated; (b) 'language' is an effective tool of communication; and (c) 'religion' can provide insights into the characteristics of culture.

1.2.1 Ethnicity

Before dealing with the concept of 'ethnicity', it is necessary to know some facts about 'race'. Genetically, race is defined as a group with genes frequently differing from those of other groups in human species. However the genes responsible for the hereditary differences between humans are few when compared with the vast number of genes common to all human beings regardless of the race to which they belong. All human groups belong to the same species and are mutually fertile. In practice, race usually refers to any of several subdivisions of mankind sharing certain physical characteristics, such as skin pigmentation, skin complexion, colour and type of hair, shape of head, stature, form of eyes and nose, and so on. The differences among races are essentially biological and are marked by the hereditary transmission of physical characteristics.

General agreement is inadequate as to the classification of such people as the Aborigines of Australia, the Dravidian people of Southern India, the

Polynesians, the Ainu of Northern Japan and so on. Most anthropologists have agreed on the existence of three relatively distinct groups: Caucasoid, Mongoloid and Negroid. The Caucasoid group, found in Europe, North Africa, and from the Middle East to North India, is characterized as having skin of pale reddish white to olive brown. The hair is light blond to dark brown. The colour of the eyes varies from light blue to dark brown. The Mongoloid group, which includes most peoples of East Asia and the American Indians, has been described as having skin of saffron to yellow or reddish brown. The hair is dark, straight. The eyes are from black to dark brown. The Negroid group, which includes the African peoples of Southern Sahara, the Pygmy groups of Indonesia, and the inhabitants of New Guinea and Melanesia, is characterized by a brown to brown-black complexion. The hair is dark and coarse, usually curly. The eyes are dark.

Unlike race, ethnicity is a social entity formed in the historical process. In practice, ethnicity is usually determined according to language rather than religion, because whereas in most cases an ethnic group uses the same or at least similar linguistic systems, it does not necessarily share religious beliefs. In brief, more than 2000 ethnic groups have been identified in the world. The ethnic distribution of the world population, however, is distinctly uneven. For example, the largest ethic group (the Han Chinese) has a population of more than one billion people, whereas the smallest (the Andmanese in India) has a population of between dozens to a few hundred. More specifically, there are more than ten million people in 67 ethnic groups; more than one million people in 202 ethnic groups; and from 100,000 to one million people in 293 ethnic groups.[3]

Box 1.1 Blood typology

Rather like the West's preoccupation with astrology, in Japan 'blood typology' is a popular means for judging a person's character. Based on 'Make Friends for Japan', a little booklet given out at the airport in Narita, the characteristics of people with various blood types are differentiated as follows:

- Type A: Calm, obeys rules, values relationships with others, very sensitive, cautious and careful.
- Type O: Strong sense of purpose, romantic, influenced by peers, good at organizing activities, very proud.
- Type B: Does things at his or her own pace, strong personality, optimistic, easy to get along with, adventurous.
- Type AB: Well aware of his or her surrounding environment, hates instinctive feelings, critical, never takes things to the limit or to the best of his or her ability, tries to be useful to other people.

Ethnic groups are not restricted to single countries. For example the Han Chinese can be found in (besides the mainland of China) almost all major countries (especially those in Southeastern Asia) and Anglo-Saxons are distributed throughout the United Kingdom, the United States, Canada, Australia, New Zealand and so on. On the other hand, there is a great range of ethnic diversities in the world, and while there is only one single ethnic group in Japan, Korea, Hungary and Romania, in most places, a nation is not a homogeneous unit but rather a collection of areas fragmented along ethnic lines. Nigeria, for example, is divided into Hausa, Ibo and Yoruba tribes and areas, as Sri Lanka is divided into Sinhalese and Tamil areas.

There is a worrying case in point. The former Soviet Union was composed of 128 ethnic groups, each with its own language, culture, history, traditions – and grievances. For decades under the soviet state these groups lived side by side in an artificial harmony imposed from above. In a very short period of time, however, the Soviet Union collapsed into 16 separate ethnic states, some of which are threatened by further ethnic divisions. The former Yugoslavia collapsed into small ethnic 'nations' and civil war broke out between divided ethnic groups. Czechoslovakia also divided along ethnic lines. This has been a continuing pattern in much of Africa as well. From Angola to Ethiopia to Sudan to Zimbabwe, tribal divisions are changing countries (Cateora and Graham, 1998, p. 142).

1.2.2 Language

Ethnicity is usually represented by linguistic identities, giving rise to the term 'ethnolinguistics'. Though complex in terms of lexicon, grammar, syntax, phonetics and so on, languages may be classified either genetically or typologically. The genetic classification assumes that certain languages are related and that they have evolved from a common ancestral language; while typological classification is based on similarities in the language structure. Before classifying the world of languages, a few points on linguistic terminology should be explained.

'Family' is a label often used for a conservative genetic classification of language, one that can be proved only when an abundance of cognates (related words) is available. 'Phylum' is a label for a liberal genetic classification that is proved with fewer cognates; it encompasses language families. A given phylum always has a greater extension than any of the families included in it, even though the term 'family' is, in practical usage, often employed to refer to a phylum.

Physical (ethnic and linguistic) differences can play a critical role in enabling members of one group to pinpoint members of the some other coalition. Early examples of this literally go back to biblical times, with tales of warring tribes distinguishing the pronunciation of certain words to establish who should be slaughtered. A more recent example is from twenty-first century Northern Ireland, where:

> ... a group of masked men [entered a school and] demanded that students produce identification or repeat the alphabet. Many Catholics pronounce the letter 'h' differently to Protestants, with an aspiration influenced by the Irish language. Students were evacuated before it became clear what was planned for people with the wrong accent.[4]

The number of languages on earth is reckoned to be approximately between 4000 and 6000 (Pinker, 1994). Although the classification of these language groups may differ, they can be roughly distinguished through the following phylums.

(1) *Indo-European phylum.* This phylum is composed of Slavic languages (including Bulgarian, Macedonian, Russian, Slovene, Serbo-Croatian, Ukrainian and so on), Germanic languages (including English, Frisian, Netherlandic-German, Insular Scandinavian and Continental Scandinavian), Romanic or Romance languages descended from Latin (including Spanish, Portuguese, French, Italian, Romanian and so on), Albanian, Celtic languages (including Irish, Welsh, Scottish), Greek languages (including Greek and Cyprian), Baltic languages (including Lithuanian and Latvian), and Indo-Iranian languages (including Hindi, Urdu, Bengali, Romany, Tajik, Persian and so on).

(2) *Sino-Tibetan phylum.* This phylum is composed of Sino-Tai languages (including Chinese, Thai, Lao and so on), Tibeto-Burman languages (including Tibetan and Burmese), Miao-Yao languages (including Miao and Yao), Zhuang-Dong languages (including Zhuang and Dong), and Karen.

(3) *Hamio-Semitic phylum.* This phylum is composed of Semitic languages (including Arabic, Hebrew, dialects of East and West Aramenian, and Modern South Arabic), Berber languages (including Guanche, Tamashek, Tamazight and so on), Cushitic languages (including Gallinya, Somali and so on), and Chadic languages (consisting of over 100 languages).

(4) *Caucasian phylum.* This phylum is composed of South Caucasian languages (including Georgian, Laz, and Svan), and Northwest Caucasian languages (including Kabardian, Abaza, Adyghian, Ubykh, Chechen, Ingush and so on).

(5) *Ural-Altaic phylum.* This phylum is composed of Uralic languages (including Mansi, Khanti and so on), Turkic languages (including Azerbaijani, Kazakh, Uighur, Uzbek, Kirgiz, Turkmen, Turkish and so on), Mongolian languages (including Mongolian and so on), and Manchu-Tungus languages (including Manchu).

(6) *Finno-Ugric phylum.* This phylum is composed of Hungarian, Norwegian, Swedish, Finnish, Russian Lapp and so on.

(7) *Dravidian phylum*. This phylum is composed of Brahui, Telugu, Tamil, Malayalam, Kannada, Gondi, Tulu, Kurukh, Kui and so on.
(8) *Nilo-Saharan phylum*. This phylum is composed of Eastern Sudanic languages (including more than 60 languages), Central Sudanic languages (including about 30 languages of which Sara, Lugbara and Mangbetu are the largest), Saharan languages (including Kanuri, Masalit, Songhai, Fur and so on).
(9) *Niger-Congo phylum*. This phylum is composed of Bantu languages (including Rwanda, Shona, Kongo, Luba-Lulua, Xhosa and so on), Mande (including Bambara, Menda, Vai and so on), Gur (Voltaic) languages (including Mossi and so on), West Atlantic languages (including Fulani, Wolof, Temne and so on), Adamawa-Eastern languages (including Sango and so on), and Kwa languages (including Twi, Yoruba, Igbo and so on).
(10) *Khoisan phylum*. This phylum includes about four dozen languages spoken in southern Africa and two click languages (Sandawe and Haza) spoken in Tanzania.
(11) *Paleo-Siberian phylum*. This phylum is composed of Luorawetlan languages (including Chukchi, Kamchadal and Koryad), Yukaghir languages (including Yukaghir, Chuvantsy and Gilyak), and Yeniseian languages (including Ket, Kott, Assan and Arin).
(12) *Austro-Asiatic phylum*. This phylum is composed of more than 50 languages (including Khmer, Mon, Vietnamese, Muong, Jahaic or Semang, Senoic or Sakai, Semelaic and so on) and some 16 or so Munda languages (including Santali, Mundari, Ho, Sora, Kharia, Korku and so on).
(13) *Austronesian phylum*. This phylum is composed of two families of approximately 500 languages, including Western Austronesian (or Indonesian) and Eastern Austronesian (or Oceanic).
(14) *Other phylums*. These languages include Japanese, Korean, Papuan, and so on.[5]

There is very uneven distribution of population among languages. The nine largest linguistic groups, which account for more than half the world population, are Chinese (19.7 per cent), English (9.2 per cent), Hindi (7.3 per cent), Spanish (5.6 per cent), Arabic (3.8 per cent), Portuguese (2.9 per cent), Russian (2.7 per cent), Japanese (2.1 per cent) and Bengali (2.1 per cent). The other linguistic groups, each accounting for more than one per cent of the world population, are French (1.9 per cent), German (1.5 per cent), Korean (1.2 per cent), Vietnamese (1.1 per cent) and Turkish (1.0 per cent). Other languages may have very few speakers.[6]

The Britannica data on language speakers needs to be evaluated with care. Since some countries collect data on ethnic or 'national' groups only, it often had to be assumed that ethnic distribution conformed roughly to the distribution of language. The above statistics should also be viewed with caution because a minority population is not always free to educate its children in its own language and because better economic opportunities often draw minority group members into majority-language communities.

Chinese-speakers, mainly concentrated on the mainland of China, Taiwan, Hong Kong and other Chinese alien communities in Southeastern Asia, account for nearly one-fifth of the world population. As a major branch of the Sino-Tibetan family of languages, Chinese is unique. Some of its outstanding characteristics include monosyllabicity and a simple phonological system, the use of tones to distinguish different meanings, and a syntax that depends on word order; it lacks inflection, grammatical gender and pluralization. Written Chinese is the only major modern writing system that uses thousands of ideographic-phonetic symbols rather than a phonetic alphabet or syllabary of a few dozen symbols. In spite of multitudinous dialects (such as Mandarin (the standard Chinese), Wu, Cantonese (or Yue), Min, Hakka, Xiang, Gan and so on), many of which are mutually unintelligible, a shared national language unites people in China. The writing system of Chinese characters inspired and profoundly influenced writing systems in Japan and Korea through a long history of intercultural communications when China served as the economic and cultural centre of East Asia. However, in terms of grammar and syntax, Japanese and Korean have no connections with Chinese.

In India around 800 different languages and over 1600 dialects are spoken. Hindi is a lingua franca as there are over 300 million speakers, of whom at least 200 million use it as a first language in the northern and central states (Saville, 2002, p. 203). Thanks to the central government's constitutional commitment, Hindi, as the official language, has been spread and developed throughout the nation. For example, in the early 1980s Hindi speakers accounted for less than 30 per cent of the Indian population; by the late 1990s, however, more than 50 per cent of the population were using Hindi as a first language (*Britannica Book of the Year,* 1998). As a result of its colonial associations, English is still regarded as a necessary second or 'associated' official language in India, especially in the southern and eastern states, where Hindi nationalism may be offensive to those who have a different language and religion (Ager, 2001, p. 27). Moreover, English also remains the language of the elite, and Indian English, as a recognizable variety, is widely accepted.

Altogether, the five major Western languages (English, French, German, Portuguese and Spanish) are spoken by approximately one-fifth of the world population, of which the native English-speakers constitute the largest part.[7] Even though the number of people with English as a first language has declined slightly during the past decades, English is still the primary language of intercultural communication, since it serves as a lingua franca for the largest group of people whose native languages are not

English. The English used by different ethnic groups throughout the world is also diversified. English is indigenized and takes on local colourations which distinguish it from British or American English and which, in extreme cases, make these 'Englishes' almost unintelligible one to another. Nigerian Pidgin English, Indian English, and other forms of English are being incorporated into their respective host cultures and perhaps will continue to differentiate themselves so as to become related but distinct languages.

A glance at the history reveals that the distribution of language speakers has reflected the distribution of economic power in the world. Latin, for example, was a universal language in Europe during the Middle Ages and the Renaissance. French was once known as the universal language of diplomacy, and English today is often said to fill such a role in world commerce. During the heyday of the Soviet Union, Russian was the lingua franca from Prague to Hanoi. The decline of Russian power has been accompanied by a parallel decline in the use of Russian as a second language. Since the late twentieth century China's economic power has stimulated the learning of Chinese in other countries. However none of these has been able to become a universal language. With the aim of making international communication simpler, numerous efforts have also been made to create artificial languages during the past centuries (see Box 1.2). But, since the vocabulary and grammar of so many artificial languages is based on those of the Indo-European tongues, non-European speakers find them hard to learn.

1.2.3 Religion

Religion is a major determinant of societal attitudes and behaviour. In the *Oxford Advanced Learner's Dictionary*, 'religion' is defined as 'belief in the existence of a supernatural ruling power, the creator and controller of the universe, who has given to man a spiritual nature which continues to exist after the death of the body' (1974, p. 712). In addition, according to the *New Columbia Encyclopedia*, religion comprises at least three aspects: (1) a system of thought, and action that is shared by a group and that gives the members of that group an object of devotion; (2) a code of behaviour by which an individual may judge the personal and social consequences of his actions; and (3) a framework of reference by which an individual may relate to a group and their universe (1975, p. 2299).

The development of human civilization has been accompanied by an increasing number of religions. In order to help understand the roles of various religions in the world economy, let us have a brief look at the basic features of Hinduism, Buddhism, Christianity, Islam, shamanism and animism.

Hinduism. Dating from 1500 BC, Hinduism is a non-creedal religion. It is a combination of ancient philosophies and customs, animistic beliefs and

Box 1.2 What is Esperanto?

Hundreds of efforts have been made to create artificial languages for international communication since the seventeenth century. Some seventeenth-century philosophers proposed the construction of a so-called philosophical language that would consist of a system of communication based on classification according to logic rather than on human speech. Several such systems were subsequently devised, but they turned out to be too difficult for most people to use and had, as well, the serious handicap of being unsuited to conversation. The first artificial language to come to prominence was Volapük. Introduced in 1880, it was created by Johann Martin Schleyer, a Roman Catholic priest of German extraction. Schleyer worked out for Volapük an alphabet, a grammar, and a vocabulary based chiefly on Latin, the Romanic languages, and the Germanic languages.

Esperanto, another artificial language, was invented by Dr Ludwig L. Zamenhof of Poland, and was first presented to the public in 1887. It has enjoyed some recognition as an international language, often being used, for example, at international meetings and conferences. In fact, an estimated 8 million people are said to speak it. The vocabulary of Esperanto is formed by adding various affixes to individual roots and it is derived chiefly from Latin, Greek, the Romanic and Germanic languages. The grammar is based on that of European languages but is greatly simplified and regular. A simplified revision of Esperanto is Ido, short for Esperantoido. Ido was introduced in 1907 by the French philosopher Louis Couturat, but it failed to replace Esperanto. Yet another artificial language, known as Interlingua, was created in 1951 by the International Auxiliary Language Association. Interlingua is derived from English and the Romanic languages in both grammar and vocabulary. It has been used at medical and scientific meetings.

Source: *The New Columbia Encyclopedia* (1975).

legends. Since a Hindu is born, not made, Hinduism is an ethnic religion and, therefore, many of its doctrines only apply to the Indian society. One important characteristic of Hinduism is the caste system. Each member of a particular caste has a specific occupational and social role, which is hereditary. Marriage is forbidden outside of the caste. Although efforts were made to weaken this system, it still has a strong hold in Indian society. Another element is *baradari*, or the 'joint family'. After marriage, the bride goes to the groom's home. After several marriages in the family, there is a large joint family. All generations of the family live together and pool their income with little distinction made between brothers and cousins. Women are completely subordinate to men, and adult men are expected to do what their fathers tell them. Veneration of the cow is perhaps the best-known Hindu custom. Another element of traditional Hinduism is the restriction of freedom for women, following the belief that to be born a woman is a sign of sin in a former life.

Buddhism. Springing from Hinduism in about 600 BC, Buddhism is one of the most influential religions in Asia. As a reformulation of Hinduism, it did not abolish caste but declared that Buddhists were released from caste restrictions. At the heart of Buddhism there are the Four Noble Truths: (1) existence is suffering; (2) suffering has a cause, namely craving and attachment; (3) there is a cessation of suffering, which is Nirvana; and (4) there is a path to the cessation of suffering, which includes the 'eight-fold path' of the right views (that is, right desires, right speech, right action, right occupation, right effort, right awareness and right contemplation). Nirvana is the ultimate goal of the Buddhist. It represents the extinction of all cravings and the final release from suffering. To the extent that such an ideal reflects the thinking of the mass of people, a Buddhist society's values would be considered antithetical to such goals as acquisitions, achievement, or affluence. From another early school of Buddhism there developed the line of thought that led toward the position advocated by Mahayana Buddhism. The Mahayana (greater vehicle) gave itself this name in polemical writings to distinguish itself from what it called the Hinayana (lesser vehicle), Theravada, and related schools. The main philosophical tenet of the Mahayana is that all things are empty, or devoid of self-nature. Geographically, Hinayana Buddhism has followers in Southeast Asia (especially in Cambodia, Myanmar, and Thailand) and in East Asia, while Mahayana Buddhism is concentrated in Southwest and Northwest China.

Christianity. Founded in Palestine by the followers of Jesus Christ in the first century, Christianity is now the most influential religion in Western society. The central teachings of traditional Christianity – which are embodied in the Bible, especially in the New Testament – are that Jesus is the Son of God, the second person of the Trinity of God the Father, the Son and the Holy Spirit; and that his life on earth, his crucifixion, resurrection, and ascension into heaven are the proofs of God's love and forgiveness of man's sins. In addition, Christians believe that by faith in Christ man may attain salvation and eternal life. In 1054 Christianity was split into two churches: Roman Catholicism and Orthodox (or Eastern Orthodox). The major differences between the two churches are that the doctrine of the Orthodox Church accepts the first seven councils while Roman Catholics recognize 21 general councils, and in the rejection by the Orthodox Church of the jurisdiction of the Bishop of Rome (the pope). Eastern Orthodox Christianity has been mainly adopted in Russia and Central Europe. Roman

Catholicism traditionally emphasized the Church and the sacraments as the principal elements of religion and the way to God. In the sixteenth century the Protestant Reformation, especially Calvinism, made some critical changes in emphasis but remained in agreement with Catholicism on most traditional Christian doctrine. The Protestants, however, stressed that the Church, its sacraments, and its clergy were not essential to salvation; rather, 'salvation is by faith alone'. Protestantism minimized the distinction between the secular and the religious life. The term Anglican describes those people and churches following the religious traditions of the Church of England, especially following the Reformation of the sixteenth century. Anglicans trace these traditions back to the first followers of Jesus, but acknowledge that schisms occurred first with the Orthodox then with the Roman Catholic churches. Unlike many Protestant churches, Anglicans maintain authority within the Church through apostolic succession. As well as the English churches, the Anglican Communion thrives in many nations of the world and has millions of members.

Islam. Islam dates from the seventh century and Islamic adherents can be found from the Atlantic across the northern half of Africa, the Middle East, and across the greater part of Asia. 'Islam' is the infinitive of the Arabic verb 'to submit'. 'Muslim' is the present participle of the same verb, thus a Muslim is one submitting to the will of Allah – the only God of the universe – of whom Mohammed is the Prophet. Muslim theology, *Tawhid*, defines the Islamic creed, whereas the law, *Shariah*, prescribes the actions of adherents. The Koran (*Qur'an*) is accepted as the ultimate guide and anything not mentioned in the Koran is quite likely to be rejected. The Five Pillars of Islam, or the duties of a Muslim, are (1) the recital of the creed, (2) prayer, (3) fasting, (4) almsgiving and (5) the pilgrimage. A Muslim must pray five times a day at definite hours. During the month of Ramadan, in the midsummer in the lunar year, Muslims are required to fast from sunrise to sunset with no food, no drink and no smoking. The fast is meant to develop both self-control and sympathy for the poor. By almsgiving the Muslim shares with the poor. The pilgrimage to Mecca is a well-known aspect of Islam. There are two major groups in Islam – namely, *Sunni* and *Shia*. While they are similar in many ways, Sunni Muslims adhere to both the Koran and *Shariah*, while Shia Muslims only believe in the Koran.

Shamanism. Shamanism originated from the Evinki people of Siberia, and literally means 'the one who knows'. Today, in the Western world, 'shaman' is often taken to mean any kind of native medicine man or woman or anyone with a strong personality and an intense stare (Horwitz, 1998). Shamanism goes hand in hand with the animist's experience of the world: first, all that is alive, and being alive embodies a spirit; second, all that is alive is connected by these spirits. Therefore, we all – humans, trees, dogs, cats, bees, stones, mountains, seas, earth and sky – are connected. Shamans believe that there exists a medium, or 'witch', between God and themselves. The witch, according to shamanism, can convey God's decrees.

Animism. As a primeval religion, the followers of animism tend to be found in remote and mountainous areas. Animists believe that hills, valleys, waterways, and rocks are spiritual beings, as are the plants and animals. Furthermore, they believe that there are other, less obvious spiritual beings not commonly associated with the phenomena of everyday experience. Animists worship the natural bodies (most of which are animals) with which they have special causal relations. Magic, a key element of animism, is the attempt to achieve results through the manipulation of the spiritual world. It represents an unscientific approach to the physical world.

According to the *World Christian Encyclopedia*, edited by David (1982), at the beginning of the twentieth century the religious composition of the world population was as follows: 26.9 per cent Western Christian,[8] 23.5 per cent Chinese folk-religionists, 12.5 per cent Hindu, 12.4 per cent Muslim, 7.8 per cent Buddhist, 7.5 per cent Orthodox Christian,[9] 6.6 per cent tribal religions, and 0.2 per cent non-religionists. Since then, the relative numerical strength of some religions around the world has changed dramatically. At the end of the twentieth century, Western Christianity was still the largest religion (27.6 per cent), followed by Muslims (23.1 per cent), non-religionists (17.7 per cent), Hindus (15.9 per cent), Buddhists (8.0 per cent), Orthodox Christians (3.2 per cent) and atheists (2.9 per cent) (*Britannica Book of the Year*, 2001).

Obviously, the largest change recorded above has been the increase in the proportion of people classified as 'non-religious' or 'atheist'. This could reflect a major shift away from religion, and the religious resurgence of the late twentieth century was yet to gather full steam. Yet this increase in non-believers is closely matched by the decrease in those classified as adherents of 'Chinese folk-religions' (usually mixed with elements of Confucianism, Taoism and Buddhism). The data do show increases in the proportions of the world population adhering to the two major proselytizing religions – Islam and Christianity – over the twentieth century. But Western Christians only experienced a moderate increase, while Muslims enjoyed a large expansion. In addition, due to the continuous population expansion in India, the numbers of Hindus also rose during the twentieth century.

It is worth noting that conversion of religious groups is a widespread phenomenon. In the Middle Ages entire Central European populations switched back and forth between Catholicism and Protestantism as the political alliances of their princes switched between the Pope and the

Emperor. In Fascist Italy many Jews converted to Catholicism to escape discrimination. In modern-day India it is extremely common for lower-caste Hindus to convert to the Muslim or Catholic faiths, in which they meet with relatively less discrimination. For most people, and for most religions, the material costs of conversion are relatively modest, amounting in many cases to geographical relocation to a locality where one can easily establish a new religious identity (Caselli and Coleman, 2002).

The existing statistical data on religious adherents are more fragmentary and less reliable than the data on language speakers. This is because the nature of affiliation with an organized religion differs greatly from country to country, as does the social context of religious practice. For example, a country in which a single religion has long been predominant will often show more than 90 per cent of its population to be affiliated, while in actual fact, no more than 10 per cent may actually practise that religion on a regular basis (*Britannica Book of the Year*, 1998, p. 775). Such a situation often leads to the under-representation of minority religions, blurring of distinctions seen to be significant elsewhere, or double counting in countries where an individual may conscientiously practise more than one 'religion' at a time.

1.3 Why culture is important

Where culture is emphasized it is often given a purely instrumental role: culture can help or hamper economic activities. When cultural attitudes thwart economic growth, they need to be eradicated, or so the reasoning goes. Culture comes into this analysis not as something valuable in itself, but as a means to the ends of fostering and sustaining economic progress. However, culture, significant as it may be as an agent of economic activity, cannot be reduced to the position of a mere promoter of or impediment to economic activities. The role of culture cannot be limited to the means towards ends, rather it is the social basis of the ends themselves.

Weber (1904) argued that religious practices and beliefs had important consequences for economic development. Nevertheless, neither mainstream or heterodox economists paid much attention to measures of culture as determinants of economic growth during the Cold War era. Since then there has been a growing tendency for researchers such as Huntington (1996), Landes (1999) and Inglehart and Baker (2000) to use a nation's culture to explain economic growth. Recently, Barro and McCleary (2003) analysed the influences of religious participation and beliefs on a country's rate of economic progress. They found that economic growth responds positively to the extent of religious belief, but negatively to church attendance. That is, growth depends on the extent of believing relative to belonging. These results accord with a perspective in which religious beliefs influence individual traits which enhance economic performance.

The application of the term 'culture' to the collective attitudes and behaviour of corporations arose in business jargon during the post-Cold War era. Unlike many such locutions it spread quickly into popular use in newspapers and magazines. However, when answering the question as to how an economy is influenced by culture, we have to remember that there was no pristine economy which was somehow later influenced by culture; rather, the economy has always been culturally influenced, from inside and outside, from the beginning (Sayer, 1997, p. 18). It is usually thought that culture influences economic outcomes by affecting personal traits such as honesty, thrift, the willingness to work hard and openness to strangers. Culture is divided into various elements that can be both a resource for and an obstacle to economic development.

Modern life has been simultaneously characterized and influenced by different cultures. Specifically, each element of a culture has a role in economic activities.[10] For example, Catholics used always to eat fish on Fridays, and milk products are popular among Hindus, many of whom are also vegetarians. Taboos against beef for Hindus or pork for Muslims and Jews are other examples. In a different way, but one that has in-depth economic implications, Islamic thinkers have sought dynamic approaches to development problem-solving within the boundaries of their own value systems. Because the *Shariah* (Islamic law) prohibits the taking of interest, 'Islamic banks' neither pay nor charge it. Since the banks must remain viable, they spread the risks flowing from their borrowing and lending by receiving a share of profits from the borrowers, and distributing proportionate shares to their depositors. Technically and ethically, such payments are not considered to be interest. Islamic banks claim that they are simply facilitating the circulation of money in ways that generate productive activities. Their example shows how a religious norm can alter 'modern' practice, instead of itself being eliminated by the dictates of modernity (Shanker, 1996).

It is necessary to be very cautious in trying to identify the role of cultural elements such as race and ethnicity in socioeconomic affairs. According to the biological tenet which sees cooperation among animals as mainly influenced by genetic similarity, socioeconomic behaviours between various groups of people can be easily differentiated. But the term 'race' is not appropriate when applied to national, religious, geographic, linguistic or cultural groups, nor can the biological criteria of race be equated with any mental characteristics such as intelligence, personality, or character. In the nineteenth and early twentieth centuries spurious theories, mainly expressed by those who were interested in emphasizing the supposed superiority of their own kind of culture or nationality, were developed about race, culture and nationality.

Language as the major tool of communication, is an obvious starting point for an exploration of differences between cultures. Every language carries a weight of values, of sensibilities, of approaches to reality – all of which insinuate themselves into the consciousness of those who speak it. To a certain extent, linguistic differences have decisively influenced global trade and marketing. Although it is not the only tool in building trusting relationships, doors usually open more quickly when knocked on by someone who speaks a familiar language. Sharing a common language, however, does not necessarily mean effective communication in technical terms. More important is the understanding of 'hidden messages' which determines the effectiveness of the communication. Proper communication takes both technical understanding of the spoken words and cultural understanding of the 'hidden meaning'. For example, when a Japanese manager says in a business negotiation 'It is very difficult' (which is a polite manner of refusal in Japanese society), the American partner would probably ask the Japanese side to find a solution, finding the expression to be more ambiguous. In contemporary Chinese society, by contrast, 'We have some difficulties' implies 'It would be OK under certain conditions.'

Compared to language, religion can provide more insights into the characteristics of a culture. What is more important, religion can have a deep impact not only on attitudes towards economic matters but also on values that influence them. Specifically, religious attitudes and values can help to determine what we think is right or appropriate, what is important, what is desirable and so on. For example, Luqmani et al. (1980) suggest a package of marketing strategies for the Muslim world, among them: 'to use religious holidays such as the end of Ramadan as the major selling time for food, clothing, and gifts'; 'to use "excessive" profits for charitable purposes'; 'to access female consumers by saleswomen, catalogs, home demonstrations'; and so on.

Some empirical researches, however, cast serious doubt on the importance of religion. For example, after examining a large cross-section of conflicts, Fox (1997) finds that in only a small minority do religious issues play more than a marginal role. Similarly, Alesina et al. (2002) find that religious fractionalization does not significantly predict the rent-seeking policy distortions usually associated with other types of ethnic fractionalization. A stark example of ethnicity (language) working better than religion as a coalition-enforcing mechanism is recounted by Horowitz (1985):

> In seventeenth century North-America, the English were originally called 'Christians,' while the African slaves were described as 'heathens.' The initial differentiation of groups relied heavily on religion. After about 1680, however, a new dichotomy of 'whites' and 'blacks' supplanted the former Christian and heathen categories, for some slaves had become Christians. If reliance had continued to be placed mainly on religion, baptism could have been employed to escape from bondage. Color provided a barrier seemingly both 'visible and permanent.'[11]

Nevertheless, it is reasonable to assume that specific cultural elements (ethnicity, language or religion) may play roles of variable importance depending on a range of internal and external conditions. More detailed empirical evidence will be provided in chapters 5 and 7.

1.4 Summary

Unravelling the determinants of economic activities promises to be one of the major research areas in the post-Cold War era. Past analyses, especially those that are quantitatively based, are mainly focused on economic variables. But there is no way in which economic activities could be conducted independently of human and cultural context. The economy is as much a cultural site as any other part of society, such as family, community or school. However, despite the importance of cultural influences on economic performance, mainstream economists have tended largely to ignore them. Cultural considerations have been cast into the underworld of developmental thought and practice.

2

Culture as a Tool for Economic Analysis

The Tao of Buddha is hard and difficult. It takes an eon of effort, patience and hard work. How can one hope to achieve Tao with little merit and little wisdom? How can one attempt to attain Tao while feeling arrogant and thinking it is easy? If one tries to do so, one tries in vain ... Drop all discursive thoughts and all attachments. Rest your mind. Like a wall, don't be influenced by internal and external factors; only then, can you enter the Buddhist Path.

(Bodhidharma, 470–543 AD)

2.1 Difficulties in global economic analysis

When referring to the spatial heterogeneity of the world economy, at least two important points must be noted. First, about 134 million square kilometres of land area (excluding Antarctica) are shared by more than 200 independent economies differing greatly in size (for example, Russia has 147,000 square kilometres, whereas Monaco has less than two square kilometres). The world economy thus is widely diversified in terms of physical environment and natural resource endowments. Second, more than 6 billion people are divided unevenly among these economies. For example, China already has a population of 1.3 billion, whereas Nauru, a small independent island in the South Pacific, only has a population of about 10,000.

The fundamental characteristics of contemporary economic issues are closely associated with the complexity of the world per se. The uneven distribution of natural and social resources has undoubtedly shaped or decisively influenced the growth pattern and process of the economic development of the world as a whole. Technically and methodologically, deeper insights into the characteristics and mechanisms of the contemporary world are hard to achieve without finding some way of sub-dividing or classifying different regions. Methods to be used for the classification of the existing economies tend to be different, depending upon the analytical purposes. Most popular would be division into the six continents:

- Asia
- Africa
- Europe
- Latin America
- North America and
- Oceania

This method to a large extent emphasizes the geographical over the socio-economic features of the world. In a similar way, the World Bank (1996) classifies all the existing economies into five groups:

- Sub-Saharan Africa
- Asia
- Europe and Central Asia
- Middle East and North Africa and
- Americas[1]

This also ignores the discrepancies within each group, since socioeconomic factors differ greatly between Europe and Central Asia, as well as between North and South America.

It may appear that the simplest method of dividing the world economy is to employ the concepts of North/South and East/West. But whereas 'North' and 'South' have universally accepted fixed reference points at the poles, 'East' and 'West' do not, and the use of such concepts to identify geographical areas is confusing. It all depends on where you stand. For example, 'West' and 'East' presumably originally referred to the western and eastern parts of Eurasia. From the American viewpoint, however, the Far East is actually the Far West. For most of Chinese history the West meant India, whereas in Japan the 'West' usually meant China (Naff, 1986).

None of the above classifications, however, can reflect the diversified natural and geographical conditions of the world. To this end, more technical criteria are needed. For example, the existing economies can be classified into three groups, using the climate zones:

- tropical
- subtropical and
- frigid

They can also be classified into three extrinsically different groups, using geographical criteria:

- landlocked
- islands or
- mixed

These two classification approaches are useful for researchers engaged with some specific purposes. For example, the climate-zone approach is usually applied for agricultural economics analyses while extrinsic geographical locations are important instruments for analysis of the spatial determinants of international trade and economic cooperation. However they are inefficient in other economic comparisons and analyses.

Economies are also diversified organizationally. For example, the existing independent countries can be divided into 17 categories of political status in the forms of governments and ruling powers. These are:

- republic (110)
- constitutional monarchy (18)
- parliamentary state (13)
- provisional military government (12)
- socialist republic (9)
- federal republic (8)
- monarchy (6)
- federal parliamentary state (3)
- Islamic republic (2)
- transitional military republic (2)
- federal Islamic republic (2)
- transitional government (1)
- federal constitutional monarchy (1)
- federation of monarchy (1)
- monarchical–sacerdotal state (1)
- constitutional monarchy under military rule (1) and
- none (1)[2]

It is true that political classifications may be helpful for those who want to conduct comparative studies of international politics and other politically related economic issues. But examples of economies with the same form of government or ruling power but with different political and economic performances can be found all over the world.

Political systems can be further classified according to the extent to which an administration or governance is intrusive, or backed by the use of force. Authoritarian regimes typically grant wide powers to law enforcement agencies; at its most extreme, this leads to a police state. Authoritarian regimes may or may not have a rule of law – in the former case, laws and procedures exist and are applied, though they may seem intrusive, unjust or excessive; in the latter case, laws do not exist, or are routinely ignored, and the actions of the government are at the whim of the leadership. Dictatorships and absolute monarchies are almost always authoritarian. Authoritarianism is distinguished from totalitarianism both in degree and scope. What is more, authoritarian administration or governance is less intrusive and, in the case of groups, not necessarily backed by the use of force. Totalitarian governments tend to be revolutionary, intent on changing the basic structure of society, while authoritarian ones tend to be conservative. Democracies are normally not authoritarian, but may exhibit authoritarian behaviour in some respects. As a result the existing economies can be roughly classified into the following types:

- totalitarian
- authoritarian and
- democratic

A controversial belief holds that countries with authoritarian regimes are more likely to be economically successful than democratic countries. Examples given to support this thesis are South Korea, Singapore, Malaysia and Taiwan, which were considered authoritarian during their period of growth. This notion of developmental authoritarianism is a central justification for the rule of the Communist Party of China. One counter-argument is that there are many instances of authoritarian nations that have not achieved rapid growth, for example the Philippines and Indonesia. In Europe, Spain under Francisco Franco's authoritarian and conservative regime was considerably less economically developed than neighbouring countries such as France, even though the latter had suffered from the devastation of World War II.[3]

The International Monetary Fund (IMF) classifies existing economies into three categories:

- advanced economies
- developing countries and
- countries in transition (IMF, 1997b, p. 147)

In addition, the following two categories are also used:

- net creditor countries and
- net debtor countries (IMF, 1997b, p. 174)

It is noticeable that the former has no clear boundaries while the latter can only be used for the purposes of international financial analyses. The World Bank has classified existing economies into three or four groups:

- low-income
- middle-income, which is further divided into
    - 'lower-middle' and
    - 'upper-middle' and
- high-income economies[4]

Classification by income level, however, does not necessarily reflect development status. Even worse, it may not be a suitable criterion by which to conduct any consistent analyses and comparisons of different groups of economies over a longer period of time as rising and falling GNP levels shift economies from one category to another.

The World Bank (1996, pp. 396–7) further classifies existing economies according to an identification of the types of international trade in which major exports are those that make up 50 per cent or more of the total exports of goods and services from one category. On the basis of these criteria, they arrive at the following classification:

- exporters of manufactures
- exporters of non-fuel primary products
- exporters of fuels (mainly oil)
- exporters of services
- diversified exporters and
- not classified by export category

This kind of classification may provide clear information about the resource endowments and industrial advantages or disadvantages for each group of economies. But it is too technical and, again, it ignores the socioeconomic differences between the various groups of the existing economies.

There is another flaw in the classifications suggested above. Economies are constantly undergoing processes of political and economic transformation. For example, politically and institutionally, the former USSR and the other economies of Central and Eastern Europe would have been characterized as socialist states before the early 1990s. Since then, however, all of them have implemented various forms of market-oriented reforms.

2.2 Economic comparison by culture

2.2.1 What is a 'culture area'?

Unlike political and economic factors, cultural factors, such as ethnicity, language, and religion, suffer relatively few changes over a comparatively long period of time. They can, therefore, serve as an important instrument for the comparative analysis of the world economy. However, given the great varieties of ethnic, linguistic, and religious groups throughout the world (as discussed in Chapter 1), the number of individual cultures is too large to be a practical tool[5] and it would be very difficult to conduct useful multicultural economic comparisons. Consequently, to facilitate multicultural economic analysis and comparison, our analytical framework will be based on a synthetic term – 'culture area'.

The concept of a 'culture area' reflects the theoretical position that each culture, on whatever level it may be analysed, must be examined with regards to its own history and the general principles of independent invention, culture borrowing, cultural integration and so on. In the *International Encyclopedia of the Social Sciences*, culture areas are defined as 'geographical territories in which characteristic culture patterns are recognizable through repeated associations of specific traits and, usually, through one or more modes of subsistence that are related to the particular environment' (1972, p. 563).

There usually exists a small and relatively homogeneous core in each culture area. Culture areas also have boundaries. The influence of a specific culture is always strongest in the core and becomes weaker from the core to peripheral areas. In theory, the boundary of a culture area can be determined as the line beyond which the influence of culture reduces to zero. However the boundaries between culture areas are not necessarily distinct; recognizable cultures within a given area may contrast with those of neighbouring ones, and if the boundaries are not sharply delineated, zones of composite culture or blended traits may make the transition from one to another a matter of gradation. Within a single area, quite different ways of life may coexist as characteristic patterns.

Although distinctions between regions based on culture are as old as mankind, the roots of the culture area concept can be traced to Europe, where the work of the German geographer Friedrich Ratzel (1844–1904) inspired the development of the *Kulturkreise* (cultural circles) school. *Kulturkreise*, which attempted to reconstruct the diffusion, or spread, of cultural traits from a few dominant cultural clusters, was associated with the German anthropologists Leo Frobenius (1873–1938) and Fritz Graebner (1877–1934). It was not in Europe, however, but in the United States that the concept of the culture area gained real social scientific cohesion. One impetus for this development was the need to make sense of the growing body of ethnographic data produced by early anthropological expeditions in the American West.

In 1917 Clark Wissler (1870–1947), an anthropologist with the American Museum of Natural History, used the culture area concept to integrate what was known about Native American communities. Wissler gathered together ethnographic data from a variety of sources and used these data to group Native American tribes based on similarities and differences in their subsistance systems, modes of transport, textiles, artwork and religious practice. As a result of this effort, he discerned a distinct geographic pattern, with groups living in proximity, or in similar natural environments, sharing many cultural traits. Wissler eventually defined nine distinct Native American culture areas, grouping tribes that shared significant traits.[6]

Even though the pioneering and classic works on the formulation and application of the culture area concept were carried out some years later (see, for example, Wissler, 1917), early studies on classification of culture areas may date back to the late nineteenth or the very early twentieth century (Driver, 1962). In 1896, O.T. Mason recognized 18 culture areas or environments in the Western Hemisphere (Kroeber, 1939, p. 7). Farrand (1904) suggested a seven-part classification of North American Indians, including considerations of both geography and culture, and discussed them at some length. Holms (1903) mapped the North American Indians into 19 geo-ethnic groups, that correspond well to the groupings in the later work of both Wissler (1917) and Kroeber (1939). Thereafter, there are a number of case studies on culture area distinctions in Asian and other cultures.[7]

2.2.2 How many culture areas are there in the world?

Before it is possible to start an economic comparison of different culture areas, it is necessary to answer the basic question: How many culture areas are there in the world?

While scholars have generally agreed in their identification of the major cultures in history and on those that exist in the modern world (see Box 2.1), there have also been significant differences of opinion.

Box 2.1 How have the world civilizations evolved?

The world civilizations have evolved through different phases, since they first emerged more than three thousand years ago. Some regions witnessed two or three generations of affiliated cultures, with the demise of one culture and interregnum followed by the rise of another successor generation. A simplified chart of the relations between major Eurasian civilizations through time is shown below.

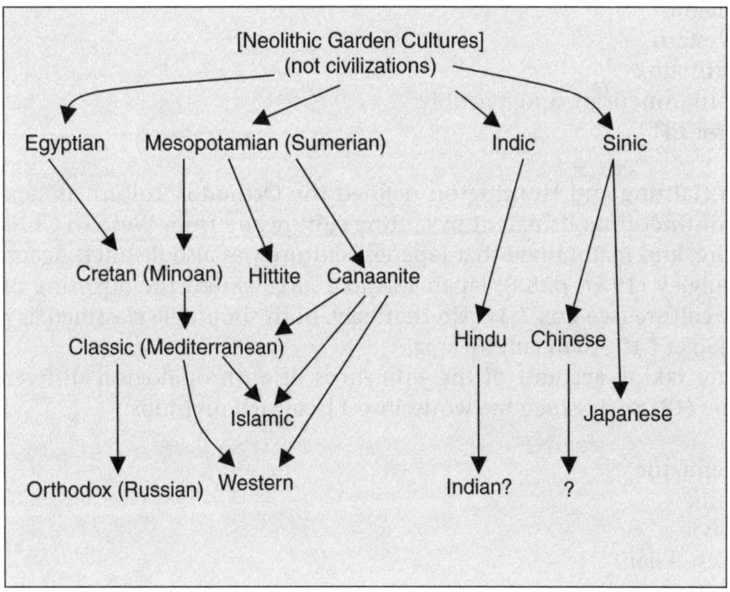

Source: Quigley (1979, p. 83).

For example, Spengler (1928) specified eight major cultures and McNeil (1963) discussed nine civilizations[8] throughout human history. Bagby (1958, pp. 165–74) saw seven major civilizations, or nine if Japan is distinguished from China and the Eastern Orthodox from the West. Rostovanyi (1993) identified seven and Braudel (1994) nine major contemporary civilizations. Quigley (1979, pp. 77 and 88) argued for 16 clear historical cases and very probably eight others, while Toynbee (1961, pp. 546–7) raised the number to 21 or 23.

Such divergent opinions depend in part, as noted by Huntington (1996, p. 44), on whether cultural groups such as the Chinese and Indians are thought to have had a single civilization throughout history or two or more closely related civilizations, one being the offspring of the other. Despite these differences, the identity of the major civilizations is not contested. As Melko (1969, p. 133) argued, there exist at least 12 major cultures in the world, seven of which no longer exist (Mesopotamian, Egyptian, Cretan, Classical, Byzantine, Middle American and Andean) and five of which still do (Chinese, Japanese, Indian, Islamic and Western).

From the perspective of intercultural politics, Galtung (1992, pp. 23–4) and Huntington (1996, pp. 45–7) developed a similar multicultural structure of seven or eight culture areas, including:

- Sinic
- Japanese
- Hindu
- Islamic
- Western
- Orthodox
- Latin American, and, possibly
- African[9]

Both Galtung and Huntington defined the Orthodox culture as separate and distinct from its parent Byzantine culture and from Western Christian culture, and maintained that Japanese culture was also distinct. According to Quigley (1979, p. 83), Japan was to a large extent the offspring of the Sinic culture (see Box 2.1). Alternatively, both should be classified as parts of a larger East Asian culture area.

After taking account of the influences of anthropological differences, Sapper (1968) classified the world into 11 cultural divisions:

- Germanic
- Latin
- Slavic
- West Asian
- Indian

- East Asian
- the inland
- African
- Malayan
- Australian and
- the North Pole

This classification only satisfies anthropologists. Political economists have usually treated Australia as part of the Western culture area and Malaysia as part of the East (or Southeast) Asian culture area. Other authors have defined a relatively small number of culture areas. For example, Kendall (1976) classified the world into six distinct culture areas:

- Western
- Islamic
- Indian
- East Asian
- Southeast Asian and
- African

In Kendall's study, the Western culture area, which is composed of four sub-culture areas (Northwest Europe, Canada, the USA, South Africa, Australia and New Zealand; the Mediterranean; Central Asia; and the former USSR), is very heterogeneous in terms of geography, political economy and culture. Quite independently, Aono (1979, pp. 48–51) developed a framework that closely parallels Kendall's (1976) on the salience to a world of six culture areas:

- East Asian
- Malayan
- South Asian
- Islamic
- African and
- European

Again, the European area is assumed to include at least three economically and geographically heterogeneous cultures (or sub-cultures) – Germanic, Latin and Slavic.

2.3 Cultural division of the world economy

Since 'culture' and 'area' are both generalized terms, their use in combination gives no real clue as to precise meaning. When comparing one culture area with another, the level of abstraction must be the same. Although many factors at the base of any recognizable culture area are ecological in nature, the culture area concept is one that conforms to the doctrine of limited possibilities rather than to a simple geographic determination. Viewed in this light and assessed according to the character of the geographic units and the degree of complexity of cultural similarities within, and differences between, units, the culture area concept takes shape as a classificatory device of marked utility in describing the cultural regions of the world.

The cultural division of the world economy may vary, usually depending on different purposes or criteria selected by researchers. Our classification of contemporary culture areas is based on the criteria by which a culture area must be contiguous (that is, one can draw a line around it on a map) and must be defined by cultural (rather than geographic) similarities. There is no universal answer to the question whether similar peoples in an area must belong to a same culture area nor to what criteria can define boundary between two culture areas. Obviously, it depends on how detailed the culture area classification is intended to be, and on which criteria are most important. Besides, the following principles are also taken into account.

First, the smallest geographical unit to be used in each culture area is country or other independent statistical area, even though different cultural identities may exist in large countries, such as India and China.[10] The reason for this is to avoid collecting large-scale sub-national (or subregional) data and information. Of course, the use of lower area-level data can make the analysis and comparison between different cultures more accurate and meaningful. But such a task seems likely to prove very costly and, perhaps, impossible, since in many countries few statistical data on cultural minorities are available. Second, the total number of culture areas to be defined in this research should be based on the principle that too many culture areas may leave us in doubt and too few tend to overwhelm our multicultural understanding of the world economy.

In sum, seven culture areas are considered for the subdivision of the world economy. They are:

- African area
- East Asian area
- Eastern Orthodox area
- Indian area
- Islamic area
- Latin American area and
- Western area

2.3.1 The African area

Africa as a whole is not recognized as a distinct culture, since the northern part of the African continent and its eastern coast belong to Islamic culture, while elsewhere European imperialism and settlements introduced Western languages and religions.[11] But, as observed by Braudel (1994) and Huntington (1996, p. 47), the Africans are increasingly developing a sense of African identity and, conceivably, sub-Saharan Africa could cohere into a distinct civilization, with South Africa possibly as its core state. The definition of the southern and central African economies as a separate culture area in our research is due to their unique ethnic identity, as well as to their history of industrialization, which is very different from that of the Islamic and European economies, all of which are geographically proximate to each other.

The African area is defined as including southern and central Africa. It has 16.67 per cent of world land area and 11.13 per cent of world population (see Figure 2.1), with an average population density of 30 persons per square kilometre.[12] The major languages used in the African area are English, French, Amharic, Portuguese and Arabic; the religious population comes from Western Christians, Muslims, and Orthodox Christians.

2.3.2 The East Asian area

Most scholars recognize the existence of either a single distinct Chinese culture dating back to 2000 BC or perhaps a thousand years earlier, or two or more Chinese cultures, one succeeding the other in the early centuries. Even though some scholars describe contemporary Japan as a distinct culture, it is also argued that Japan was to a large extent the offspring of Chinese culture, emerging during the period between AD 100 and 400, and in turn influential to some extent on Chinese culture during Japan's economic upsurge in the twentieth century. Therefore it is reasonable to combine Japanese and Chinese culture under the heading of a single 'East Asian' culture.

The Southeast Asian economies are classified into the 'East Asian area' in view of the fact that, besides Taiwan and Singapore whose ethnic majorities are Chinese, ethnic Chinese living in other Southeast Asian economies have made considerable contributions to them. For example, during the late twentieth century, the ethnic Chinese in the Philippines contributed to 35 per cent of the total domestic sales with a meagre 1 per cent of population. With only 2–3 per cent of Indonesia's total population, the ethnic Chinese held 70 per cent of its domestic private capital; and in Indonesia 17 of the 25 top enterprises were controlled by the Chinese. With 10 per cent of the total population of Thailand, the ethnic Chinese possessed nine of the ten largest business groups and produced half of the country's GNP. The ethnic Chinese shared about one-third of the total population but almost monopolized the economy of Malaysia.[13]

With 12.65 per cent of land area, the East Asian area has 33.62 per cent of the world population. The major languages used in the East Asian area are Chinese, Japanese, Korean, Vietnamese, Thai and English.

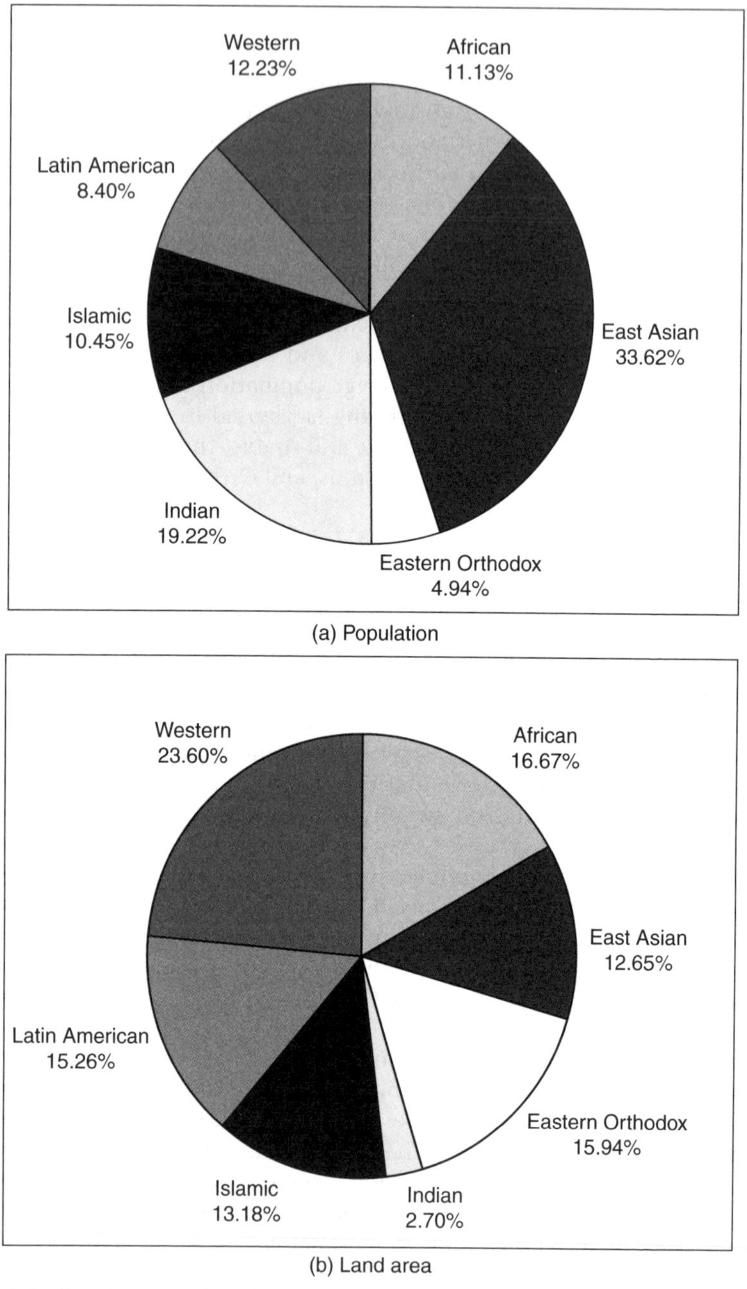

Figure 2.1 Population and land area shares by culture area

Source: Calculated by the author based on (1) Population Division and Statistical Division of the United Nations Secretariat for population and (2) *World Atlas* (1994, pp. 2–6) for land area.

Non-religionists account for the largest share of population,[14] followed by Buddhists, Muslims, Western Christians and atheists.

2.3.3 The Eastern Orthodox area

Although a part of its parent Byzantine culture and closely related to Western Christianity, the Eastern Orthodox Church has been treated as a separate religion since the sixteenth century (for more details about the differences between Eastern Orthodox and Western Christianity, see Chapter 1, section 1.2.3). It is therefore more appropriate and useful to distinguish the Eastern Orthodox countries as a single culture area, especially for the purpose of drawing political and economic comparisons between them and Western Europe, Asia and the Islamic world.

With 15.94 per cent of world land area and only 4.94 per cent of world population, the Eastern Orthodox area is the least dense culture area in the world, averaging only 14 people to each square kilometre of land. The major languages spoken in the Eastern Orthodox area are Russian, Ukrainian, Romanian, Greek, Serbo-Croat, and Armenian. Though classified as the Eastern Orthodox area, Orthodox Christianity only attracts slightly more than one-third of the believers in the area, while non-religionists make up nearly half of the total population, followed by Western Christians, and Muslims.[15]

2.3.4 The Indian area

Indian culture is generally referred to as Indic or Hindu. In one form or another, Hinduism has been central to the culture of the subcontinent of South Asia since the second millennium BC. Even though Indian culture is at the core of this area, some small Buddhist and Islamic communities as well as several other smaller cultural minorities are also included. The reason for this is their geographic and linguistic proximity to the Indian (but not to any other culture's) core.

With the smallest portion of world territory (2.70 per cent) but the second largest population (19.22 per cent), the Indian area is the most populous culture area in the world; for each square kilometre of land there are as many as 316 people. The major languages spoken in the Indian area are Hindi and Bengali. Western colonialism has left a legacy of some English and French speakers still in this area. Hinduism is the mainstream religion, with almost two-thirds of the total population adhering to it. The other religions in this area include Islam, Western Christianity, Buddhism and Sikhism.

2.3.5 The Islamic area

Originating in the Arabian peninsula in the seventh century AD, Islam rapidly spread across North Africa and the Iberian peninsula and also eastward into central Asia, the subcontinent, and Southeast Asia. The reason why we do not classify Indonesia and Malaysia as part of the Islamic area in this book is their peripheral location far from the Arabic cores and their looser Southeast Asian variety of Islam; further, their people and culture are a mixture of indigenous, Muslim, Hindu, Chinese and Christian influences.

The Islamic area is defined as northern Africa, the Middle East and adjacent Islamic states in central Asia. It has 13.18 per cent of world land area and 10.45 per cent of world population. The major languages spoken are Arabic, Turkish, English, French and Russian. In the Islamic area, as its name shows, Muslims account for the majority of the total population, followed by Western and Orthodox Christians.

2.3.6 The Latin American area

Although an offspring of European culture, Latin America has evolved along a very different path from the Western nations. As a result Latin America has been generally recognized as having a distinct identity that differentiates it from the Western nations, especially from those that are Anglo-dominated.

Among the major differences between the Latin American area and the Anglo-dominated North American area is that the majority of Latin Americans are more culturally collectivistic than the North Americans; or, in other words, North Americans are more culturally individualistic than the Latin Americans. For example, in their comparison of Latin American (Brazil) and North American (the USA) cultures' preferences of styles of negotiation, Pearson and Stephan (1999) find that Brazilians favour styles of negotiation that express concern for the outcomes of others, whereas Americans favour styles of negotiation that reflect a concern for their own outcomes.

The Latin American area has 15.26 per cent of world land area and 8.40 per cent of world population. The major languages spoken are Spanish, Portuguese and French. In terms of religion the area is homogeneous: Western Christianity accounts for the majority of the population in the Latin American area, while the remaining religions (such as Islam, Hinduism, and Judaism) and non-religion combined account for less than 5 per cent of the total population.

2.3.7 The Western area

Historical evidence suggests that Europe gradually pulled ahead of the rest of the world from the sixteenth century. As a result, European culture has influenced many non-European areas, some of the which themselves became Westernized.[16] Mainly due to its strong influence throughout contemporary history, the Western area is the only one defined here that has a diverse geography. It includes not only the Western Hemisphere economies (except Latin America) and the traditionally defined 'West' European nations, but also those that are geographically distant from the Western core, such as Australia and New Zealand in the South Pacific, and Israel in the Middle East. These countries have closer cultural linkages with the Western area than with any other areas.

With 23.60 per cent of world land area and 12.23 per cent of world population, the Western area has the lowest population density. The major languages spoken are English, German, French, Italian, Spanish, Polish, Dutch, Portuguese, Hungarian, Czech and Swedish. Western Christianity is the largest religion in the Western area, with more than 80 per cent of the total population adhering to it, followed by non-religionists, Muslims, Jews and Orthodox Christians.

2.4 Summary

The culture area concept is a means of organizing a vast amount of variegated ethnographic data into comprehensive units within a classificatory system. It depends on a number of criteria or determinants in the isolation of units. In theory, major considerations in recognizing these areas and sub-areas are ecological zones, patterns of cultural integration and correlations between the independently diffused traits, among others. In practice, however, because the factors by which a culture is determined or influenced are so numerous, the cultural classification of diversified economies is an extremely difficult task. Therefore, it is necessary to simplify the multicultural division of the world economy.

The classification of human groups into culture areas has been critiqued on the grounds that the bases for these classifications, such as similar farming systems or pottery styles, are always arbitrary. Despite this limitation, the organization of human communities into cultural areas remains a common practice throughout the social sciences. Today, the definition of culture areas is enjoying a resurgence of practical and theoretical interest as social scientists conduct research on processes of cultural globalization (Gupta and Ferguson, 1997). The most obvious drawback of culture areas is that, in reality, cultural variation tends to be continuous rather than abrupt. Cultural groups near boundaries thus become 'intermediate'. Also, many traits cut across culture area boundaries: cultural variation is complex and not easily reduced to geographical patterns. Despite these problems, the culture area concept is extremely useful as a device for organizing ethnographic diversity, so that it may be taken account of and general patterns investigated.

Culture area analysis has been widely used by both anthropologists and cultural geographers, primarily because it facilitates comparisons between regions, assists in the historical reconstruction of economic and cultural developments and lends itself to questions about the impact of the natural environment on the form of human cultures. In this chapter, we have proposed a framework of seven culture areas for the cultural division of the world economy. Of course, our discussion of the cultural make-up as well as the culture areas derived therefrom is not definitive and perhaps would not satisfy anthropologists. However, as discussed in Chapter 1, language and religion are the most important elements in representing a culture. Besides, it has been much easier for us to collect the linguistic and religious data than the other cultural data. This information will help in preparation of the cross-national panel data of cultural index, which are needed in the quantitative analysis of cultural influences on economic activities.

A multicultural comparison of the world economy will be conducted in the next chapter, with some emphases on the economic differences between various culture areas.

3
Multicultural Economic Comparisons and Differences

> We who are strong in the faith ought to help the weak to carry their burdens. We should not please ourselves. Instead, we should all please our brothers for their own good, in order to build them up in the faith. For Christ did not please himself. Instead, as the Scripture says, 'The insults which are hurled at you have fallen on me.' Everything written in the Scriptures was written to teach us, in order that we might have hope through the patience and encouragement which the Scriptures give us. And may God, the source of patience and encouragement, enable you to have the same point of view among yourselves by following the example of Christ Jesus, so that all of you together may praise with one voice the God and Father of our Lord Jesus Christ.
>
> (Romans 15:1–6)

3.1 About statistical data

A problem for multicultural economic comparisons for the period since World War II is that the world economy has been organized according to various different statistical systems. In many market economies, national income statistics have been compiled according to the United Nations' System of National Accounts (SNA). As a key indicator derived from the SNA, gross national product (GNP) is the total value of the entire final products and services generated during a defined period of time. GNP is the sum of two components: gross domestic product (GDP) and net income from abroad. GDP measures the final output of goods and services produced by the domestic economy. Net income from abroad is income in the form of compensation of employees, interest on loans, profits and other factor payments that residents receive from abroad, less payments made for labour and capital. Most countries have estimated their GDP indicators by the production method. This method sums the final outputs of the various sectors of the economy (for example, agriculture, manufacturing and services), from which the value of the inputs to production has been subtracted.

However, in most centrally planned economies (CPEs), national accounts were based on the material product system (MPS) whose most important aggregate is net material product (NMP) and national income (NI). NMP comprehensively covers value added in the 'material' sectors of production during a defined period of time; while NI is the total of all income received by all factors in productive activities carried out in their territories. The sum of the outputs of all separately enumerated production units multiplied by the relevant prices of outputs is called gross value of social product (GVSP). As GVSP also includes the values of intermediate products that are simply the material costs for consecutive production units, values of products were counted more than once. Obviously, the use of the GVSP concept could result in a series of negative effects. This is particularly true when using the GVSP as an indicator to evaluate the sizes and efficiencies of economies, as a part of it is contributed by intermediate products and is thus irrelevant to social welfare.

The estimation of GDP data left many unpersuaded in economies that are under transition from the centrally planned system to a market system. With the exception of the data on the tertiary sector, the NMP data were transformed to GDP data through simple multiplication by a conversion factor, a process that was held by many to be inadequate. In fact, since a socialist accounting system does not take account of the output value of the service sector, historical records of this sector were very fragmentary. The GDP data at constant prices are inextricably linked to the real NMP data collected by the old system. Unlike the market economies, in which real GDP is derived using a system of price indices, in centrally planned systems the basic production units at the lowest level of the statistical reporting system are responsible for computing the real output value based on a catalogue of fixed prices given from above. Even though they were prepared by analysts who were attempting to make measures of GDP with the same criteria as those used for Western countries, it seems likely that the GDP growth figures of Bulgaria, Romania and former Yugoslavia from 1950 to the mid-1980s have exaggerated the economic performance of these countries (Maddison, 1996, p. 125). Since the late 1980s, during which time the socialist economies were undergoing major transition, their growth may be understated because the authorities have not found it easy to monitor all the new private activities.[1]

The application of the multifarious monetary systems in different economies is another hurdle in the study of multicultural economic issues. In general, there are three options for converting the nominal values of GNP or GDP into comparable values. The first, and also the simplest, option is to use exchange rates. But exchange rates are mainly a reflection of purchasing power over internationally tradeable items. For these goods inter-country price differences are reduced because of possibilities for trade and specification. For example, in poor countries where wages are low, non-tradeable items, such as haircuts, building construction or other services are generally cheaper than in high-income countries, so that there is a general tendency for their exchange rates to understate purchasing power. The other problem with exchange rates is that they are often powerfully influenced by capital movements and in the past decades have been too volatile to serve as reliable indicators of purchasing power.

The second methodology appears in the *World Bank Atlas*. According to this method, the GNP estimates for one year are determined via the following steps. First, the GNP in constant market prices and national currency units is converted to GNP measured in constant average prices for the year and the two preceding years. This is done by multiplying the original constant price series by the weighted-mean domestic GNP deflator for the base period (that is, by the ratio of total GNP in current prices to total GNP in constant prices for the three-year period). In the second step, the GNP measured in constant three-year average prices in national currency is converted to US dollars by dividing that GNP by the weighted-mean exchange rate for the base period. The weighted-mean exchange rate is the ratio of the sum of GNP in current prices to the sum of the GNP divided by the annual average exchange rate in national currency per US dollar for the three years. The last step is to convert the GNP measured in constant average three-year US dollars to one measured in current US dollars by multiplying that GNP by the implicit US GNP deflator for the base period. In general, the *Atlas* method of averaging three years of exchange rates smooths fluctuations due to the currency market and provides a more reliable measure, over time, of overall income than do estimates based on a single year's exchange rate. But it, again, does not overcome the obstacles for international economic comparisons.

The last approach is to use purchasing power parity (PPP) converters. The PPP approach was developed through cooperative research between some national statistical offices and international agencies over the past few decades.[2] GDP and GDP per capita using PPP are estimates based on the purchasing power of currencies rather than on current exchange rates. This conversion factor, the PPP, is defined as the number of units of a country's currency required to buy the same amounts of goods and services in the domestic market as one US dollar can buy in the United States. The computation involves deriving implicit quantities from national accounts expenditure data and specially collected price data and then revaluing the implicit quantities in each country at a single set of average prices. Because the same international price averages are used for every country, cross-country comparisons reflect differences in quantities of goods and services free of price-level differences. This procedure is designed to bring cross-country comparisons in line with cross-time real value comparisons that are based on constant price series.

Although considerable progress has been made in standardizing cross-national economic data, one should be very careful when interpreting economic indicators on the international level. Inter-country and inter-temporal comparisons using economic data involve complicated technical problems that are not easily resolved; therefore, readers are urged to consider these data as characterizing major differences between economies rather than as precise, quantitative measurements. For example, the UK and the USA place major reliance on information on income flows which is derived from tax sources, whereas Germany relies more on output information from industrial surveys. Measurement of output in high-tech industries can also be tackled in different ways. For example, when a country introduces a hedonic index for computers, which takes much better account of characteristics such as memory capacity and speed of operation, the new price index falls much more sharply than its predecessor.[3] As a result GDP growth rates differ.

3.2 Macroeconomic indicators

Notwithstanding repeated interruptions to the process of world development in the twentieth century, substantial progress has been achieved. At the beginning of the century the average per capita GDP of the world was only $1263 (at 1990 constant price). In the following decades it rose only slowly, to $2138 by the year 1950 (Maddison, 1996, table G-3). Since the 1950s, however, the world economy has grown at a much faster rate than ever before. Even though the economic growth of some former socialist economies in Central and Eastern Europe and the former Soviet Union was slow-footed during the early 1990s, due both to the limitations of the old system and to the risks of the structural changes being undertaken, the average per capita GDP of the world as a whole has risen to more than $6000 in 2000, amounting to approximately three times that in 1950 and five times that in 1900.[4]

The rapid economic expansion has been underpinned by continued solid growth in the developed countries, such as the United States, and a broadening recovery across continental Western Europe. Also, robust growth trends have been found in some parts of the developing world, particularly in China and India. Previous experience might suggest that a moderation of world growth is likely to occur at some point, as historically economic expansion has usually been followed by recession. But the International Monetary Fund (IMF) has given three reasons for believing that the economic expansion can be sustained. First, there are relatively few signs of the tensions and imbalances that usually presage significant downturns in the business cycle. Second, cyclical divergences remain sizeable among the advanced economies. Third, the recovery that is in progress in the transition countries seems likely to continue to strengthen, while the growing number of successful economies in the developing world are providing both new markets and increased production capacities (IMF, 1997a, p. 2).

Despite the steadiness of economic growth in the world as a whole, considerable differences still exist between countries. For example, many poor economies, particularly those of Sub-Saharan Africa and Central Asia, are still facing deep poverty and economic stagnation. As a result of the diverse growth processes national and regional income levels have differed throughout the world.

Interculturally, economic output (represented by GNP) has not been proportionally distributed. Specifically, the Western area contributed some 60 per cent, followed by the East Asian area, with 23 per cent, while the remainder was shared by the Latin American (7 per cent), Islamic (4 per cent), Eastern Orthodox (2 per cent), African (2 per cent) and Indian (2 per cent) areas. In terms of per capita values, the Western area was the highest, with an average per capita GNP of more than $20,000; in contrast, the six other culture areas as a whole had an average per capita GNP of less than $5000, with the Indian area being the lowest.[5]

It is worth noting that different methods can result in different cross-cultural scenarios. For example, when the exchange rates and *World Bank Atlas* methods are used, the Indian area appears to have the lowest per capita GNP (that is, $396 and $373, respectively), followed by the African ($778 and $521, respectively) and Islamic ($1877 and $1466, respectively) areas; by way of contrast, when the PPP method is used, the African area becomes the poorest in terms of per capita GNP ($1499), followed by the Indian ($1600) and Islamic ($3597) areas (see Table 3.1).

The economic differences, represented either by per capita GNP or GDP, mainly resulted from the different conversion factors used by each method. Except for Nigeria, the per capita GDP data of those African economies for which data are available were understated in 1995 if

Table 3.1 Estimation of per capita GNP, by culture area

Culture area	**Exchange rate (199 economies)**	***World Bank Atlas*** **(167 economies)**	**PPP rate (151 economies)**
African	778	521	1,499
East Asian	3,373	3,808	4,984
Eastern Orthodox	2,487	2,363	4,048
Indian	396	373	1,600
Islamic	1,877	1,460	3,597
Latin American	4,229	3,956	6,769
Western	22,579	23,344	22,113
World	4,948	5,201	6,278

Source: Calculated by the author based on United Nations (2001) and World Bank (2001).

exchange rates are used to convert their per capita GDP into US dollars. A comparison of the PPP and exchange rates methods also reveals that the per capita GDPs of Norway, Switzerland, Denmark, Sweden, Germany, Finland, Austria, Ireland, Australia, the Netherlands, France, New Zealand, the United Kingdom and Belgium were overstated if calculated via the exchange rate method; in contrast, the per capita GDPs of Italy, the United States, Croatia, Lithuania, Canada, Latvia, Estonia, Israel, Spain, Hungary, Slovenia, Poland, Portugal, the Slovak Republic, Malta and the Czech Republic were understated.[6] Finally, the number of economies examined by each method may also affect the outcome (in Table 3.1, 199, 167 and 151 economies are selected in the exchange rate, *World Bank Atlas* and PPP methods, respectively).

Next, let us look at how these multicultural economic situations change over time. To make data collection easier, we use Maddison's (2003) estimates on the GDP of 56 major economies.[7] Altogether these economies account for about one-fourth of the total number of economies, 87 per cent of total population and more than 99 per cent of GDP of the world as a whole.[8] The per capita GDPs of the seven culture areas from 1950 to 2000 can be roughly divided into three groups by income level. In the early 1950s the Western area, with a per capita GDP of more than G-K$6000, was defined as the high-income group; the Latin American and Eastern Orthodox areas, each having an average per capita GDP of G-K$2000–3000, were defined as the middle-income group; and the African, East Asian, Islamic and Indian areas, each with an average per capita GDP of G-K$500–1000, were defined as the low-income group. Fifty years later, while the Western area has more than doubled its per capita GDP, the African and Indian area GDPs remain almost unchanged. Particularly worthy of note is the East Asian area, which has raised its per capita GDP level sixfold from 1950 to 2000, making it possible for the area to move from the low-income group to the middle-income group.

Bearing in mind the considerable cross-cultural differences in the world economy, we may further ask the following questions: Why has the Latin American area, after having enjoyed faster economic growth in the 1960s and 1970s, kept its per capita GDP almost unchanged since the 1980s? Why have the African and Indian areas experienced much slower economic growth than either the Western or the East Asian areas? We will discuss these issues in detail in Chapter 4.

3.3 Real living standards

Living standards are, and should be, the final outcomes of economic growth in the human world. A basic indicator reflecting living standards is 'daily calorie supply per capita' which is calculated by dividing the calorie equivalent of the food supplies in an economy by the population. Food

Box 3.1 A millennial perspective of the world economy
In *The World Economy: a Millennial Perspective* (2001), Professor Angus Maddison provides a comprehensive view of the long-term economic growth and GDP levels of major nations (see figure below).

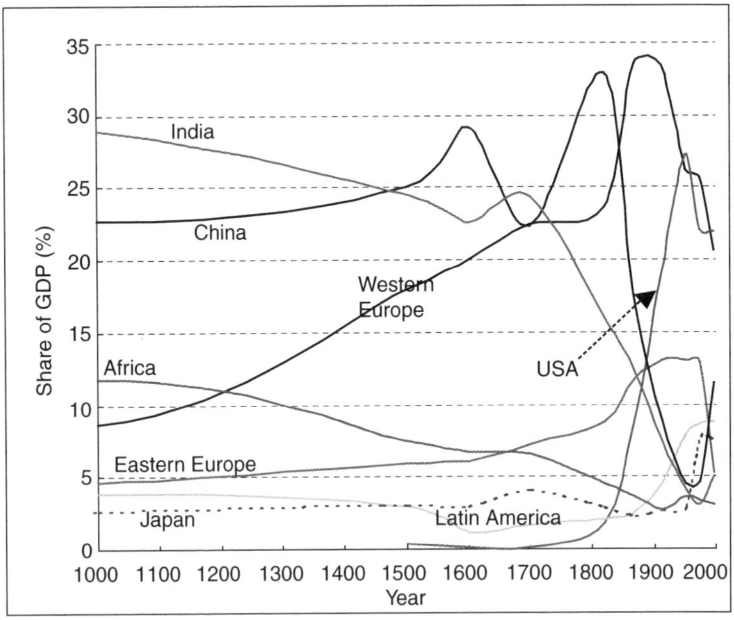

Source: Based on Maddison (2001, p. 261).

supplies comprise domestic production, imports less exports and changes in stocks; they exclude animal feed, seeds for use in agriculture and food lost in processing and distribution. 'Daily calorie requirement per capita' refers to the calories needed to sustain a person at normal levels of activity and health, taking account of age and sex distribution, average body weights and environmental temperatures.

The standards of living differ greatly across all culture areas (see Table 3.2). Except for the African area, the daily per capita calorie supply has met or exceeded the total requirements in all culture areas. For example, in the Western and Eastern Orthodox areas, the daily per capita calorie supplies as percentages of total requirements are 135 per cent and 131 per cent, respectively. The daily per capita calorie supplies as percentages of total requirements of the East Asian, Islamic and Latin American areas, though lower than that of the Western and Eastern Orthodox areas, are greater than 100 per cent. It should be noted that due to the

Table 3.2 Major indicators related to living standards in the 1990s, by culture area

Indicator		African area	East Asian area	Eastern Orthodox area	Indian area	Islamic area	Latin American area	Western area
(1) Daily per capita calorie supply as a percentage of total requirements[a]		94	114	131	100	115	114	135
(2) Life expectancy at birth (years)[b]	Male	50	68	63	62	64	66	73
	Female	53	72	72	62	67	73	80
(3) Population per doctor (persons)[c]		8,203	1,196	240	12,662	1,016	769	339
(4) Population per nurse (persons)[d]		2,298	1,306	91	6,857	485	527	132
(5) Daily newspapers per 1000 inhabitants[e]		12	155	93	12	42	74	221
(6) Television receivers per 1000 inhabitants[f]		35	275	350	54	112	205	613

Notes

a. 118 economies are included in analysis for the most recent year available, between 1988 and 1990.
b. 197 economies are included in analysis for 1995–2000.
c. 97 economies are included in analysis for the most recent year available, between 1990 and 1993.
d. 73 economies are included in analysis for the most recent year available, between 1990 and 1993.
e. Expressed in number of copies per 1000 inhabitants in 1996.
f. Based on estimates of the number of receivers in use in 1996.

Sources: (1) Population Division and Statistics Division of the United Nations Secretariat, obtained from www.un.org; (2) WRI (1999); and (3) UNESCO (1999).

unavailability of data for most Orthodox economies, only three economies (Bulgaria, Greece and Romania) are included in our analysis. The actual average daily per capita calorie supply as a percentage of total requirements of the Eastern Orthodox area would be reduced substantially if all economies were included since the rest of the Orthodox economies have a much lower average income level than the three in the sample.

Another significant indicator of real living standards is 'life expectancy at birth'. In demography, 'life expectancy at birth' is a measure of the number of years newborn children would be expected to live if subject to the mortality risks prevailing for a cross-section of population at the time of their birth. Usually, a higher living standard will, *ceteris paribus*, result in a longer life expectancy. Among all the seven culture areas, the Western area has the longest life expectancy at birth (73 years for men and 80 years for women), followed by the East Asian (68 years for men and 72 years for women) and Latin American (66 years for men and 73 years for women) areas; in contrast, the African area has the shortest life expectancy (50 years for men and 53 years for women) (see Table 3.2).

While real living standards can benefit from economic growth, they are also determined by other economic and social factors. The lack of social and human progress in China is analysed by Sen (2004) in a case study which draws comparisons between China and an Indian state, Kerala

> At the time of economic reforms, when China had a life expectancy of about 67 years or so, the Indian state of Kerala had a similar figure. By now, however, Kerala's life expectancy of 74 years is very considerably above China's 70. Going further, if we look at specific points of vulnerability, the infant mortality rate in China has declined very slowly since the economic reforms, whereas it has continued to fall very sharply in Kerala. While Kerala had roughly the same infant mortality rate as China – 37 per thousand – at the time of the Chinese reforms in 1979, Kerala's present rate, below 14 per thousand, is less than half of China's 30 per thousand (where it has stagnated over the last decade).

With its daily per capita calorie supply just meeting total requirements, the Indian area has the same level of life expectancy (62 years) for both men and women, demonstrating a quite different pattern from the other culture areas. Altough they have the same level of daily per capita calorie supply as a percentage of total requirements, men's life expectancy in the East Asian area is longer than that of the Latin American area, while women's life expectancy in the Latin American area is longer than that of the East Asian area (see Table 3.2). Whether or not this means that the standard of living for women relative to men in the Latin American area is higher than that in the East Asian area still needs to be investigated in detail.[9]

The indicators that are mainly responsible for health include, besides income level, population per doctor and population per nurse. Naturally, the smaller the population cared for by each doctor and each nurse, *ceteris paribus*, the better the implications for health care in a culture area. But what constitutes a 'qualified' doctor or nurse often varies from country to country, making consistent international comparisons difficult. For example, it has been suggested that it is not always clear whether a 'doctor' in some poor and backward nations will actually be a licensed doctor who has received a regular education at medical school (Hwang, 1993, pp. 123–39).

According to Engel's Law, the proportion of total expenditure on food and other basic necessities drops as income level rises. Expenditure on education, leisure recreation and others, on the other hand, is seen to be more income-elastic. Due to the data unavailability of many key indicators, we look at only two indicators: circulation of daily newspapers (expressed in number of copies per thousand inhabitants) and number of television receivers per thousand inhabitants. Table 3.2 shows that the Western area has the largest number of daily newspapers and television receivers per thousand inhabitants (221 and 613, respectively), whereas the African and Indian areas have the smallest numbers of newspapers and television receivers per thousand inhabitants, approximately one-seventeenth to one-eighteenth those of the Western area, respectively.

Nevertheless, it is necessary to be cautious in applying Engel's Law to cross-national analysis. Statistical data show that countries with the same or similar income levels can have very variable consumer expenditure patterns, while countries with different income levels may demonstrate the same or similar consumer expenditure patterns – which does not conform with Engel's Law. For example, according to the World Bank (1993, pp. 256–7), expenditure on food ranges from 38 per cent in Kenya to 64 per cent in Tanzania (both are lower-income economies) and from 25 per cent in Hungary to 35 per cent in Argentina and South Korea (both are upper-middle-income economies); for clothing and footwear, from 7 per cent in Peru to 16 per cent in Thailand (both are lower-middle-income economies); for rent, fuel and power, from 8 per cent in Tanzania to 17 per cent in Bangladesh (both are lower-income economies) and from 7 per cent in Thailand to 23 per cent in Iran (both are lower-middle-income economies); for medical care, from 2 per cent in Senegal to 6 per cent in Iran (both are lower-middle-income economies); for education, from 1 per cent in Bangladesh to 10 per cent in Kenya (both are lower-income economies); for transportation and communication, from 9 per cent in Japan to 14 per cent in Canada and the USA (all are high-income economies), from 5 per cent in Senegal to 10 per cent in Peru (both are lower-middle-income economies) and from 2 per cent in Tanzania to 7–8 per cent in India and Peru (all are lower-income economies).

It seems very likely that only non-economic factors can account for the above variations.

3.4 Economic differences

3.4.1 General tendency

As a result of diversified natural and social conditions, economic differences have persisted for very many years throughout the world. In the early 1980s, the per capita GNP of the richest economy (the United Arab Emirates) was $23,770, or just less than 300 times that of the poorest economy (Chad, $80). In the late 1990s, however, the per capita GNP gap between the richest (Luxembourg, $37,785) and the poorest economy (Democratic Republic of the Congo, $52) widened enormously to more than 700 times.[10]

The income gap between the fifth of the people living in the richest countries and the fifth in the poorest countries was 74 to 1 in 1997, up from 60 to 1 in 1990 and 30 to 1 in 1960. Before the early twentieth century, too, inequality grew rapidly: the income gap between the top and bottom countries increased from 3 to 1 in 1820 to 7 to 1 in 1870 and 11 to 1 in 1913. By the late 1990s the fifth of the people living in the world's highest-income countries had 86 per cent of the world's total GDP, 82 per cent of the world's total export markets, 68 per cent of the total foreign direct investment and 74 per cent of the world's telephone lines (today's basic means of communication); by contrast, the bottom fifth just had a meagre 1 per cent or so in each category.[11]

Cross-national economic differences can be measured by different comprehensive methods, such as the coefficient of variation (CV), the Gini coefficient (GINI), the standard error (SE), the weighted mean error (MW) and so on. In most cases, these methods are consistent with each other. For tractability, here we use only the CV as the index of economic differences. In 1997 the CV of the world economy was 1.298 when the exchange rate-based per capita GNPs of 199 economies are included; alternatively, it was 1.688 when the *World Bank Atlas*-based per capita GNPs of 167 economies are included. We can see that the cross-national differences should be reduced considerably when the PPP-based per capita GNPs are taken into account, since, as discussed in Section 3.2, the PPP converters tend to increase the levels of per capita GNP for most of the low-income economies and, at the same time, reduce those for most of the high-income economies. The CV of the PPP-based per capita GNPs of 151 economies was 1.089 in 1997, which was lower than derived from both the exchange rates-based and *World Bank Atlas*-based per capita GNPs (see Table 3.3).

Table 3.3 CVs of per capita GNPs by culture area

Culture area	Exchange rate (199 economies)	*World Bank Atlas* (167 economies)	PPP rate (151 economies)
African	2.055	1.538	1.036
East Asian	1.402	1.859	1.203
Eastern Orthodox	1.325	1.437	0.742
Indian	2.037	0.644	0.502
Islamic	1.416	1.069	0.719
Latin American	0.832	0.734	0.490
Western	0.572	0.635	0.443
World	1.398	1.688	1.089

Note: The measurement of the coefficient of variation (CV) is expressed by:

$$CV= \sqrt{\frac{\Sigma(x_i - \bar{x})^2}{N}} \Big/ \bar{x}$$

Where x_i = per capita GNP of country i; $\bar{x} = \Sigma x_i/N$, $x_i = 1, 2, 3, \ldots$ and N; N = total number of observations.

Sources: Calculated by the author based on United Nations (2001) and World Bank (2001).

The inverted-U hypothesis on the relationship between income distribution and economic development was first proposed by Kuznets (1955), who suggested that inequality tends to widen during the initial stage of economic development, with a reversal of this tendency in the later stage.[12] There is mixed evidence for this hypothesis. A number of cross-sectional studies (such as Paukert, 1973; Cline, 1975; Chenery and Syrquin, 1975; Ahluwalia, 1976; Deininger and Squire, 1998) support this hypothesis. However studies by Fields (1991), Jha (1996) and Eichera and Garcia-Penalosab (2001) show that there is no tendency for poorer countries to yield increased rather than decreased inequality or for richer countries to yield decreased rather than increased income inequality. Using cross-national data from before the 1950s, Williamson (1965) finds that the international economic growth process has followed an inverted-U pattern. Can this pattern be used to explain the world development process over the recent decades?

On the basis of the per capita GDPs of the 56 major economies, we can roughly measure the cross-national economic differences from 1950 to 2000. In 1950 the CV was 0.841. Cross-national economic differences narrowed slightly thereafter, by about 10 per cent until 1981, except for 1955 and 1959 in which the CV jumped to 0.954 and 0.984, respectively. Since 1981, however, cross-national economic differences have widened steadily and they were estimated to reach 0.821 by the year 2000, which is about 9 per cent higher than that in 1981 (see Figure 3.1). Williamson's pattern may be used roughly to describe cross-national economic differences for

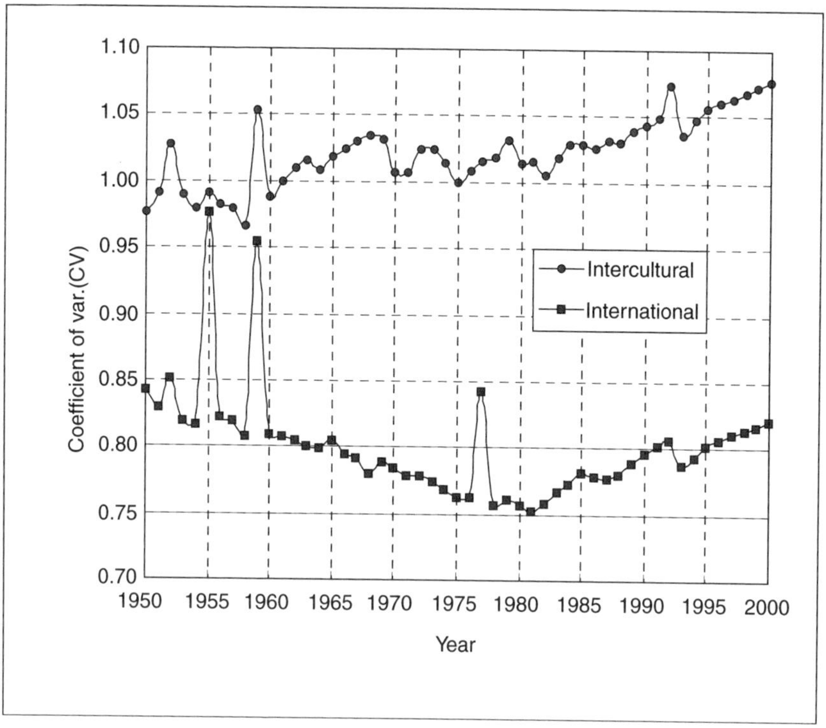

Figure 3.1 Global economic differences, 1950–2000

Source: Calculated by the author based on Maddison (2003).

the 1950s and 1960s. However, viewing the cross-national economic growth process for the 1950–2000 period, we cannot obtain an inverted-U pattern.

In general the world's economic differences mentioned above are composed of two parts – intracultural and intercultural. Specifically, the intracultural economic difference is the sum of the economic differences within each individual culture area; the intercultural economic difference is the sum of the economic differences between all culture areas. Let us analyse this in more detail.

3.4.2 Intercultural difference

The necessary first stage of an investigation into intercultural economic differences is a dynamic examination of the economic gaps between the poorest and richest culture areas. In 1950 the per capita GDP (at 1990 constant prices) of the Western area was G-K$6143 which was 10.38 times that of the Indian area; it was estimated that the Western area's per capita GDP

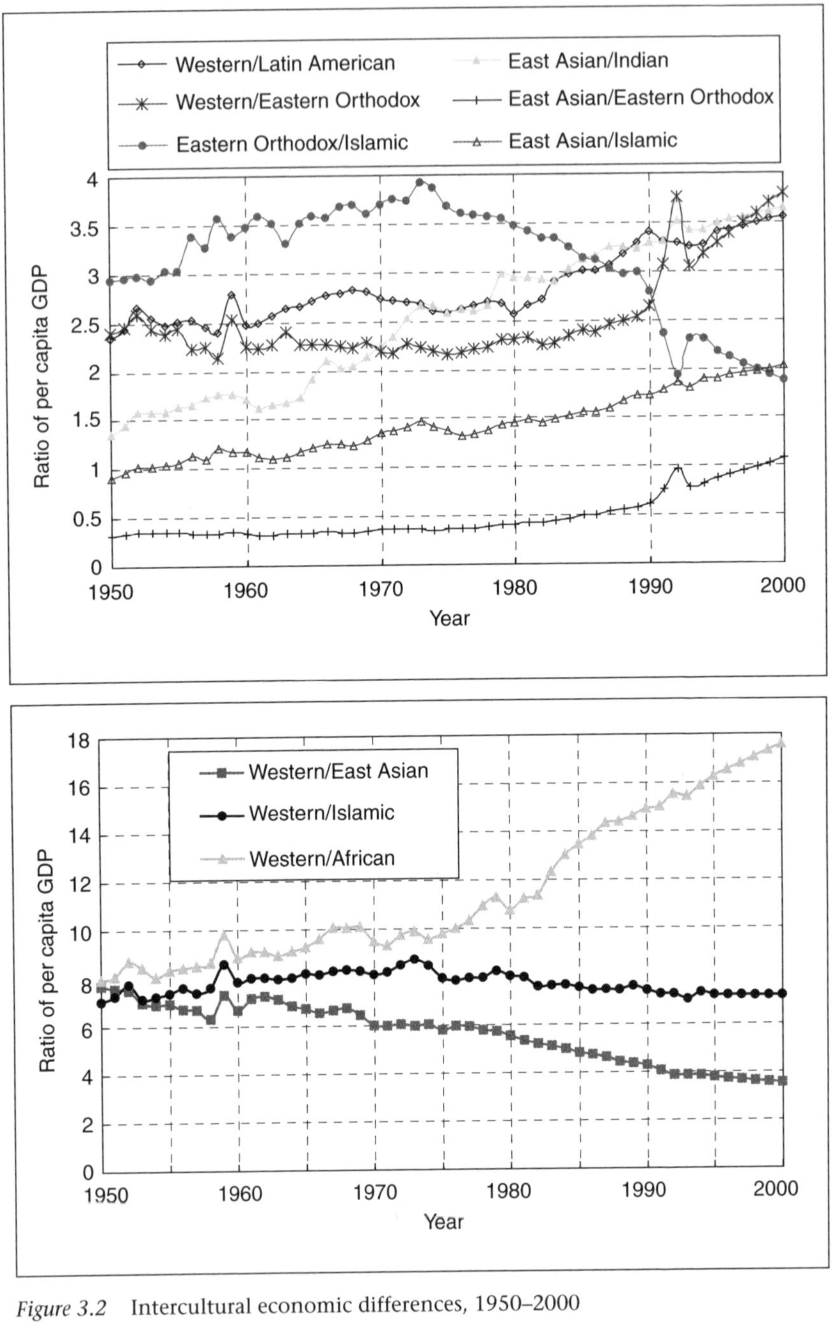

Figure 3.2 Intercultural economic differences, 1950–2000

Source: Calculated by the author based on Maddison (2003).

(at 1990 constant prices) would rise to G-K$19,331 in 2000, amounting to 17.59 times that of the African area (as shown in Figure 3.2). Obviously, the economic gap between the poorest and richest culture areas widened during this period. But how about the final results of intercultural economic differences after all culture areas are taken into account?

The intercultural economic difference of the world as a whole can be measured using the cross-cultural data of per capita GDP (as shown in Figure 3.2). Our result shows that the widened divergence exists for the period from 1950 to 2000: the CV was only 0.98 in 1950 while it rose to 1.08 in 2000 (see Figure 3.1). Although their CV indicators have not changed greatly, the intercultural economic gaps between some culture areas demand particular attention. Specifically, intercultural economic differences have demonstrated different patterns since World War II. On the one hand, per capita GDP gaps narrowed between the Western and East Asian and Eastern Orthodox and Islamic areas; on the other hand, the per capita GDP gaps widened between the Western and African, East Asian and Eastern Orthodox and Western and Latin American areas. The only exception is the Western/Islamic per capita GDP ratio which remained almost unchanged from 1950 to 2000 (see Figure 3.2).

Of all the intercultural economic gaps, that of the Western area with both the African and the East Asian areas needs to be further explained. In 1950 the per capita GDP ratios of the Western area to both the African and the East Asian areas were among the highest (each around eight). Since then, however, the Western/African ratio has increased significantly, whereas the Western/East Asian ratio has decreased steadily. In 2000 they rose to about 18 and fell down to less than four, respectively (see Figure 3.2). Some possible sources for these economic differences will be examined in Chapter 4.

3.4.3 Intracultural difference

The economic difference (measured by the CV index) of each culture area is shown in Table 3.3. After all per capita GNP values are converted into nominal US dollars, the African area had the largest economic difference (2.055), followed by the Indian (2.037), Islamic (1.416) and East Asian (1.402) areas; by way of contrast, the Western area had the smallest economic differences (0.572), followed by the Latin American area (0.832). In terms of the PPP-based per capita GNPs, however, the East Asian area had the largest intracultural economic difference (1.203), followed by the African area (1.036); by way of contrast, the Western area had the smallest intracultural economic difference (0.443), followed by the Latin American (0.490) and Indian (0.502) areas.

How have the intracultural economic differences changed across culture areas and over time? Our estimated results show that the Indian area had the smallest intracultural economic differences in 1950, followed by the Eastern Orthodox and Western areas; in contrast, the African area had the

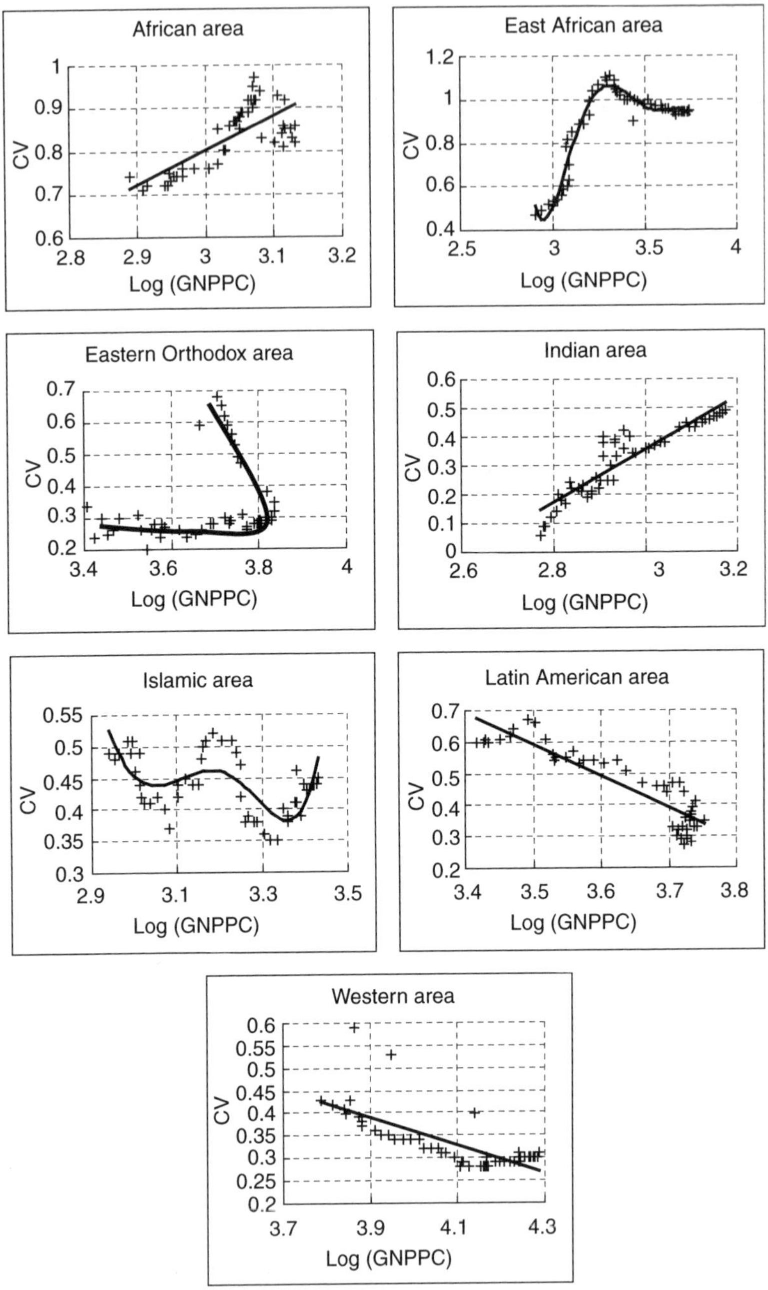

Figure 3.3 Scatter diagrams of CV against log (GNPPC), by culture area

Sources: Drawn by the author based on United Nations (2001), World Bank (2001) and Maddison (2001).

largest intracultural economic differences, followed by the Latin American and East Asian areas. However, by 2000, the Western area would enjoy the smallest intracultural economic difference, followed by the Latin American and Islamic areas. By way of contrast, the East Asian area would have the largest intracultural economic difference, followed by the African area.[13]

The determinants of intracultural economic difference are assessed by considering the CV index of a panel of countries observed from 1950 to 2000. Figure 3.3 shows a scatter diagram of these values against contemporaneous values of the log of per capita GNP (GNPPC) for each culture area. It is obvious from the scatter of plot of the East Asian area that a Kuznets curve would show up as an inverted-U relationship between the CV value and the log of GNPPC (that is, intracultural economic difference first increases and later decreases during the process of economic development). This relationship, however, doesn't exist in the other culture areas. For example, the value of intracultural CV tends to rise with respect to the log of per capita GNP in the African and Indian areas and to fall with respect to the log of the per capita GNP in the Latin American and Western areas. What is more ambiguous is the relation between the value of intracultural CV and the log of per capita GNP in both the Eastern Orthodox and Islamic areas. Specifically, the curve in the Islamic area shows that the intracultural economic divergence may be either positively or negatively related to the log of per capita GNP, depending on income level; and that in the Eastern Orthodox area suggests that the intracultural economic divergence may either remain almost unchanged with respect to, or be negatively related to, the log of per capita GNP.

3.4.4 Decomposition of the economic differences

The common tool for decomposition of the economic differences has been the Theil index. The simplest form of Theil index (I_0) is expressed as follows:

$$I_0 = \frac{1}{N}\sum_i \log\left(\frac{x}{x_i}\right) \tag{3.1}$$

where x_i is the economic indicator (such as income level and per capita GDP) of the ith country (region) ($i = 1, 2, \ldots$ and N); x is the mean value of all x_i; N is the number of countries (regions).

Mathematically, if the N countries (regions) are divided into M culture areas ($M \leq N$), I_0 can be further decomposed into two parts (I_{0A} and I_{0B}):[14]

$$I_0 = I_{0A} + I_{0B}, \text{ where } I_{0A} = \frac{1}{N}\sum_k N_k I_0^k \text{ and } I_{0B} = \frac{1}{N}\sum_k N_k \log\left(\frac{\mu}{\mu_k}\right). \tag{3.2}$$

where I_{0A} and I_{0B} denote the intracultural and intercultural economic differences, respectively; I_0^k is the Theil index of the kth culture area (it is

Table 3.4 Decomposition of the world's economic differences, selected years from 1950–2000

Year	Theil index (I_0)	Intracultural difference (I_{0A})	Intercultural difference (I_{0B})
1950	80.63 (100.00)	46.28 (57.40)	34.35 (42.60)
1960	76.74 (100.00)	44.92 (58.53)	31.82 (41.47)
1970	78.03 (100.00)	54.21 (69.47)	23.82 (30.53)
1980	66.73 (100.00)	51.61 (77.34)	15.12 (22.66)
1990	72.23 (100.00)	59.93 (82.97)	12.30 (17.03)
2000	91.80 (100.00)	74.45 (81.10)	17.35 (18.90)

Notes: All figures are multiplied by 1000; figures within parentheses are percentages.

calculated by Equation (3.1)); μ_k is the economic indicator (such as income level and per capita GDP) of the *k*th culture area ($k = 1, 2, \ldots$ and M); μ is the mean value of all μ_k; N_k is the number of countries (regions) of the *k*th culture area (where $N_k<N$ and $N_1 + N_2 + \ldots + N_M = N$). Using the above methodology, we can estimate the indicators of intracultural and intercultural differences (I_{0A} and I_{0B}), respectively.

As shown in Table 3.4, the Theil index of the per capita GDPs for the 56 major economies was U-shaped between 1950 and 2000. This indicates that economic differences increased during the last decades of the twentieth century, which is consistent with the pattern illustrated in Figure 3.1. After having decomposed the Theil index, we may find that the intracultural difference (I_{0A}) has always contributed a larger amount to the Theil index (I_0) than the intercultural difference (I_{0B}).

Specifically, I_{0A} experienced significant increases during most of the years monitored; in contrast, I_{0B} was reduced. The intracultural economic difference produced only 57.4 per cent of the economic differences of the world as a whole in 1950, while this figure rose to 81.1 per cent in 2000. Naturally, the share of intercultural economic difference in the total economic differences of the world as a whole (that is, I_0) decreased, from 42.60 per cent in 1950 to 18.90 per cent in 2000. We can see that the only exception was that from 1990 to 2000 the share of intracultural economic difference to I_0 decreased slightly from 82.97 per cent to 81.1 per cent and that of intercultural economic difference to I_0 increased from 17.03 per cent to 18.9 per cent.

3.5 Summary

In this chapter, a dynamic comparison of the world economy has been conducted via seven culture areas – African, East Asian, Eastern Orthodox, Indian, Islamic, Latin American and Western. It is generally admitted that the Western area has the highest income level and standard of living. By contrast, the Indian area – or, if measurement is made using the PPP method the African area – has the lowest income level and, naturally, the lowest standard of living. During the period from 1950 to 2000, as a result of either relatively fast economic growth in the high-income culture areas or relatively slow economic growth in the low-income culture areas, the multicultural economic inequalities have widened. Particularly noteworthy is the fact that, while both were located at the bottom of the world economy during the early 1950s, the East Asian area has raised its per capita GDP far more significantly than the African and Indian areas.

The results derived from this chapter show that in 1950 the Indian area had the smallest intracultural economic differences, followed by the Eastern Orthodox and Western areas; in contrast, the African area had the largest intracultural economic differences, followed by the Latin American and East Asian areas. However, by 2000 the Western area would enjoy the smallest intracultural economic difference, followed by the Latin American and Islamic areas; by way of contrast, the East Asian area would have the largest intracultural economic difference, followed by the African area.

A series of questions can be derived from this chapter. They include, inter alia: Why has the economic development process of the seven culture areas become so different from each other? What are the inherent causes for the differing patterns of the existing culture areas? Furthermore, from the standpoint of political economics, we still lack any convincing evidence to answer other questions, such as: Why was the ancient civilization of India so tardy in fully exploiting possibilities for growth? Why have some East Asian economies had such high growth rates? Why is the African area still stuck at the income level that most of the Western economies had more than a century ago? Last but not least, there are more puzzles for international economic theorists and practitioners. They include, for example: Why has Germany not attracted more foreign direct investment (FDI) than the UK? Why has France sustained a better foreign trade performance than Italy?

Existing economic theories and evidence in development experience conflict with one another in some circumstances. As a result cultural influences on the world economy – no matter whether they are positive or negative – should be further clarified.

4
Causes for Intercultural Economic Differences

> The blind men were asked to feel an elephant and report what they thought it was. The first blind person examined and manipulated the tail, noting its size and frayed end. It is a rope, he exclaimed! The second blind person concentrated on the leg, noting the knobby skin and its huge size. He concluded it was the trunk of a tree and a large one at that. The third blind person handled the elephant's trunk the best he could because it wiggled and waggled. He reported that what was in front of him was a snake and it was pretty spry.
>
> (An old fable)

4.1 Physical capital

Natural resources once figured prominently as a production factor in studies of economic growth. At times, natural resources (such as land, climate, biology, water, minerals and energy) have indeed been the primary component among the factors that influence social and economic activities. But early pessimists like Malthus (1798) and Ricardo (1817) were probably wrong about the importance of scarce natural resources as a retardant of growth.[1] This is most obviously evidenced in the fact that, in spite of the enormous increase in the world population, and given the unchanged human biological needs for food, the proportion of employment in agriculture has dropped enormously. After having examined the development process of the world as a whole for the twentieth century, especially for the postwar period, it seems unlikely that there exists to any extent a positive correlation between economic growth and endowment of natural resources.

Neoclassical theory emphasizes capital accumulation (or saving) and changes of exogenous inputs such as technology and population.[2] According to this theory, an economy's growth rate will, in the long term, simply equal the rate of growth of labour and capital plus technological innovation. In many neoclassical growth models, a country's economic growth rate tends to be inversely related to its starting level of per capita income. In particular, if countries are similar with respect to structural parameters for preferences and technology, then poor countries tend to grow faster than rich countries. Thus, there is a force that promotes convergence in levels of per capita income across countries throughout the world. Clearly the main element behind the convergence in neoclassical economic growth models is diminishing returns to reproducible capital. Poor countries with low ratios of capital to labour have high marginal products of capital and thereby tend to grow at high rates. This tendency for low-income countries to grow at high rates is reinforced in extensions of the neoclassical models that allow for equilibrating mobility of labour, capital and technology. Using neoclassical theory, Gould and Ruffin (1993) also conclude that over time the per capita incomes of rich and poor countries will converge due to the law of diminishing returns.

However it seems that the above hypothesis on economic convergence is inconsistent with the evidence obtained in a number of case studies. For some countries, especially mature ones, such as the USA, Japan and some western European countries, the cross-regional convergence of per capita incomes has indeed occurred (Barro and Sala-i-Martin, 1995, ch. 11), but in a number of others (especially in the developing countries, such as China (Zhao, 2001), India (Nair, 1985) and Indonesia (Hill and Weidemann, 1989), to list but three), one can only find a divergent pattern of per capita incomes. Moreover, some cross-country studies have also indicated that per capita growth rates have little correlation with the starting level of per capita product. For example, Summers and Heston (1988) use data from 98 countries and find that the average growth rate of per capita gross domestic product (GDP) from 1960 to 1985 is not significantly related to the 1960 value of real per capita GDP (the correlation is only 9 per cent).[3] Possibly due to this judgement, Lucas (1988) and Rebelo (1991) assume that the growth rate of per capita GDP is independent of the starting level of per capita GDP.

During the last decades of the twentieth century investment as a ratio of GDP has experienced a wide range of fluctuations (see Figure 4.1a). In the late 1960s, for example, the lowest ratio of investment to GDP in the developing countries was less than 17 per cent, while the highest ratio was above 25 per cent in 1975 and 1977. This suggests that the developing countries must have experienced different economic performances, particularly given (in comparison to the developed countries) their weakness in well-trained human resources and lack of advanced technologies (both of which, as will be discussed later, are also strong driving forces for economic development). A comparison between developed and developing countries may help us to reach the conclusion that, except for a few years, the ratios of investment to GDP have tended to become convergent since the 1960s.

(a)

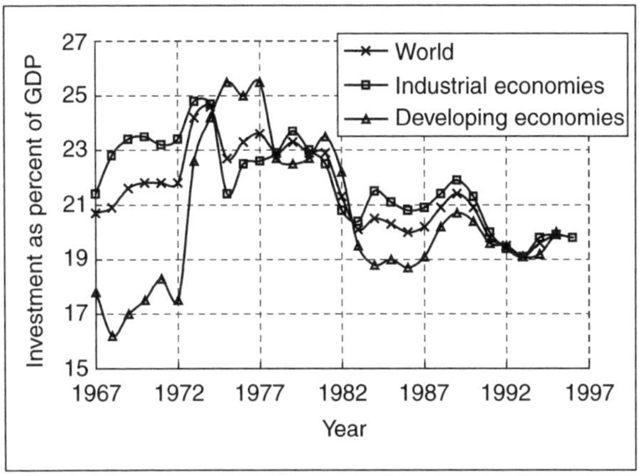

(b)

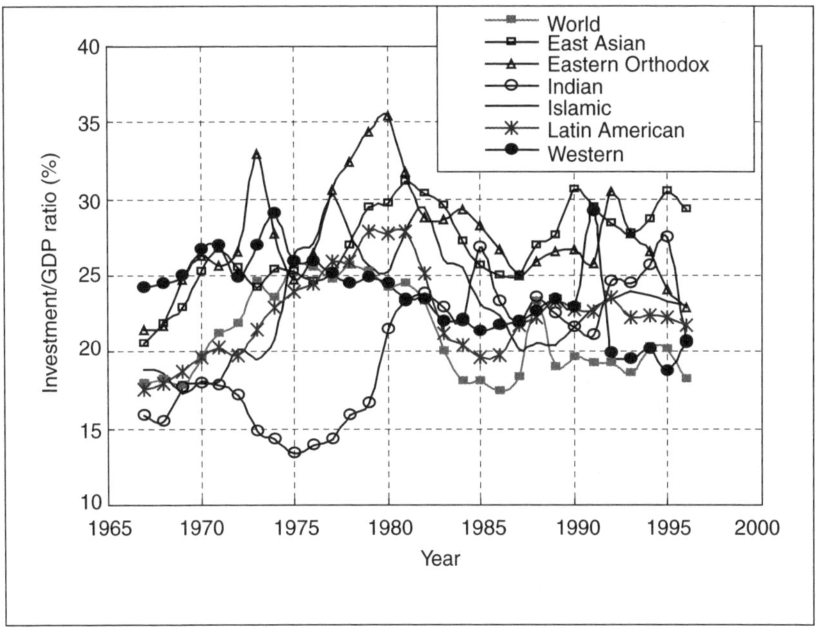

Figure 4.1 Investment/GDP ratios, 1967–96

Source: Based on IMF (1997b, pp. 152–5).

Interculturally, the investment/GDP ratios have demonstrated different patterns during the past decades, as shown in Figure 4.1b. The Western area had put the highest portion of GDP into capital construction before the early 1970s. During most of the 1970s and 1980s the Eastern Orthodox area took the lead, with its investment as a percentage of GDP surprisingly reaching the highest level in 1980. After 1990, apart from 1992 and 1993, the East Asian area began to lead other culture areas. Nevertheless, of the seven culture areas, the African and Indian areas had the lowest ratios of investment to GDP, which may explain, at least partially, their relatively low economic growth rates during the past decades.[4] During 1967 and 1981 the Indian area had the lowest ratios of investment to GDP; while during 1982 and 1996 the African area had the lowest ratios of investment to GDP.

Figure 4.1b also indicates that capital accumulation, though remaining at the highest level of intercultural differences during 1973 and 1980, generally followed a slightly convergent process during the 1967–96 period. According to neoclassical theory, as a result of the convergence of capital accumulation among all the culture areas, the intercultural economic differences should, *ceteris paribus*, have been reduced accordingly. Figure 3.2, however, does not confirm this assumption. Therefore, other factors must have contributed to the divergent growth pattern of the world economy.

4.2 Human capital

> If you plan for a year, sow a seed; if for ten years, plant a tree; if for a hundred years, teach the people. You will reap a single harvest by sowing a seed once and ten harvests by planting a tree; while you will reap a hundred harvests by teaching the people.
>
> (Guan Zhong, 551–479 BC)

Information about the economically active population, a term defined by economists as 'all men or women who simply work for the production of economic goods and services during a specific period', can be found in Table 4.1. Briefly in the 1990s more than 40 per cent of the world population was employed, of whom one-third or more were female employees; each individual worked, on average, 736 hours per year. Particularly noteworthy are the gender differences between culture areas. For example, the female labourers of the Indian and Islamic areas comprised only 16.5 per cent and 18.3 per cent of their total labourers, respectively. These figures were much lower than that of the Eastern Orthodox area (44.4 per cent), the Western area (42.5 per cent) and the rest. If there are no other convincing reasons for this seriously unbalanced employment pattern between males and females it might plausibly be taken to imply that women have not been placed in a position of equality in Indian and Islamic societies. It is also noticeable that the East Asian area had an incredibly high level of per capita annual labour input (947 hours), compared with the others, especially the African (608 hours), Latin American (643 hours), Western

(709 hours) and Eastern Orthodox (717 hours) areas. The high labour input of the East Asian area may help us to understand, at least in part, its rapid economic growth during this period.

However a huge labour force does not sufficiently represent an advantage in human resources for economic development, particularly when a country is undergoing transformation from an agricultural society, mainly using traditional methods of production to an industrial society, which requires not only new and advanced technologies but also well-trained personnel. A well-educated and law-abiding population that possesses a strong work ethic is the sine qua non of modern economic growth. A striking feature of the world economy in the twentieth century was the enormous increase in the average level of education. Before the nineteenth century the majority of the population was illiterate in almost all countries. Since then, universal enrolment in primary education has become obligatory in advanced countries. As a result the proportion of people receiving secondary and higher education has risen steadily.[5]

Education as a factor of production was first stressed by Schulz (1961) in his analysis of human capital and has since been rediscovered by 'new' growth theorists (see Section 4.3). Data on education stock should be readjusted before an international comparison is conducted, because educational systems usually differ from country to country. Nevertheless, primary school enrolment ratios have often been used as a crude proxy in the new growth literature, though it is sometimes not an internationally comparable measure for changes in human capital.[6] In the mid-1990s gross primary school enrolment ratios were 89 per cent for males and 82 per cent for females, an average of 86 per cent, for the total population of primary school age (see Table 4.1). Interculturally, the Western area had the highest gross enrolment ratio (104 per cent),[7] followed by the East Asian (96 per cent) and Latin American (89 per cent) areas; in contrast, the African area had the lowest gross enrolment ratio (only 53 per cent), followed by the Indian (72 per cent) and Islamic (73 per cent) areas. It is also worth noting that there were larger differences between gross enrolment ratios of males and females in the Indian (81 per cent for male and 63 per cent for female) and Islamic (79 per cent for male and 67 per cent for female) areas than in the other culture areas.

A glance at the world's development process reveals information that tends to contradict current growth theories. There is no doubt that the success of economies in achieving faster growth has been facilitated by the relatively higher inputs in education. But there are exceptions, for example, during the 1960s the Philippines had a higher level of education than South Korea, but sustained, at the same time, a much lower rate of economic growth than the latter. In the early 1960s these two countries displayed similar major macroeconomic indicators (such as GDP per capita, investment per capita and average saving rate) except that the Philippines

Table 4.1 Characteristics of human capital, by culture area, 1990s

Item	African	East Asian	Eastern Orthodox	Indian	Islamic	Latin American	Western	World
Proportion of female labour (%)[a]	38.1	37.3	44.4	16.5	18.3	26.6	42.5	36.2
Ratio of employment to population (%)[a]	39.3	44.0	42.0	34.6	30.1	33.1	44.5	40.5
Per capita labour input (in hours)[a]	608	947	717	762	736	643	709	736
Gross enrolment ratios[b]	53	96	86	72	73	89	104	86
(1) Male	58	98	85	81	79	89	104	89
(2) Female	50	94	86	63	67	90	105	82

Notes
a. Calculated by the author based on Maddison (1996, table J-1).
b. Gross enrolment in primary education.
Source: UNESCO (1999).

had a higher level of education than South Korea. During the following decades, however, South Korea maintained a much faster economic growth than the Philippines. Other evidence comes from China whose cross-provincial data on educational level and economic development were not positively correlated in the 1980s.[8]

4.3 Technological innovation

Technological innovation has been the most fundamental element in promoting, either directly or indirectly, economic development and social change. Although it is very difficult to measure its short-term impact precisely, no one would reject the idea that technological progress is changing the world at an incredibly high rate. The most obvious contributions are in transport and communications where crude means (such as horses, carriages and handwritten letters) have been superseded by superjets, telephones and faxes, as well as by increasingly efficient computer networks, including the Internet which is becoming the most important means for transmitting information.[9] Mobile telephones, computer networks and other technological inventions which were once considered to be either impossible or useless, are now becoming the necessities of our daily life.

Before the early twentieth century, technological innovation had been contributed mainly by individual inventors or small-scale entrepreneurs. But now the great bulk of it – such as the space shuttle and the Internet, to list but two – is conducted by prominent firms with substantial budgets, as well as by governments. As a result the process of technological innovation has become more complicated than ever before. Specifically, technological and related products are positively related to capital stock of, and personnel engagement in, technological innovation. In addition, technological innovation is also related to educational levels, as the content of education changes over time to accommodate to the growing stock of knowledge. There has been a proliferation of specialized intellectual disciplines to facilitate the absorption of knowledge and to promote its development through research.

Personnel engagement in technological innovation is unevenly distributed among culture areas (see Table 4.2). On the one hand, the Eastern Orthodox and Western areas had 2998 and 2709 scientist and engineers per million population, respectively; on the other hand, the Indian, African and Latin American areas had only 149, 221 and 258 scientists and engineers per million population, respectively. Research and development (R&D) is indispensable not only for the advancement of new technologies

Table 4.2 Selected R&D indicators by culture area,1990–95

Culture area[a]	**Scientists and engineers per million population**	**R&D/GNP (%)**		
		Exchange rates[b]	***Atlas* method**[c]	**PPP rates**[d]
African (7)	221	0.54	0.56	0.45
East Asian (12)	848	2.41	2.40	1.34
Eastern Orthodox (6)	2998	0.78	0.79	0.77
Indian (1)	149	0.80	0.80	0.80
Islamic (7)	367	0.58	0.62	0.60
Latin American (11)	258	0.51	0.50	0.49
Western (28)	2709	2.19	2.20	2.15
World (72)	1007	2.07	2.08	1.61

Notes

a. Figures within parentheses are numbers of economies included.

b. GDP of 1995 is used for weighting.

c. GNP of 1995 is used for weighting; only 6 economies are included in the Islamic area.

d. GDP of 1995 is used for weighting; only 11 and 26 economies are included for the East Asian and Western areas, respectively.

Source: Calculated by the author, based on WRI (1999, pp. 236–7) and UN (1996, table 5.1).

and products, but also for the improvement of those that already exist. A rough calculation of the 72 sampled economies indicates that during 1990 and 1995 annual R&D expenditures averaged 2.07 per cent, 2.08 per cent or 1.61 per cent of total GNP, depending on which measurement – exchange rates, the *World Bank Atlas* method or PPP rates – is applied (see Table 4.2). An intercultural comparison of R&D expenditures simply shows that the R&D/GNP ratio was largest for the East Asian area (if the exchange rates and *Atlas* method are used for weighting) and for the Western area (if the PPP rates are used for weighting). In all cases, nevertheless, the R&D/GNP ratios of the Latin American and African areas were the smallest (approximately one-fourth that of the East Asian area or Western area).

A state's policies, particularly economic incentives, are important influences on the long-run economic growth rate. In endogenous growth theory, technological innovation is treated as endogenously determined by the accumulation of human capital, research and development (R&D), learning-by-doing and so on. Clearly, human capital plays a special role in a number of endogenous growth models. In Romer (1990), for example, human capital is treated as a key input to the research sector in which new products or ideas that underlie technological innovation are generated. As a result countries with greater initial stocks of human capital will experience more rapid growth. In the international case, the spread of new ideas across countries also plays an important role in economic growth. As Nelson and Phelps (1966) suggest, a larger stock of human capital makes it easier for a country to absorb new products or ideas that have been discovered elsewhere. Therefore, a follower country with more human capital tends to grow faster because it catches up more rapidly with the technological leader.

Using the models that emphasize the importance of the educated population, Griliches (1979) and Romer (1990) conclude that convergence of per capita incomes between rich and poor countries is not inevitable, because growth will tend to be faster in the countries where workers are better educated and policies that align social and private rates of return are implemented. Barro (1991) uses school enrolment rates as proxies for human capital and shows that, for a given starting value of per capita GDP, a country's subsequent growth rate is positively related to these measures of initial human capital and, given the human capital variables, subsequent growth is substantially negatively related to the initial level of per capita GDP. Thus, in this modified sense, Barro supports the convergence hypothesis of neoclassical growth models (a poor country tends to grow faster than a rich country), but only for a given quantity of human capital. In other words, only if the poor country's human capital exceeds the amount that typically accompanies the low level of per capita income.

The new growth model is insightful for explaining the continuous growth of the developed nations, which use the most advanced tech-

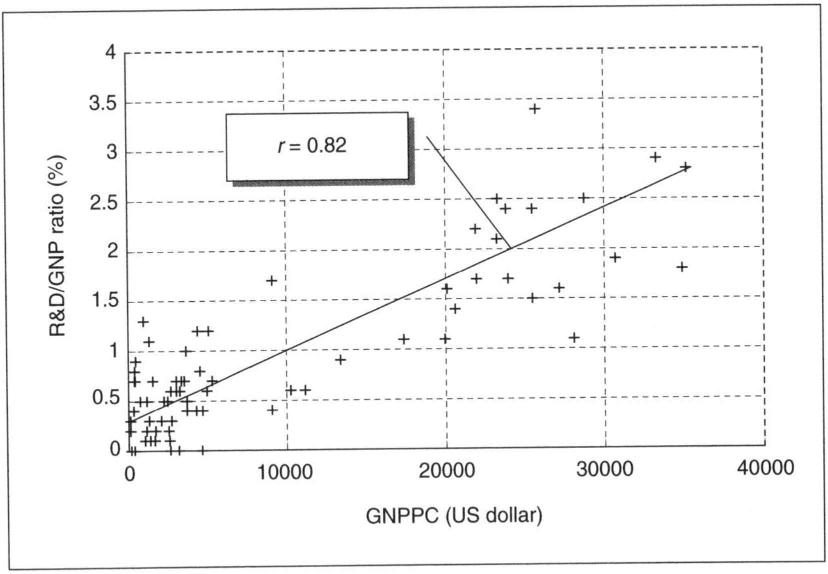

Figure 4.2 Correlation between the R&D/GNP ratio and GNP per capita

Source: As for Table 4.2.

nologies. However the theory cannot easily explain the extraordinary growth and convergence of the newly industrialized economies (NIEs) in Asia – including South Korea, Taiwan, Hong Kong, Singapore and recently China – during the last three decades of the twentieth century (see Pack, 1994; and Grossman and Helpman, 1994). For example, China made rapid economic growth although the ratio of R&D to GNP fell considerably from the mid-1980s to the mid-1990s. China's cross-provincial data do not offer any statistical support to a significant correlation between the R&D/GNP ratio and per capita GNP in China (Guo, 1999, p. 108).

The evidence from a panel of nations indicates that the positive correlation ($r = 0.82$) between the R&D/GNP ratio and per capita GNP (see Figure 4.2) demonstrates that the higher the level of per capital GNP, the larger the ratio of the R&D to GNP, and vice versa. This correlation also plausibly indicates that, *ceteris paribus*, high-income economies should always enjoy – as a result of rapid technological progress – higher growth rates than low-income economies. Obviously, this cannot be used to interpret convincingly the process of the narrowing gap between the advanced economies and the successful followers (such as Japan, then Taiwan, South Korea and mainland China) throughout the twentieth century. In other words, other reasons must exist for some, if not all, developing economies to have grown faster than the advanced economies. One of them may derive from international trade through which developing countries can enjoy the advantage of being able to introduce new technology from advanced countries and can therefore expect rapid technological progress and industrialization.

4.4 Political and institutional bases

If we are to explain why economic growth rates have been so diverse among nations, it is necessary for us to consider political and institutional influences. Institutions in economic research are analysed as formal (laws, regulations) and informal (customs, traditions, norms) rules that structure and simplify human interactions within a society. Historically, institutions have been devised by human beings to create order and reduce uncertainty in exchange. They evolve incrementally connecting the past with the present and the future (North, 1991). According to new institutional economics, the economic system, like other production factors required in economic development, is a special kind of scarce resource and should be treated thus. The economic system of any nation is the mechanism that brings together natural resources, labour, technology and the necessary managerial talents. Anticipating and then meeting human needs through production and distribution of goods and services is the end purpose of every economic system. While the type of economic system applied by a nation is usually artificially decided, it is also to a large extent the result of historical experience, which becomes over time a part of political culture.

Historical evidence suggests that the Western countries gradually pulled ahead of the rest of the world from the sixteenth century.[10] Northern Italy and Flanders played the leading role from the sixteenth to the seventeenth centuries, the Netherlands from then until the end of the eighteenth century, the UK and Germany in the nineteenth and the USA since then. The main institutional characteristics of Western society that have favoured its development can be broadly summarized as follows: (1) the recognition of human capacity to transform the forces of nature through rational investigation and experiment and (2) the ending of feudal constraints on the free purchase and sale of property, followed by a whole series of developments which gave scope for successful entrepreneurship (Maddison, 1996, p. 50).

However, country situations differ greatly throughout the world and it is difficult to reach any generalized conclusion about the influence of deeper layers of causality. For this we need individual country narratives. At the same time, it is also worth noting that Western-style institutions may not work well in other economies, which may have different demographic, cultural and historical conditions. For example, considering the four systems (British, French, German and Scandinavian) which La Porta et al. (1999) use to categorize the origins of nations, Lin (2001) suggests that the

French and German legal systems are more favourable to the economic growth of less-developed nations than those of British and Scandinavian origin.

Since the fall of the socialist system in 1990, old institutions which had provided a degree of economic and social stability to society have been rapidly destroyed and new market-oriented ideologies have spread rapidly throughout the economic environment of the former Soviet Union. By the late 1990s, however, while many elements of a market-based formal framework had been established, its implementation was often weak. The enforcement of new laws and regulations has been constrained by the presence of old informal institutions – the strong bureaucracy, the weak respect for law, informal networking and other social factors, which were historically rooted in the behaviour of Soviet society. As a result the speed and sequencing of economic reforms, which were important at the beginning of the transition, seem to be becoming less important in comparison with the necessity of institutional transformation.

During the twentieth century the failure of the centrally planned economies (CPEs) to keep pace with their market-oriented counterparts demonstrated clearly enough that planning entire economies at the central government level is not a productive path to long-term development. But the experiences of East Asia, especially of Japan, South Korea and China make clear that it is possible for a country to have an interventionist government and still enjoy extremely rapid economic growth over a period of decades. Nevertheless, certain policies that helped Japan develop in the 1950s and 1960s, generated growth in East Asia in the 1970s and 1980s and, more recently, sparked China's economic boom in the 1980s and 1990s were specific to the time and place. They may not have worked well in other countries, nor are they likely to be appropriate in the opening decades of the twenty-first century.

Various attempts have been made to provide a theoretical and empirical explanation of economic growth at the 'institutional' level.[11] It is, however, very difficult to conduct any meaningful economic comparison between a large number of economies with different political, historical and cultural backgrounds. Following Gastil's (1987, p. 210) division of countries into economic systems with respect to the role of government, Barro (1991), for example, tried to differentiate quantitatively the primarily socialist, mixed socialist and free enterprise and primarily free enterprise economies. His estimated coefficient for socialist economies is negative on growth but that for mixed systems is essentially zero. Because the division of economic systems into groups is subjective and because there are only nine 'socialist' countries in the sample, these results are not very reliable.

Using a country narrative approach, Rodrik and his collaborators have tried to explore the respective roles of microeconomic and macroeconomic policies, institutions, political economy and initial conditions in driving patterns of technological convergence and accumulation in selected countries (see Rodrik, 2003) for detailed analysis of these country narratives). However, application of the analytic narrative approach, as Rodrik (2003, pp. 2–3) confessed, could be clouded by preconceptions of the institutional influences on economic growth in each country.

Might political stability be a better factor to explain the engines for economic development than the political system? To measure political stability, Barro (1991) included two variables (the number of revolutions and coups per year and the number of political assassinations per million population per year). Using Banks's (1979) data set, Barro found that each of these variables is significantly negative for economic growth. So what determines political stability? Naturally, economic factors, such as economic growth and income distribution, may play a very critical role. Londregan and Poole (1989), for example, found a negative association between economic growth and political instability. But what is the primary cause driving this political and economic feedback loop? In fact, although Barro's (1991) results do reflect a positive influence of growth on political stability, rather than (or in addition to) the effects of stability on growth, it still needs further statistical proofs for the hypothesis that economic growth more decisively influences political stability rather than the opposite.

To conclude, existing growth theories and evidence in development experience are conflicting. Furthermore, from the standpoint of political economics, we still lack any convincing evidence to explain, for example, why Latin America's economic performance has been worse than North America's. Why were the ancient civilizations of Asia so tardy in fully exploiting possibilities for growth? Why is the African area stuck at the income level that most Western economies had more than a century ago? Nor can we find any convincing evidence for the differing economic performances between countries that have the same or similar geographic, economic or political conditions.

4.5 External and boundary conditions

In the *Wealth of Nations* (1776), Adam Smith explained not only the critical role that the market played in the relocation of a nation's resources but also the nature of the social order that it achieved and helped to maintain. Applying his ideas about economic activity within a country to specialization and exchange between countries, Smith concluded that countries should specialize in and export those commodities in which they had an absolute advantage and should import those commodities in which the trading partner had an absolute advantage. Each country should export those commodities it produced most efficiently because the absolute labour required per unit was less than that of the prospective trading partner.

According to Smith, there is a basis for trade because nations are clearly better off specializing in their lower-cost commodities and importing the commodities that can be produced more cheaply abroad.

Although Smith's ideas were crucial for the early development of classical thought and for altering the view of the potential gains from international trade, it was David Ricardo who expanded upon Smith's concepts and demonstrated that the potential gains from trade were far greater than Adam Smith had envisioned in his concept of absolute advantage. In *The Principles of Political Economy and Taxation* (1817), Ricardo noted that industry locates where the greatest absolute advantage exists and that labour and capital move to the area where productivity and returns are the greatest. This movement would continue until factor returns were equalized. Internationally, however, the story is quite different. While international trade can take place on the basis of absolute advantage, given the international immobility of the factors of production, gains from trade on the basis of comparative advantage can occur as well.

During the first half of the twentieth century economic contacts and exchanges between many countries were interrupted time and again due to international tensions, especially the two world wars (from 1914 to 1918; and from 1939 to 1945, respectively). Since the late 1940s and fostered by global and regional interdependence in terms of flows of information, technology, capital, people and cultural influences, the degree of interaction between different parts of the world has grown greatly. For example, in 1950, the ratio of exports to GDP was only a meagre 7 per cent; by 2000, however, it rose to about 18 per cent.[12] This growth has been important because it enables countries to benefit from exporting those commodities it can produce more cheaply and importing those that can be produced more efficiently abroad.[13]

Interculturally, foreign trade performance has differed greatly in the world. At the end of the twentieth century, the Western area had the largest per capita value of foreign trade (more than $8000), followed by the East Asian and Latin American areas (each with nearly $1500), the Eastern Orthodox and Islamic areas (each with less than $1000), and the African (less than $300) and Indian (less than $100) areas.[14] It is obvious that a strong correlation exists between per capita GNP and per capita value of foreign trade. As rising per capita GNP may lead to improvements in transportation technology (which reduces costs and makes distance less significant) and international competitiveness, it will promote the export of goods and services. In the meantime, the importation of consumption goods also increases with respect to income level.

The determinants of intercultural trade may also be different from those of intracultural trade. As shown by the East Asian case study in Table 4.3, geographical factors (expressed by the natural log of distance between trade partners) have a significant influence on external trade (that is, trade with

Table 4.3 Determinants of internal and external trade in East Asia

Explanatory variable	Trade with internal economies	Trade with external economies
Constant	–13.371 (2.837[a])	–11.711 (1.380[a])
$\ln(GNP_iGNP_j)$	1.123 (0.103[a])	1.306 (0.023[a])
$\ln(GNPPC_iGNPPC_j)$	–0.076 (0.125)	–0.097 (0.031[a])
$\ln(DISTANCE_{ij})$	0.016 (0.312)	–0.730 (0.147[a])
$LANGUAGE_{ij}$	1.537 (1.752)	6.464 (1.289[a])
$RELIGION_{ij}$	2.322 (1.011[b])	0.560 (0.301[c])
R square	0.408	0.622
F-statistic	34.29	877.84
Number of observations	254	2669

Notes:
(1) Dependent variable is the natural log of bilateral trade in 1995 (in thousand US dollars).
(2) Except LANGUAGE and RELIGION (which, as defined in Equation (7.4), denote each trade partner's linguistic and religious similarities, respectively), all other explanatory variables are measured in the natural log form.
(3) The East Asian economies include Brunei, Cambodia, China (mainland), Hong Kong, Indonesia, Japan, Korea (North), Korea (South), Laos, Malaysia, Myanmar, Philippines, Singapore, Thailand, and Vietnam.
(4) Figures within parentheses are standard errors.
[a], [b] and [c] denote statistically significant at the 1%, 5% and 10% levels, respectively.

Source: Guo (2006).

non-East Asian economies). The estimated coefficient of external trade on distance (–0.730, which is statistically significant at the 1 per cent confidence level) suggests that a 1 per cent increase in distance will reduce the amount of trade with the non-East Asian economies by 0.730 per cent. However the estimated coefficient of internal trade on distance is not only very small (0.016) but also statistically insignificant even at the 10 per cent level, showing that geographical factors have almost no effect on trade within East Asian economies. What is more interesting are variations in the influences of linguistic and religious patterns on internal and external trade. For example, the linguistic influences on East Asia's trade with external economies are more significant than those on internal economies. By contrast, the religious influences on East Asia's trade with internal economies are more significant than those on external economies. These results suggest that, in East Asia, religion should be more important in the determinants of internal trade than language, while language should be more important in the determinants of external trade than 'religion'.[15]

4.6 Cultural issues

The term 'cultural pattern' refers to the way in which people relate to one another. This differs to some extent from society to society. The primary kind of cultural pattern is based on kinship. In most societies, a family unit includes only the father and mother and the unmarried child (children); but it can also be larger, including more relatives, as in India and some African economies. In the Democratic Republic of Congo those who call themselves brothers include those who would be called cousins and uncles in other parts of the world. The extended family fulfils several important social and economic roles. It provides mutual cooperation, psychological support and a kind of economic insurance or social security for its members. In a world of tribal warfare and primitive agriculture, this support was invaluable. However, in modern societies, this kind of family system becomes inefficient in promoting economic development, due, at least in part, to the lack of individual incentives for capital accumulation and control over population growth. In fact, many African and Indian economies achieved quite respectable rates of GDP growth during the late twentieth century, but their welfare impact was to a large extent eaten away by explosive population expansion which was faster than in the rest of the world and shows little sign of deceleration.[16]

In India the joint family system (*baradari*) (as discussed in 'Hinduism' in Section 1.2.3 of Chapter 1) is generally accepted as having not only stimulated population growth but also restricted capital accumulation. The caste system is another obstacle to India's economic development. In a particular caste, each member has a specific occupational and social role, which is hereditary. This hierarchical system to a large extent segregates the population into mutually exclusive groups, which prevents people from raising productivity by changing their economic activities. This gives no allowance for aptitude, intelligence or new ideas in allocating jobs and little possibility of firing someone for inefficiency. During British rule 56,000 kilometres of railway were built and irrigation was extended eightfold in India. Conquerors of India, however, were neither absorbed into Hindu culture nor were able to modify this caste system. Instead, they simply added themselves as another layer to a complex system of social segregation and siphoned their profits out of India. Consequently, there was little growth in per capita national income in India during their rule. When the British left, most of the Indian population were still illiterate.[17]

Western nations have achieved considerable success in recent centuries. Unlike many other religious adherents, such as Buddhists and Taoists, Western Christians, especially the Protestants, eliminated the distinction between secular and religious life. Hard work was enjoined to glorify God; achievement was the evidence of hard work; and thrift was necessary because the produced wealth was not to be used selfishly. Accumulation of

Box 4.1 Max Weber (1864–1920)

Max Weber was born in 1864 in Erfurt and died in 1920 in Munich. After early studies in the history of commercial law, he established himself as one of the leading figures in a new generation of historical political economists in the Germany of the 1890s. He was appointed to chairs in political economy at Freiburg in 1894 and at Heidelberg in 1896. A nervous breakdown in 1898 led to his withdrawal from academic teaching, but did little to impair the flow of his writing. In 1904, he took over the editorship of the *Archiv für Sozialwissenschaft und Sozialpolitik*, the leading academic journal in social economics, devoted to the exploration of the interrelationship between economy on the one hand, and law, politics and culture on the other.

In his famous study *The Protestant Ethic and the Sprit of Capitalism* (1904), Weber argued that the profit-maximizing behaviour so characteristic of the bourgeoisie, which could be explained under fully developed capitalist conditions by its sheer necessity to survival in the face of competition, could not be so explained under the earlier phases of capitalist development. It was the product of an autonomous impulse to accumulate far beyond the needs of personal consumption, an impulse which was historically unique. Weber traced its source to the 'worldly asceticism' of reformed Christianity, with its twin imperatives of methodical work as the chief duty of life, and to the limited enjoyment of its product. The unintended consequence of this ethic, which was enforced by the social and psychological pressures on the believer to prove (but not earn) his salvation, was the accumulation of capital for investment.

Source: *New Palgrave: a Dictionary of Economics* (2001, vol. 4, p. 887).

wealth, capital formation and the desire for greater production became a Christian duty.[18] Furthermore, the Protestant Reformation led to greater emphasis on individualism and action as contrasted with the more ritualistic and contemplative approach of Catholicism. The result of this was a downgrading of the role of the Church and a consequent upgrading of the role of the individual. Thus, among Western nations a system of nation-states emerged in close propinquity, with significant trading relations and relatively easy intellectual interchange in spite of their linguistic and cultural differences. Finally, the Western family system, which was different from that in many other parts of the world, involves control over fertility and limited obligations to more distant kin and, as a result, reinforces the possibilities for accumulation.

By analysing the role of cultural factors in the Western economies, we can further track its influence elsewhere. For example, the Anglo-Saxon genotype is based on individualistic behaviour and competitive pragmatism, which is reflected in the liberal economic systems of the USA, Great Britain and other European countries. Given the historic differences between the European countries, one might, however, distinguish between the 'bourgeois' culture of Germany, which implies the existence of industrial, or applied, activities and the 'aristocratic' culture of Great Britain, which reflects the significant interest of British entrepreneurs in management, law and finance. The 'bourgeois' type of economic activity also typifies the Netherlands, Sweden, Switzerland and the north of Italy, where it coincides with regions influenced by the Protestant ethic (Maslichenko, 2004).

Although most economies in the Latin American and Eastern Orthodox areas are more closely related to Western culture than to any others, their economic performances have been poorer than those of the Western world. It seems very likely that the heavy-handed regulatory tendencies in government, chronic inflation, a long history of debt default and fiscal irresponsibility and long-standing political instability were important in keeping Latin American growth and levels of income well below those of North America.[19] However, it is worth noting that the Eastern Orthodox area enjoyed some record growth before the 1980s, when a series of economic difficulties interrupted the progress of many Orthodox economies toward transition from the centrally planned system to a market-oriented one. While some economies in this area have returned to the normal path of growth, the substantial recovery of the Eastern Orthodox area as a whole will need more time.[20]

It would be true to say that the material and industrial success of the modern West had its basis in certain natural, historical and cultural conjunctures. The natural and geographical advantages (such as adequate water and temperate climate, among others) that gave most of the Western nations an economic advantage was also available in the Eastern Orthodox and Latin American areas. According to current growth theories (as discussed in the previous sections of this chapter) an economy will tend to grow (or at least stop declining) as soon as all of its necessary production factors are properly arranged. This should have been true for many Eastern Orthodox economies, given their rich natural resources and the well-educated manpower that they inherited from the Soviet Union. However many Eastern Orthodox economies have been critically entangled in problems in geopolitics, ethnicity and religion during the process of economic transition. It appears more and more likely that it is these factors that have blocked the social and economic development agendas of some, if not all, of these nations since the end of the Cold War.[21]

The ethical beliefs of Confucianism have consistently remained within the bounds of a set of orthodox principles governing interpersonal relationships in most of the East Asian economies. They have been officially applied to all strata of society: loyalty, filial piety, benevolence, righteousness, love, faith, harmony and peace. As a result, East Asia has developed a different culture in relation to economic development from the rest of the world, in response to its own particular environment and social conditions. For instance, unlike the majority of Westerners, East Asians in general care more about their spiritual interests (including the richness of spiritual life and harmonization of feeling) than about material matters. All of this has determined or at least partially influenced East Asia's economic life and structure, the result of which is a particular economic culture.

Cultural and economic relations, however, may still be seen as unconnected in East Asia. Despite its ancient civilization and technological breakthroughs, East Asia lagged far behind the Western nations during the nineteenth and most of the twentieth centuries, partly, it was argued, because of the Confucians' contempt for trade. The following were also blamed for East Asia's backwardness: the attachment to the family becomes nepotism; the importance of interpersonal relationships rather than formal legality becomes cronyism; consensus becomes wheel-greasing and corrupt politics; conservatism and respect for authority become rigidity and an inability to innovate; much-vaunted educational achievements become rote-learning and a refusal to question those in authority; and so on. Since the 1980s, however, it has also been argued that those same intellectual and social traditions, now subsumed into a broader concept – 'Asian values', as they have been called – helped explain remarkable economic success in East Asia and prepared the region for global dominance in what was to be the 'Pacific century'.

'Asian values' vary from country to country. Although Japan imported not only Chinese characters but also Buddhism and Confucianism from China, the adoption of the external religions came only after the authorities decided they would not conflict with Shinto (the way of the gods). Unlike Western religions, Shinto has no scriptures or commandments. It does have customary practices, including ancestor worship adopted from Confucianism. Among the most important aspects of modern Shinto are (1) reverence for the special or divine origin of Japanese people and (2) reverence for the Japanese nation and the imperial family as head of that nation. The impact of modern Shinto on Japanese life is reflected in an aggressive patriotism. The mobilization of the Japanese and their behaviour during the Second World War are examples of that patriotism. The economic success of the second half of the twentieth century is due, at least partially, to the patriotic attitude of all those working in Japanese enterprises. The family spirit has largely carried over to the firm, which has meant greater cooperation and productivity. Some Eastern religions (such as Buddhism and Chinese Taoism) seek virtue through passivity. Shinto, by contrast, stresses the search for progress through creative activities.[22]

Chinese culture is perhaps the most sophisticated in the East Asian area. Its religious package, aiming at a harmonious balance between Confucianism, Buddhism and Taoism, worked well for a long period. Probably because of this, the Chinese remained intoxicated by past prosperity and still proudly treated China as the 'central kingdom' (*zhongguo*) of the world, even when it lagged economically far behind the Western nations. This kind of ethnocentrism and self-satisfaction resulted in a long period in which China was a typical autarkic society. With regards to the cultural differences between the Chinese and Japanese economies, Maddison (1996, p. 53) argues that:

> In China, the foreigners appeared on the fringes of a huge country. The ruling elite regarded it as the locus of civilization and considered the 'barbarian' intruders as an irritating nuisance. In Japan, they struck in the biggest city, humiliated the Shogun and destroyed his legitimacy as a ruler. The Japanese had already borrowed important elements of Chinese civilization and saw no shame in copying a Western model which had demonstrated its superior technology so dramatically.

4.7 Summary

This chapter has taken an intercultural look at the influences of various factors (including capital accumulation, human resources, technological innovation, political and institutional bases, external and boundary conditions and cultural context) on the divergence of the world economy. Since World War II, mainstream development thinking has evolved towards a broad pragmatism. As with many subjects, a deeper understanding of development involves the recognition that sweeping beliefs are often incomplete, that layers of complexity are buried not far beneath the surface and that wisdom is often contingent on the particular conditions of time and place.

Furthering the understanding of the determinants of economic development promises to be one of the major areas of research in the post-Cold War era. In recent decades both experience and intellectual insight have pushed development thinking away from debates over the role of states and markets and the search for a single, overarching policy prescription. Investment in physical and human capital, for example, should encourage economic growth and as a general rule, the empirical evidence presented in this chapter supports this proposition. But in a number of cases, high rates of investment and educational attainment have not been enough to deliver rapid growth. It is difficult to ignore the fact that people's behaviour patterns vary with distinct cultural backgrounds. Naturally, one would ask to what extent these variations are important for economic analysis in general and economic growth in particular. Are there significant influences of cultural traditions and behavioural norms on economic success and achievement? This is a subject in which much interest has been taken by sociologists and historians as well as economists. If we want to pay attention to cultural influences on economic performance in general and business behaviour in particular, a certain amount of scepticism toward lofty theories may not be improper. And yet the justified scepticism toward cultural theory does not give us enough reason to reject altogether the manifest influence of culture on human behaviour (Sen, 2000).

Earlier analyses on the determinants of economic development, especially those that are quantitatively based, are mainly focused on economic variables. Despite the significant existence of cultural influences on economic performance, mainstream economists have failed to embrace them, although there is no way in which economic activities could be conducted independently of cultural context. The economy is as much a cultural site as any other part of society – family, community or school. Culture's significance for development will always be greater than that of a mere promoter of or impediment to economic growth.

5
A Contribution to Economic Growth in Culturally Diverse Nations

> Mankind were one community, and Allah sent (unto them) prophets as bearers of good tidings and as warners, and revealed therewith the Scripture with the truth that it might judge between mankind concerning that wherein they differed. And only those unto whom (the Scripture) was given differed concerning it, after clear proofs had come unto them, through hatred one of another. And Allah by His Will guided those who believe unto the truth of that concerning which they differed.
>
> (Al-Baqarah, 2:213)

5.1 What is cultural diversity?

In Webster's Dictionary, 'diverse' is defined as 'the state or quality of being different or varied; a point of difference; property of being numerically different; condition capable of having various traits composed of unlike or distinct elements'. The term 'cultural diversity' used here describes a wide range of ethnic, linguistic, religious and other cultural groupings. It is generally assumed that while all persons share some traits with all others, all persons also share other traits with only some others, and all persons have still other traits which they share with no one else. Following this assumption, each person may be described in three ways: via the universal characteristics of the species; the sets of characteristics that define that person as a member of a group; and the person's idiosyncratic characteristics. Diversity also sometimes implies clashes of values, goals and interests, which can lead to highly conflictual debates, anger, frustration, mistrust and hostility. When attempting dialogue in a conflict situation, the experience might be negative, discourage people from further interaction, and increase mistrust.

How to classify cultural groups is a difficult and politically charged issue. For the United States the Census Bureau provides a classification of racial groups into five categories: (i) white, (ii) black, (iii) American Indian, Eskimo, Aleutian, (iv) Asian, Pacific Islander, and (v) other (including Hispanic). Some studies also look at 'ancestry' or ethnic origin, most often defined in this context as the country of birth of the American individual (for instance, Western European, Eastern European and Indian).

Ethnic diversity does not necessarily coincide with either linguistic diversity or religious diversity. For instance, most Latin American countries are relatively homogeneous in terms of language but less so in terms of 'ethnicity' or 'race'. Fearon (2003) and Alesina et al. (2003) have compiled various measures of ethnic diversity which try to tackle the fact that the difference amongst groups manifests itself in different ways in different places. The two classifications are constructed differently. Alesina et al. (2003) do not take a stand on what characteristics (ethnicity, language or religion) are more salient, but adopt the country breakdown suggested by original sources, mainly the *Encyclopedia Britannica*. Fearon (2003, p. 198) instead tries to construct a list of 'relevant' ethnic groups which 'depend on what people in the country identify as the most socially relevant ethnic groupings'.

Another notable fact is that each cultural element (ethnicity, language, or religion) may play a different role in the synthesized measure of cultural diversity. For example, religion may contribute a large portion to cultural diversity in the Balkan states and the Middle East, while ethnicity as a key factor in cultural make-up differs within South Asia and between China, Japan and Korea. Nevertheless, language is the most important index when the cultural differences within the western European nations are analysed (see Box 5.1). There is also an argument that religion per se should be a relatively weak source of cultural diversity. For most people, and for most religions, the material costs of conversion are relatively modest, amounting in many cases to geographical relocation to a locality where one can easily establish a new religious identity (Caselli and Coleman, 2002).

Cultural data are only roughly reported in existing statistical yearbooks. Since some countries only collect data on ethnic or 'national' groups, ethnic distribution often had to be assumed to conform roughly to the distribution of language communications. However this approach should be viewed with caution, because a minority population is not always free to educate its children in its own languages and because better economic opportunities often draw minority group members into the majority-language communities (*Britannica Book of the Year 1996*, p. 770). Furthermore, the data on religious adherence are relatively more fragmentary and less reliable than the data on language speakers. This is because the nature of the affiliation (with an organized religion) differs greatly from country to country, as does the social context of religious practice.

Posner (2004) argues that the current data suffer from a 'grouping problem' at two different levels. On the one hand, many groups are aggregated into a single category while they are distinct political actors – even enemies – at national level. The most striking example of this concerns the Tutsis and the Hutus in Rwanda, which are aggregated into a single category

Box 5.1 A story about the birth of the euro

On 12 December 1995, leaders from the European Union were meeting in Madrid, Spain, to discuss whether or not 'ECU' was to be used as the name of the forthcoming single currency. When the meeting reached midway, German chancellor Helmut Kohl suddenly stated: 'ECU as the name of the single currency is not acceptable to Germans. Its pronunciation is very similar to that of the German word "cow".'

In December 1978, when the leaders of the European Community decided in Brussels to start the European monetary system, the European currency unit was set up in order to stabilize the exchange rates of its member states. Interestingly, the abbreviation of the European Currency Unit, or ECU, is exactly the same, in both pronunciation and spelling, as the French word '*ecu*' (an ancient French coin). In French, 'ecu' refers to a shield used by French cavaliers in ancient times. A currency named after a shield would give people a feeling of strength. The start of the European single monetary system and the establishment of the ECU were proposed by the then French president and, therefore, worked to the particular satisfaction of France.

When the meeting came close to launch time, the Spanish premier, González said: 'I have consulted with some fellows that "EURO" is relatively acceptable.' This time, the Greeks complained that the pronunciation of 'euro' is very similar to that of 'urine' in Greek, a word that is even worse than 'ecu' in German. But they were not able to provide better proposals. At last, with the support of Chirac, a compromise was reached: euro was decided for the name of the EU's single currency.

'Banyrwanda'. At the opposite extreme stand a number of groups that are listed as separate linguistic categories, but whose distinction has no political or economic relevance. Posner thus proposes a classification based on 'politically relevant ethnic groups', defined as groups that can influence economic policy decisions either directly or indirectly (for example, by threatening to remove politicians from power). However it is difficult to argue that the realized structure of power at a given point in time is exogenous and can be used as an underlying determinant of the definition of ethnic groups. To date, it is still unclear how to integrate linguistic or 'ethnic' differences with other dimensions that make the latter politically or economically salient.

5.2 How cultural diversity is measured

There are different ways to measure cultural diversity. The simplest method is derived from the number of cultural groups: thus, the cultural diversity of a society is positively related to the number of cultural groups involved. But this ignores the influence of population composition among the cultural groups. For example, two societies may have the same number of cultural groups, but that in which population is equally distributed among all cultural groups might be more culturally diverse than one in which population is unevenly distributed among a cultural *majority* and much smaller cultural minorities. To demonstrate this point, let us consider an extreme case in which the cultural majority accounts for almost 100 per cent of the total population, while each of the minorities retains only a tiny share. Such a society can only be defined as culturally homogeneous, no matter how many minority groups exist.

The second method defines cultural diversity in relation to the population ratio of the largest cultural group. In many cases, the lower the ratio of the largest cultural group, the greater the cultural diversity it implies. However, as it only takes account of one (that is, the largest) cultural group, this method may miscalculate the cultural diversity when two or more large cultural groups exist simultaneously in a country (or region). Furthermore, depending on criteria used, these methods may result in conflicting measurement on cultural diversity. For example, from the linguistic perspective, India, the United States, China, the Philippines, Mexico and Russia are the most culturally diversified in terms of number of linguistic groups; while India, Cameroon, Togo, Zambia, France, South Africa and Uganda are defined as the most culturally diversified in terms of population ratio of the largest linguistic group. From the religious perspective, South Africa, the United States, Taiwan, Canada, India, the United Kingdom and New Zealand are the most culturally diversified in terms of number of religious groups; while New Zealand, Malawi, Samoa, Australia, Suriname and Ghana are defined as the most culturally diversified in terms of population ratio of the largest religious group.[1]

There are a number of papers in the literature that proxy for diversity using the ethnolinguistic fractionalization index, which measures the probability that two individuals who meet at random will be from different ethnolinguistic groups (Mauro, 1995; Easterly and Levine, 1997; La Porta et al., 1999; Bluedorn, 2001; Alesina and Ferrara, 2005; and Montalvo and Reynal-Querol, 2005). Specifically, the ethno-linguistic fractionalization (ELF) measure is defined as follows:

$$\mathrm{ELF} = 1 - \sum_{i=1}^{N} s_i^2 \qquad (5.1)$$

where s_i is the share of group i over the total of the population. This index represents the probability that two randomly drawn individuals from the unit of observation (say, country) belong to different ethnic groups and reaches a theoretical maximum of 1 when every individual belongs to a different group. This measure implies that a country composed of, say,

100 equally sized groups is more fractionalized than a country with two equally sized groups.

But many hypotheses and arguments in the literature refer not just to measures of ethnic diversity like this one, but to more fine-grained conceptualizations of ethnic structure. For example, Horowitz (1985) and others say that ethnic conflict is more likely in countries with an ethnic majority and a large ethnic minority, as opposed to homogeneous or highly heterogeneous countries. Based upon the theoretical results of Esteban and Ray (1994), Montalvo and Reynal-Querol (2002) propose the following polarization index (PI):

$$\mathrm{PI} = 1 - \sum_{i=1}^{N} \left(\frac{1/2 - s_i}{1/2} \right)^2 s_i \tag{5.2}$$

where s_i is the share of group i in the population. The index PI reaches maximum when two equally sized groups face each other and declines as the configuration of groups differs more and more from this half and half split.

Lian and Oneal (1997) use a comprehensive diversity score (CDS) based on the formula developed by Molinar (1991):

$$\mathrm{CDS} = \frac{(\sum_{i=1}^{N} \rho_i^2) - \rho_l^2}{(\sum_{i=1}^{N} \rho_i^2)^2} \tag{5.3}$$

where ρ_i is the percentage of the ith group and ρ_l is the percentage of the largest cultural group; N is the total number of ethnic groups. Obviously, the larger the value of ρ_l, the smaller the CDS.

Although the understanding of cultural diversity may vary according to the perspective taken, the number of cultural groups and their populations should be taken into account simultaneously. To this end, the measurement of cultural diversity index (DIV) can be further simplified as follows:

$$\mathrm{DIV} = N^{(1 - \rho_l)} - 1 \tag{5.4}$$

where N denotes number of cultural groups; ρ_l is population ratio of the largest cultural group (that is, the majority) to the total population. In Equation (5.4), DIV is positively related to N but negatively related to ρ_l. Specifically, when $N = 1$ (or $\rho_l = 1$), DIV = 0.

Several other methods can also be used to measure cultural diversity. For example, a larger population is likely to be less homogeneous, since the average preference distance between individuals is likely to be positively correlated with the size of a country (Dahl and Tufle, 1973; Alesina and Spolaore, 1997). But this is not effective when universally used as an index of cultural diversity.

Table 5.1 gives a few examples (labelled A–K) of how these measures work in a set of economies with differing cultural structures.

Table 5.1 Diversity examples

Type	Structure	Eq. (5.1)	Eq. (5.2)	Eq. (5.3)	Eq. (5.4)
A	Perfectly homogeneous[a]	0	0	0	0
B	(.95, .05)	0.10	0.19	0.00	0.04
C	(.8; .2)	0.32	0.64	0.09	0.15
D	(1/2, 1/2)	0.50	1.00	1.00	0.41
E	(.75, .20, .05)	0.40	0.70	0.12	0.32
F	(.55, .30, .15)	0.59	0.87	0.65	0.64
G	(1/3, 1/3, 1/3)	0.67	0.89	2.00	1.08
H	(.49, .17, .17, .17)	0.67	0.78	0.81	1.03
I	(1/4; 1/4; 1/4; 1/4)	0.75	0.75	3.00	1.83
J	(.48, .01, .01, .01, ...)	0.76	0.50	0.09	6.88
K	Perfectly heterogeneous[b]	≈1[c]	≈0[c]	N–1	≈N[c]

Notes
a. There is only one cultural group.
b. There are N cultural groups, each of which has a share of $1/N$ in population.
c. Only when N is large enough.

Montalvo and Reynal-Querol (2002) show that the PI index is highly correlated with the ELF at low levels of the ELF, uncorrelated at intermediate levels, and negatively correlated at high levels. In a cross-country regression analysis, they find that ethnic polarization has a positive impact on the likelihood of civil war, and a negative effect on a country's growth rate. They do not find an independent effect of ethnic fractionalization. Using a different data set, Alesina et al. (2003) compare the results of the polarization index PI and the fractionalization index ELF, and find that fractionalization works slightly better as a determinant of policies and economic outcomes. While the apparent inconsistency between the two sets of results may be due partly to different parameterization and partly to different data sources, it is difficult to gauge the statistical significance of the difference due to the high correlation between the two measures at low levels of fragmentation (Alesina and Ferrara, 2005).

There are arguments that the CDS is superior to the ELF because it better reflects the distance between the two largest groups without overstating the influence of the largest (Rae, 1967, p. 120; Taagepera and Shugart, 1989, p. 210; Molinar, 1991; and Lian and Oneal, 1997). However, most problematic is that the CDS formula (Equation 5.3) is not sensitive for the measures of cultural diversity in countries in which there is only one major cultural group. For example, the cases C (0.8, 0.2) and J (0.48, 0.01, 0.01, 0.01, ...)

have different cultural structures (see Table 5.1), but they have the same diversity score (0.09). Besides, Table 5.1 shows that the CDS index is not correlated with the other indexes.

Even though each formula has its own advantage, Equation (5.4) is the easiest in application since it does not need the data on population shares for all cultural groups. By contrast, Equations (5.1), (5.2) and (5.3) will meet difficulties in application, especially when a large number of panel data are selected.

5.3 Costs and benefits of cultural diversity

5.3.1 A simple model

Alesina and Ferrara (2005) provide a model that helps to clarify the pros and cons of ethnic diversity. They find that (i) the potential benefits of heterogeneity come from variety in production; and (ii) the costs come from the inability to agree on common public goods and public policies. One testable implication is that more heterogeneous societies may exhibit higher productivity in private goods but lower taxation and lower provision of public goods (in relative terms). Several important aspects are missing in the above model. Of particular note is that while provision of pure public goods may be lower in more fragmented communities, the amount of publicly provided 'private' goods – especially those that can be targeted to specific groups – may be larger. Another important topic that the authors do not investigate directly in their model is that an increase in diversity would simply lead to smaller jurisdictions. In practice this process may be peaceful or not, at the extreme leading to violent civil wars (see, for example, Fearon and Laitin, 2003).

In order to clarify the relationship between economic performance and cultural diversity, let us stipulate an economy with N cultural groups. For simplicity, the N cultural groups are further assumed to be represented by N equally sized culture areas (this will make the cultural diversity index a monotonous positive function of the variable N). Each culture area is different and independent from the others in terms of various cultural identities (such as language, religion and other cultural beliefs and values). Furthermore, to make our analysis clearer and more concrete, let us use five assumptions:

1. All necessary production factors (such as labour force, capital, technology, natural resources and information) are both scarcely and unevenly distributed within the economy.
2. The production factors can flow more freely within each culture area than between the N culture areas of the economy when $N \geq 2$.
3. Each of the N culture areas has at least one comparatively advantageous (or disadvantageous) sector over the other(s) when $N \geq 2$.

4. Transport and communication cost within each culture area is too small to influence the preference of the culture area in allocating its production factors.
5. The objective of each culture area is to maximize its well-being.

In fact, assumption 1 is not ad hoc in the real economic world. Assumption 2 basically characterizes all economic activities in which culture-related barriers exist. Since each culture area is different and independent from the others in terms of cultural identity, intercultural economic cooperation is more difficult and costly than intracultural economic cooperation. In the real world, assumption 3 is the sine qua non for the culture areas to develop intercultural cooperation after the culture-related barriers are removed or reduced. Technically, assumption 4 allows the intracultural cooperation to become profitable within each of the N culture areas when N decreases (or, in other words, when the size of each culture area increases). Finally, assumption 5 serves as an indispensable condition under which the output levels of each culture area and of the economy as a whole can be maximized.

On the basis of the above assumptions, we can induce the following results.

Proposition 1 *Intercultural dependence within an economy usually grows with respect to the number of culture areas involved in the economy*. In other words, the economic dependence of each culture area on the outside world is negatively related to its size.

Proof. Suppose that the degree of economic dependence and the size of the culture area are denoted by R and S ($S = \pi r^2$, where r denotes the average radius of the culture area), respectively. Deriving the differential of R with respect to S, we have:

$$\frac{\partial R}{\partial S} = \frac{\partial R}{\partial r} \cdot \frac{\partial r}{\partial S} = \frac{1}{2\pi r} \cdot \frac{\partial R}{\partial r} \qquad (5.5)$$

It is always set in economics that the degree of economic dependence (R) should decrease with respect to distance, so does the latter with respect to r. Finally, Equation (5.5) becomes $\partial R/\partial S<0$. As a matter of fact, since the number of culture areas (N) and the average size of each culture area (S) are negatively related to each other for the given economy, we have

$$\partial R/\partial N>0. \qquad QED$$

While intercultural dependence may increase opportunities to promote economic development, it also raises risks and transactional costs. This totally depends on the internal and external conditions concerned. As a result some economies will inevitably face frustrations in dealing with intercultural relations, and these frustrations will be magnified for small culture areas. But such culture areas stand to gain more from intercultural trade and finance than their larger counterparts, since they face tighter resource and market size constraints. At the same time these economies may feel any disruption generated in the global economy far more intensely.[2] Accordingly, the stability of multicultural economic relations follows.

Proposition 2 *Multicultural economic relations usually become less stable with respect to the number of culture areas involved.* In other words, the overall stability of multicultural economic relations is negatively associated with the number of culture areas involved.

Proof. Theoretically, if different groups of people have markedly differing attitudes as well as different cultural values, the adoption of a common standard and the socioeconomic coordination between them are not likely to be emphasized. From the political perspective, different culture areas may articulate their political demands by creating new parties or polarizing existing ones. As a result political systems with a small number of parties are more likely to offer moderate, comprehensive policies that reflect the interests of the nation rather than particular factions.

Suppose the stability of economic relation between any pair of culture areas is expressed by r_j ($0 \leq r_j < 1$). Thus, the overall stability of multicultural relations (R) of an economy with N culture areas can be expressed by the product of all r_j of the culture areas included in the economy, that is,

$$R(N) = \prod_{j=1}^{\sum_{i=1}^{N-1} i} r_j \tag{5.6}$$

In Equation (5.6), 'Π...' is the sign of the product of '...'; $\Sigma_{i=1}^{N-1} i$ denotes the number of cultures in pairs. To make the expression simpler, let $r_j = r$ for all j. Then, Equation (5.6) becomes

$$R(N) = r^{\sum_{i=1}^{N-1} i} \tag{5.7}$$

Obviously, Equation (5.7) shows that, since the value of r ranges between 0 and 1, the overall stability of multicultural economic relations is negatively associated with the number of culture areas involved, that is, $R(N) < R(N-1) < \ldots R(3) < R(2)$. *QED*

Proposition 3 *The output level of an economy with different culture areas usually decreases with respect to the number of culture areas involved, if the culture-related barriers exist.* In more precise words, the largest output of the economy with N culture areas (expressed by F_N^*) is lower than that of the economy with $N-1$ culture areas (expressed by F_{N-1}^*), that is,

$$F_N^* < F_{N-1}^* < \ldots F_i^* < \ldots < F_2^* < F_1^*, \text{ where } F_i^* > 0 \text{ and } i=1, 2\ldots \text{ and } N. \qquad (5.8)$$

Proof. See Appendix 1.

Proposition 4 *Intercultural economic cooperation usually becomes more profitable with respect to the number of culture areas involved.* In other words, after all the culture-related barriers are removed, the increase of output of an economy with N culture areas is larger than that of the economy with $N-1$ culture areas.

Proof. Suppose that the total output of all the N sub-areas in the economy now becomes F^{**}. Since the culture-related barriers are removed, the largest outputs of all types of multicultural economies are now the same, that is, $F_N^{**} = F_{N-1}^{**} = \ldots F_2^{**} = F_1^*$, where F_1^* (that is, the largest output of the 1-dimension (1-d) cultural system) is as defined in Model (A1.1). As a result the increase of output of the economy involving N culture areas becomes:

$$F_N^{**} - F_N^* = F_1^* - F_N^* > 0. \qquad (5.9)$$

After combining Formulas (5.8) and (5.9), we have $F_1^* - F_N^* > F_1^* - F_{N-1}^* > \ldots F_1^* - F_i^* > \ldots > F_1^* - F_2^* > 0$.

QED

5.3.2 Implications of the model

A long line of assumptions have been made about the influences of cultural diversity on economic development. Much of it, as stated by Hagen (1986) and Cullen (1993), is attributed to the variety of competing demands on political and economic capital that must be met or on the difficulty that disparate groups have in communicating or co-operating. This hypothesis may trace back to a biological basis in which cooperation among animals is importantly influenced by genetic similarity (Wilson, 1980). It is very easy to understand that culturally diverse societies are associated with political instability which, as indicated in Nordlinger (1972) and Lijphart (1990), adversely affects economic development.

The detrimental influence of cultural diversity on economic development may be transmitted by a proliferation of political parties which interjects elements of political instability or political fragmentation into society. For example, Hannan and Carroll (1981) consider that the effectiveness of democratic institutions may be reduced if different groups in a society articulate their demands by creating separate political parties or by polarizing existing ones.[3]

While there may be several reasons for high illiteracy (which is a clear obstacle to economic development), it is likely that the imposition of different languages may be one of the reasons why literacy rates remain low in multicultural areas. For example, in Andhra Pradesh, India's biggest state, the official language is Hindi; however, Urdu-speaking Muslims make up at least 15 per cent of the population, and constitute 50 per cent or more of the population in some large western cities such as Meeruta. Literacy rates in Andhra Pradesh rose from 21.2 per cent to only 45.11 per cent between 1961 and 1993, whereas in Kerala, where there is relatively little language conflict, the rise was from 46.8 per cent to 90.59 per cent (Saville, 2002, p. 203).

By way of contrast to the above hypotheses, there are also views on the positive effects of cultural diversity on economic growth. The potential benefits of heterogeneity come from variety in production (Alesina and Ferrara, 2005). Cultural diversities exist spatially and temporally, between and within nations in terms of economic availability, opportunities, access to power, resources and human existence. Although every cultural group runs the risk of being stereotyped because of shared commonalities, no group, culture or person remains static or lives in isolation. Instead, all societies have interacted. History reveals similarities in societal structures, and differences in behaviour and stages of development. Societies can and do benefit from the diversity and plurality of cultures that are discovering their own peculiarities and idiosyncrasies.

Technological and educational advances have contributed significantly to a better understanding and appreciation of cultures that have appeared in the world. As a result '[cultural diversity will] allow all individuals to lead a life that is decent, dignified and wise, without losing their identity and sense of community, and without betraying their heritage' (WCCD, 1995). If the WCCD's view is correct, then cultural differences do not necessarily mean violence, but should be something to be cherished. Already, native languages are beginning to be re-evaluated, traditional knowledge rediscovered and local economies revitalized. In fact, a world without the 'other' would be a world of stagnation, for, in culture as in nature, diversity holds the key to innovation and creative, nonlinear solutions (Shanker, 1996).

5.4 Cultural diversity, income inequality and growth

5.4.1 Cultural diversity and economic growth

A number of scholars have empirically assessed the influence of cultural diversity on economic growth (Easterly and Levine, 1997; Bluedorn, 2001; Montalvo and Reynal-Querol, 2005; Alesina and Ferrara, 2005). The primary argument suggests that diverse states are more susceptible to development-inhibiting internal strife than are their homogeneous counterparts (Lijphart, 1977; and Lemco, 1991). Following Tocqueville (1873), Duetsch

(1953) and Banks and Textor (1963), Adelman and Morris (1967) gather the data for 74 less-developed countries from 1957 to 1962 and rank each country on a 10-point ordinal scale of diversity. Their results, based on factor analysis, support their hypothesis: homogeneous countries typically had higher growth rates. Haug (1967) finds a negative correlation between per capita GNP and cultural diversity based on the data of 114 countries in 1963. Reynolds (1985) compares 37 less-developed countries from 1950 to 1980 and, again, indicates that cultural diversity results in lower growth rates. He suggests that this may be due to a sense of alienation among peoples. In other words, reaching a consensus on policies favourable to economic development, especially for the long term, may be difficult when groups have different interpretations of the past and different goals for the future.

Among the existing studies on the correlation between cultural diversity and economic development, Lian and Oneal (1997) demonstrate quite a different scenario. They use data from 98 countries from 1960 to 1985 and find that the growth rate in per capita GDP is not significantly related to ethnic, religious and linguistic differences. They then try to investigate whether the influence of cultural diversity on economic development might be indirect through the intervening factors of political instability or political fragmentation, which also shows no correlation. Obviously, their result could support an assumption that political instability and social conflict – with which economic development is closely associated – are not related to cultural difference. This assumption might be confirmed by the fact that the proliferation of political groups can actually be stabilizing because it allows centrist parties to become arbiters in coalition governments (Horowitz, 1971).[4]

There are methodological reasons for the different results of the existing studies. Adelman and Morris (1967), for example, consider three indicators for cultural diversity (language, religion and ethnicity) and weight linguistic attributes most heavily: countries where over 85 per cent of the population spoke the dominant language, over 90 per cent were of the same race and the society was bounded by a common religion were put in the most homogeneous group; countries in which 50 per cent or fewer of the people spoke the same language were rated least homogeneous. In addition to language, race and religion, two non-ascriptive characteristics (sectionalism and interest articulation) are examined in Haug (1967). Again, Haug emphasizes a country's linguistic characteristics vis-à-vis ethnic and religious divisions. Other studies, such as Hannan and Carroll (1981), Bollen and Jackman (1985) and Esman (1990), neglect one or more aspects of cultural diversity, focusing on either ethnic or ethnolinguistic cleavages. More recently, Lian and Oneal (1997) calculate each country's ethnic, linguistic and religious diversity score and then standardize the three measures of diversity by dividing each country's score by the highest score in that category to attain an average of these three standardized components.

However, there are reasons to believe that these predictions of the correlation between cultural diversity and economic development might have been misleading. One could be that the periods selected in these analyses were (or at least partly encompassed) the high tide of the Cold War, a time when global or regional economic development could only be a very special case and needs to be carefully investigated on this basis. Huntington (1996, p. 125) pointed out that countries could make choices according to their ideological preferences. It might, therefore, be wrong to apply Cold War era results to the post-Cold War period.

Using a model of a community with *K* different types of a total population of *N* individuals, Alesina and Ferrara (2005) find that the potential benefits of heterogeneity come from variety in production; and the costs come from the inability to agree on common public goods and public policies. One testable implication is that more heterogeneous societies may exhibit higher productivity in private goods but lower taxation and lower provision of public goods (in relative terms). The benefits in production from variety in skills are more likely to be relevant for more advanced societies. While in poor economies ethnic diversity may not be beneficial from the point of view of productivity, it may be so in rich ones.

5.4.2 Income inequality and economic growth

A substantial literature has analysed the effects of income inequality on macroeconomic performance, as reflected in rates of economic growth.[5] Most argue that greater income inequality is actually an impediment to economic growth. A seemingly plausible argument points to the existence of credit market failures such that people are unable to exploit growth-promoting opportunities for investment (see, for example, Benabou, 1996; Aghion et al., 1999; Barro, 2000). With limited access to credit, the exploitation of investment opportunities depends on individuals' levels of assets and incomes. Specifically, poor households tend to forgo human capital investments that offer relatively high rates of return. In this case, a distortion-free redistribution of assets and incomes from rich to poor tends to raise the quantity and average productivity of investment. With declining marginal products of capital, the output loss from the market failure will be greater for the poor. So the higher the proportion of poor people there are in the economy the lower the rate of growth (Ravallion, 2001, p. 1808).

A second way in which inequality could affect future growth is through political channels. The degree of inequality could affect the median voter's desired pattern of policies or it could determine individuals' ability to access political markets and participate in costly lobbying. If the mean income in an economy exceeds the median income, then a system of majority voting tends to favour redistribution of resources from rich to poor.[6] As the median voter's distance from the average capital endowment in the economy increases with the aggregate inequality of wealth, he or she will be led to approve a higher tax rate. This in turn could reduce incentives for productive investment, resulting in lower growth. If this is correct, democratic societies with a more unequal distribution of wealth should be characterized by exploitation of the rich by the poor – that is, high taxes and, consequently, low investment and growth, whereas undemocratic ones with similar characteristics would not (Deininger and Squire, 1998).

Indeed, the negative effects of income inequality might exist in almost every sphere of human life. But there also exists evidence that supports the view that income inequality could encourage economic growth – both directly and indirectly. The most intuitive thesis is that a lower degree of inequality would mean a greater amount of redistribution from rich to poor. It is this redistribution that would become an impediment to the creation of incentives for people (especially the poorest and richest groups of them) to work hard (Li and Zou, 1998). There is also a positive view for the effect of inequality on economic growth: if individual saving rates rise with the level of income, then a redistribution of resources from rich to poor tends to lower the aggregate rate of saving in an economy. Through this channel, a rise in income inequality tends to raise investment.[7] In this case, greater inequality would enhance economic growth. However, there is also an argument that inequality may lead to higher fertility rates, which in turn could reduce economic growth (Perotti, 1996).

Worsening inequality of wealth and income motivates the poor to engage in crime, riots and other disruptive activities (see, for example, Hibbs, 1973; Venieris and Gupta, 1986; Gupta, 1990; and Alesina and Perotti, 1996). In a civilized world the existence of millions of starving people is not only unacceptable from an ethical point of view but can hardly be expected to lead to peace and tranquillity. As a consequence, it is widely believed that inequality could become an impediment to economic development. Unfortunately, the existing empirical analyses, using data on the performance of a broad panel of countries, have yielded conflicting results. Perotti (1996) and Benabou (1996), for instance, report an overall tendency for income inequality to generate lower economic growth in cross-country regressions, whereas some panel studies, such as that of Forbes (1997) and Li and Zou (1998), find relationships with the opposite sign. Nevertheless, Deininger and Squire (1998) provide evidence in support of the view that inequality retards economic growth in poor countries but not in richer countries. Using a large quantity of time-series and cross-national data, Barro (2000) also supports this hypothesis.[8] However other carefully conducted researches, such as Eichera and Garcia-Penalosab (2001) and Ravallion (2001), among others, provide little evidence to support the above views.

5.4.3 Summarizing the implications

Many theories exist for assessing the effects of income inequality and cultural diversity on economic growth – both negative and positive (see Table 5.2 for a summarized statements of these effects). The problem is that most of these theories tend to have offsetting effects and that the net effects on growth, which depend entirely on the internal and external conditions and environment concerned, are ambiguous. For example, while income inequality and cultural diversity raise risks and costs for economic transactions between different groups of people, including the rich and poor or those with different cultural values and religious beliefs, they may also become incentives and even productive factors contributing to technological innovation and economic development.

Alesina and Ferrara (2005) highlight three 'microfoundations' underlying the nonlinear relationship between cultural (ethnic) diversity and economic performance. First, diversity can affect economic choices by directly entering individual preferences. Second, diversity can affect economic outcomes by influencing the strategies of individuals. Even when individuals have no taste for or against homogeneity, it may be optimal from an efficiency point of view to transact preferentially with members of one's

Table 5.2 Theoretical effects of income inequality and cultural diversity

	Negative effects	**Positive effects**
Income inequality	Inequality motivates the poor to engage in crime, riots and other disruptive activities (Hibbs, 1973; Venieris and Gupta, 1986; Gupta, 1990; Alesina and Perotti, 1996); inequality may lead to higher fertility rates, which in turn could reduce economic growth (Perotti, 1996); rise in inequality tends to reduce the average productivity of investment (Barro, 2000).	Higher inequality tends to induce stronger incentives for people to work hard (Li and Zou, 1998); rise in inequality implies a higher level of saving rates, which tends to raise investment and to enhance economic growth (Barro, 2000).
Cultural diversity	Cultural diversity reduces the effectiveness of democratic institutions (Hannan and Carroll, 1981); rise in cultural diversity tends to increase the cost for intercultural communication and mistrust in economic cooperation (Bollen and Jackman, 1985; Huntington, 1993; Montalvo and Reynal-Querol, 2003); inability to agree on common public goods and public policies (Alesina and Ferrara, 2005).	Cultural diversity holds the potential for innovation and creative, nonlinear solutions (Shanker, 1996); potential benefits of heterogeneity come from variety in production (Alesina and Ferrara, 2005); comparative economic advantages tend to exist between culturally dissimilar economies rather than between culturally homogeneous places (Guo, 2004).

own type if there are market imperfections. Finally, diversity may enter the production function. People differ in their productive skills and, more fundamentally, in the way they interpret problems and use their cognitive abilities to solve them. This can be considered the origin of the relationship between individual heterogeneity and innovation or productivity. An elegant formalization of the third microfoundation is provided by Hong and Page (1998), who prove two key results on this point. First, a group of 'cognitively diverse' problem solvers can find optimal solutions to difficult problems; second, under certain conditions a more diverse group of people with limited abilities can outperform a more homogeneous group of high-ability problem solvers. The intuition is that an individual's likelihood of improving decisions depends more on having a different perspective from other group members than on an individual's own high expected score.[9]

The goal of this section is to study the joint effects of income distribution and cultural diversity on economic growth. It is important, therefore, to explore the conditions that might diminish the negative effects of inequality and cultural factors as nations perhaps overcome barriers to intranational economic activities or, more significantly, attain a reduction in violence, as sources of growth-inhibiting friction. The negative effects of income inequality and cultural diversity on economic development would become very small if diverse groups learned to live with each other and pursue their differences peacefully. This leads to the presumption that socially stable and economically harmonious societies will be less sensitive to the measures of income inequality and cultural diversity than others.

5.5 Evidence from a panel of nations[10]

5.5.1 Analytical framework and data

In past literature relating to the determinants of economic growth, income inequality and cultural diversity have been treated separately. In this section, we try to investigate their joint effects on economic growth. Our task is to clarify (1) the cultural conditions under which income inequality encourages (retards) economic growth; and (2) the economic conditions under which cultural diversity encourages (retards) economic growth. Our empirical work considers average growth rates of real per capita GDP over two decades, from 1980 to 1989 and from 1990 to 1999. We define these periods as those of the Cold War and the post-Cold War, respectively. What we intend to do is to see if the determinants of economic growth are different in the two periods.[11]

Our analytical model is based on Barro's (2000) findings on the determinants of economic growth. In Barro's model, which was estimated by the three-stage least squares (3SLS) technique, 11 explanatory variables (the log of real per capita GDP and its square, the ratio of government consumption to GDP, a subjective index of the maintenance of the rule of law, a subjective for democracy (electoral rights) and its square, the ratio of inflation, the years of schooling, the log of total fertility rate, the ratio of investment to GDP, and the growth rate of the terms of trade) are used. In order to avoid possible estimation errors resulting from multicolinearity, we will only focus on how the growth rate that remains unexplained in Barro's model is related to GINI (Gini coefficient, representing income inequality) and DIVERSITY (cultural diversity, including language and religion).

As suggested in Section 5.4, the effects of income inequality and cultural diversity on economic growth, both positive and negative, may be offsetting. Consequently, the regressions might not be statistically significant. In order to clarify the conditions under which economic growth can be both positively and negatively related to income inequality and cultural diversity, we allow the influences of the DIVERSITY and GINI variables on growth to depend on each other. To this end, the DIVERSITY and GINI variables are now entered into the growth model both individually and jointly as a product. We also allow income level (measured by natural log of per capita GDP, or lnGDPPC) and DIVERSITY (or GINI) as joint explanatory variables in the growth model.

The dependent variable is defined as the average growth rates of real per capita GDP which remain unexplained in Barro's baseline panel regression (2000, p. 12, table 1).[12] The real per capita GDP, the data for which come from the IMF *World Economic Outlook* (various years), is measured in 1985 US dollars for all sample nations. The data for the Gini coefficients come from a revised version of the World Income Inequality Database (WIID2 Beta), available at the website of the World Institute for Development Economics Research (WIDER): www.wider.unu.edu/wiid/wiid.htm. Our empirical work considers the average level for all annual Gini coefficients available within each period. When national data are absent, regional (urban or rural areas) data are used.

The data on the linguistic and religious diversity indexes are calculated based on Equation (5.4). To save time in data collection, we will not calculate the period average data for cultural diversity indexes. Instead, we only collect the mid-period data. Specifically, we collect the cultural data for two years: 1985 for the period 1980–89 and 1995 for the period 1990–99 (see Appendix 2 for a full set of diversity indexes of the existing economies in 1995). This will not affect our panel regressions since population shares among cultural groups do not usually undergo any significant changes within a ten-year period. Table 5.3 shows the descriptive statistics of all the variables considered in this research.

The framework includes countries with vastly different social, economic and cultural conditions. The attractive feature of this broad sample is that it encompasses great variation in the explanatory variables that are to be evaluated. Our view is that it is impossible to use the experience of one or a

Table 5.3 Descriptive statistics for the explanatory variables

Period	Variable	Number of observations	Minimum	Maximum	Mean	Std. deviation
1980–89	LANGUAGE	97	0.000	44.554	2.249	5.467
	RELIGION	97	0.001	4.594	0.742	0.916
	GINI	84	0.274	0.677	0.433	0.101
1990–99	LANGUAGE	97	0.000	19.352	1.354	2.864
	RELIGION	97	0.001	4.072	0.505	0.671
	GINI	84	0.219	0.649	0.417	0.102

Notes: The linguistic and religious diversity indexes (LANGUAGE and RELIGION) are measured at 1985 (to represent the period 1980–89) and 1995 (to represent the period 1990–99). The Gini coefficients (GINI) are period averages for all the Gini coefficients available.

few countries to get an accurate empirical assessment of the long-term growth implications from a set of social, economic and cultural variables. However one drawback of this kind of diverse sample is that it creates difficulties in measuring variables in a consistent and accurate way across countries and over time.

The other empirical issue, which is likely to be more important, is the sorting out of directions of causation. From a longer perspective of human history, the extent of cultural diversities (especially in terms of religion, which appears in our model as the explanatory variable) is the final result of economic development (which appears in our model as the dependent variable). But we argue that within a shorter period of time this kind of causation is very weak.

5.5.2 Results of estimation

Our baseline panel regressions in Tables 5.4 and 5.5 do not yield any overall relation between growth and income inequality for the 1980s and 1990s as a whole. But the estimated coefficients on income inequality (GINI) become statistically significant when the panel regressions are based on the data from the 1980s and the 1990s separately. Specifically, the income inequality (GINI) tends to retard growth in the 1980s (with an estimated coefficient of –11.202 in Table 5.4 or of –10.690 in Table 5.5) and to encourage growth in the 1990s (with an estimated coefficient of 6.861 in Table 5.4 or of 6.902 in Table 5.5). The above results are similar to Barro's (2000) findings when the full (that is, from 1980 to 1989 and from 1990 to 1999) samples are considered in a single regression, but different from his findings when the 1980–89 and the 1990–99 samples are considered in separate regressions.

By way of contrast to the findings reported by other researchers, the regressions reported in Tables 5.4 and 5.5 provide different patterns of rela-

Table 5.4 Effects of income inequality and linguistic diversity on growth rates

Period	Explanatory variable	Coefficient	Std. error	Sig. level
1980–89/ 1990–99	(Constant)	0.565	0.875	0.520
	GINI	–2.429	2.020	0.231
	LANGUAGE	–0.033	0.045	0.467
	Number of observations	161		
	R squared	0.013		
1990–99	(Constant)	–3.238	1.224	0.010
	GINI	6.861	2.782	0.016
	LANGUAGE	–0.060	0.049	0.227
	Number of observations	78		
	R squared	0.090		
1980–89	(Constant)	3.958	1.118	0.001
	GINI	–11.202	2.628	0.000
	LANGUAGE	0.078	0.089	0.382
	Number of observations	83		
	R squared	0.184		

Notes: Based on OLS regressions. The dependent variable, the unexplained part of the growth rate of real per capita GDP, is determined by the baseline panel regression in Barro (2000, p. 12, table 1). See notes to Table 5.3 for information about the explanatory variables.

Table 5.5 Effects of income inequality and religious diversity on growth rates

Period	Explanatory variable	Coefficient	Std. error	Sig. level
1980–89/ 1990–99	(Constant)	0.509	0.892	0.569
	GINI	–2.514	2.019	0.215
	RELIGION	0.052	0.239	0.830
	Number of observations	161		
	R squared	0.010		
1990–99	(Constant)	–3.229	1.239	0.011
	GINI	6.902	2.803	0.016
	RELIGION	–0.198	0.284	0.489
	Number of observations	78		
	R squared	0.078		
1980–89	(Constant)	3.725	1.167	0.002
	GINI	–10.690	2.626	0.000
	RELIGION	0.251	0.390	0.521
	Number of observations	83		
	R squared	0.180		

Notes: Based on OLS regressions. See notes to Table 5.4 for other information.

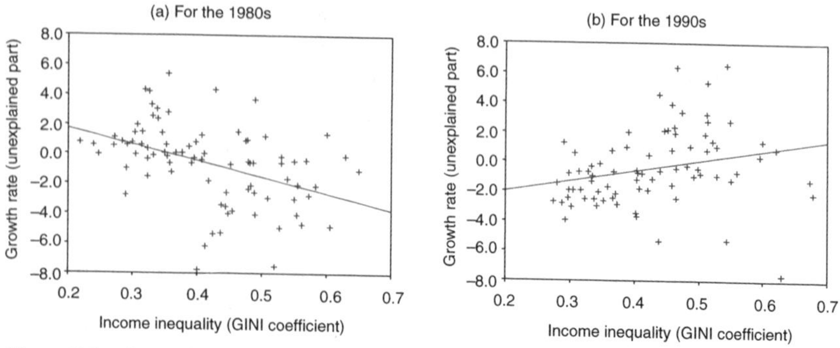

Figure 5.1 Growth rate versus income inequality

tion between economic growth and income inequality for the 1980s and 1990s (see also Figure 5.1 for the scatter diagrams).[13] Since the 1980s and 1990s were defined as the Cold War and the post-Cold War periods, respectively, the question arises as to whether the findings are determined to any extent by Cold War policies. Since countries may make choices in terms of ideological preferences (Huntington, 1996, p. 125), the determination of economic activities during that period might be distorted, or at any rate, different from that of the post-Cold War period. Following this analytical logic, we would also believe that during the Cold War era cultural influences on economic activities might be largely reduced, if not dismissed.

In both tables 5.4 and 5.5, the estimated coefficients on linguistic and religious diversity (denoted by LANGUAGE and RELIGION, respectively) are statistically insignificant for the samples of the 1980s and the 1990s as a whole. But there is an indication that the linguistic and religious diversities tend to encourage growth in the 1980s more than in the 1990s; or they tend to retard growth in the 1990s more than in the 1980s. Unfortunately, since none of the estimated results are statistically significant at the 10 per cent confidence level, they cannot be used to provide strong evidence for the relationship between cultural diversity and economic growth.

Might there be any forms of nonlinear relation between growth and cultural diversity? Our regressions show that the coefficients on linguistic diversity (LANGUAGE) and on its interactive term with income inequality (LANGUAGE*GINI) are statistically insignificant for both the 1980–89 and the 1990–99 periods (the regressions are omitted here). We suspect that linguistic barriers do not impact on economic activities in the 1990s, or, if they do, have become insignificant, in contrast to the previous estimates by Adelman and Morris (1967), Haug (1967) and Reynolds (1985). The reason for this might be that educational and technological advances have to a certain extent reduced linguistic barriers, especially for international and intercultural economic activities in the developed economies (Guo, 2004.)

Table 5.6 Nonlinear effects of income inequality and religious diversity on growth rates

Period	Explanatory variable	Coefficient	Std. error	Sig. level
1980–89/	(Constant)	0.470	1.228	0.702
1990–99	GINI	-2.689	2.830	0.344
	RELIGION	3.160	2.389	0.188
	RELIGION*lnGDPPC	-0.267	0.149	0.075
	RELIGION*GINI	-2.106	3.387	0.535
	Number of observations	161		
	R squared	0.032		
1990–99	(Constant)	-5.214	1.740	0.004
	GINI	11.338	4.012	0.006
	RELIGION	5.508	2.845	0.057
	RELIGION*lnGDPPC	-0.282	0.168	0.098
	RELIGION*GINI	-7.904	4.045	0.054
	Number of observations	78		
	R squared	0.126		
1980–89	(Constant)	4.618	1.637	0.006
	GINI	-13.110	3.831	0.001
	RELIGION	0.643	3.895	0.869
	RELIGION*lnGDPPC	-0.206	0.265	0.440
	RELIGION*GINI	3.513	5.954	0.557
	Number of observations	83		
	R squared	0.193		

Notes: Based on OLS regressions. The explanatory variables RELIGION*lnGDPPC and RELIGION*GINI are the products of RELIGION and the natural log of per capita GDP and of RELIGION and GINI, respectively. See notes to Table 5.4 for other information.

By way of contrast, our regressions show that the coefficients on income inequality (GINI), religious diversity (RELIGION) and on their interactive terms are statistically significant for the 1990–99 period, though not for the 1980–89 period (see Table 5.6).[14] This suggests that economic growth may be related to a religious variable. More interesting results emerge in our regressions when the effect of religious diversity on economic growth is allowed to depend on the level of income inequality measured by the Gini coefficient.

As intuited from Figure 5.2, religious diversity tends to encourage economic growth for income inequality (represented by Gini coefficient) to be less than a break-point value of inequality (represented by GINI*)[15] (see Figure 5.2a) and tends to retard economic growth for income inequality to be larger than GINI* (see Figure 5.2b). This result may be supported by the following presumptions. On the one hand, lower inequality economies will be less sensitive to the measures of cultural diversity than higher inequality

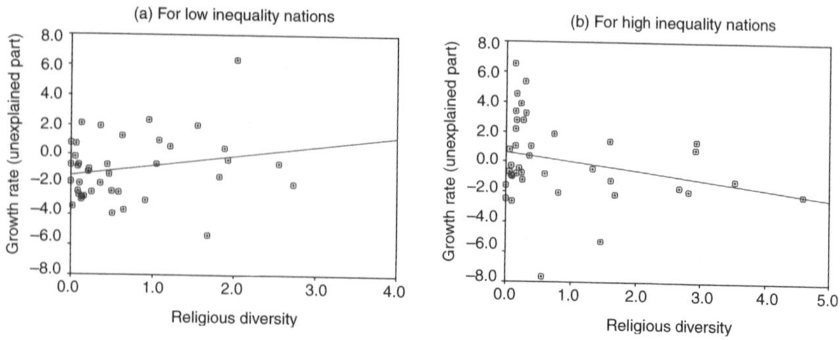

Figure 5.2 Growth rate versus religious diversity, 1990s

economies in which cultural diversity leads to barriers to intranational trade or, more significantly, to violence. On the other hand, higher cultural diversity implies greater comparative economic advantages for low inequality places.

These results have far-reaching implications. For a long time, there has been serious concern that societal conflict arises from cultural dissimilarity (Huntington, 1993). Ultimately, this may to some extent be traceable to a biological basis, since in most circumstances cooperation among animals is importantly influenced by genetic similarity (Wilson, 1980). As a result ascriptive ties are said to dampen coalition building and to inhibit compromise across groups (which cross-cutting cleavages promote), thus increasing chances for social conflict (Bollen and Jackman, 1985). But our empirical evidence indicates that the above hypothesis might not be completely copied into human societies, at least during the post-Cold War period. In fact, the high level of religious diversity of a country is usually positively related to another cultural variable – religious similarity of the country with the outside world, which usually plays an important role in foreign trade.[16]

The major concern here is that we are trying to identify the roles of inequality and cultural variables whose effect on economic growth is indirect. When the effect of income inequality is allowed to depend on the level of economic development, measured by the natural log of real per capita GDP, none of our regressions on the interactive term GINI*lnGDPPC (to save space, we omit the estimated results here) shows any statistical significance for the 1980s and 1990s samples.[17]

As stated in Section 5.4, there have been different views as to the effects of income inequality on economic growth. Our regressions, shown in Table 5.6, suggest that for the 1990s income inequality tends to encourage economic growth for religious diversity indexes (DIVERSITY) below 1.434 and tends to retard growth for religious diversity indexes above 1.434.[18]

Since there are quite few nations with a religious diversity index higher than 1.434 (see Figure 5.3b), we still need more statistical evidence that

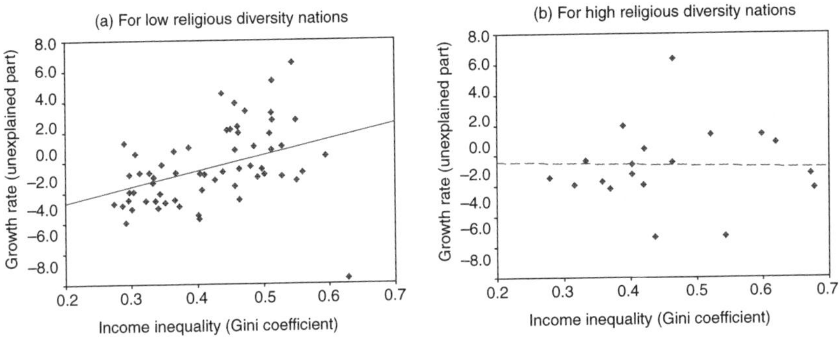

Figure 5.3 Growth rate versus income inequality, 1990s

supports the view that income inequality (GINI) retards economic growth in nations with higher religious diversity indexes. Nevertheless, Figure 5.3a does provide some evidence to support the view that income inequality (GINI) tends to encourage economic growth in nations with lower religious diversity indexes.

In our regressions (see Table 5.6) income inequality is found to be a key factor that could change the direction of the religious influences on economic growth in the 1990s (if not in the 1980s). As a summary, we can divide some typical nations in the sample into four categories according to religious diversity and income inequality (see Table 5.7):

(I) Low diversity and low inequality. This category includes Morocco, Ireland, Denmark, Portugal, Greece, Belgium, Norway and Sweden.
(II) High diversity and low inequality. This category includes New Zealand, the United Kingdom, the Netherlands, Canada, Germany and South Korea.
(III) Low diversity and high inequality. This category includes Colombia, Paraguay, Ecuador, Senegal, Thailand, Algeria, Mauritania and Turkey.
(IV) High diversity and high inequality. This category includes Lesotho, Zimbabwe, Malawi, Central African Republic, Zambia, Cameroon, Kenya, Nigeria and Malaysia.

According to our estimated results, higher religious diversity could become a source of productive factors contributing to economic growth for low inequality nations (shown in Category II); but in nations in Category IV, high inequality could seriously affect economic growth. In Category III, income inequality could generate higher economic growth since there are very few, if any, intercultural barriers within each religiously homogeneous nation. But it seems that the nations listed in Category I still need stronger economic incentives (or, higher income inequality) or religious diversities in order to promote their domestic economies.

Table 5.7 A quadrantal classification of selected nations

	Low income inequality	High income inequality
Low religious diversity	Morocco (0.001, 0.368); Ireland (0.059, 0.365); Denmark (0.093, 0.352); Portugal (0.055, 0.346); Greece (0.095, 0.327); Belgium (0.087, 0.297); Norway (0.085, 0.296); Sweden (0.098, 0.274)	Colombia (0.058, 0.559); Paraguay (0.084, 0.528); Ecuador (0.054, 0.513); Senegal (0.092, 0.491); Thailand (0.075, 0.481); Algeria (0.005, 0.463); Mauritania (0.003, 0.456); Turkey (0.002, 0.456);
High religious diversity	New Zealand (4.594, 0.370); United Kingdom (2.674, 0.358); Netherlands (1.930, 0.333); Canada (2.722, 0.316); Germany (1.210, 0.307); South Korea (1.823, 0.300)	Lesotho (1.669, 0.677); Zimbabwe (1.604, 0.672); Malawi (2.919, 0.620); Central African Rep. (1.594, 0.598); Zambia (1.522, 0.570); Cameroon (1.464, 0.544); Kenya (2.941, 0.521); Nigeria (2.032, 0.464); Malaysia (1.325, 0.463)

Note: Figures within parentheses are the religious diversity indexes (in 1995) and the Gini coefficients (1990–99 averages), which are calculated based on *Britannica Book for the Year 1996* (pp. 774–7) and the World Income Inequality Database (WIID2 Beta, available at www.wider.unu.edu/wiid/wiid.htm), respectively.

5.6 Summary

Explaining growth is one of the most important tasks for economists. This chapter is part of an upsurge of empirical work on economic growth and tries to shed some light on the relative merit of models emphasizing the significance of cultural influences. On the basis of the data of a panel of countries for the period 1980–99, we develop a model of economic growth with respect to, either individually or in an interactive term, cultural diversity and income inequality. We find that high inequality tends to retard growth in the 1980s and to encourage growth in the 1990s. Although we have not found evidence for the relation between linguistic diversity and economic growth (which is consistent with the findings of Lian and Oneal, 1997), our estimated results do suggest that the growth rate of real per capita GDP is related to religious diversity under certain circumstances.

The indication that economic development is more strongly related to religious diversity than to linguistic diversity may be reasonable: since most governments have endeavoured to promote their official languages, fewer and fewer people – most of whom are either illiterates or economically inactive – meet linguistic difficulties in communicating nationally.[19] As a result the influence of linguistic diversity on economic development becomes less significant than that of religious diversity. If our results are correct, the make-up of cultural diversity should be much more complicated than either emphasizing language (as Alelman and Morris, 1967, and Haug, 1967, suggested) or treating language and religion equally (as Lian and Oneal, 1997, suggested).

Our regressions provide evidence to support the view that the world economy has been more significantly influenced by religious diversity in the post-Cold War period than was the case during the Cold War. While it is easy to understand why economic activities have been determined by religious diversity since the end of the Cold War, we find that, for the 1990s, religious diversity tends to retard growth in high inequality nations and to encourage growth in low inequality places. We also find some evidence to support the view that inequality tends to encourage growth in nations that are homogeneous in regard to religion. But we still need more statistical explanations for the negative relation between inequality and growth in nations with high religious diversity indexes.

The above evidence supports the presumption that the lower inequality economies will not only be less sensitive to the measures of cultural diversity than higher inequality economies in which cultural diversity leads to barriers to intranational trade or, more significantly, to violence, but that they can also benefit from the comparative economic advantages in the present, culturally diverse world. These results could be good news for global and regional leaders who have been troubled by problems in dealing with cultural clashes. Hopefully, cultural diversity will come to be a positive factor for economic development.

6
Cultural Influences on International Economic Analysis (I)

> There is 'true' Knowledge. Learn thou it is this: to see one changeless life in all the lives, and in the separate, one inseparable. There is imperfect Knowledge: that which sees the separate existences apart, and, being separated, holds them real. There is false Knowledge: that which blindly clings to one as if 'there were all, seeking no cause, deprived of light, narrow, and dull, and dark.'
>
> (*Sankhya-Yog*, the Book of Doctrines)

6.1 A critique of contemporary theories on trade

It has been broadly assumed that a country's economic dependence on the outside world is negatively related to its land area.[1] This may be illustrated unambiguously by the relationship between the supply and demand of some basic resources for countries differing in size (land area).[2] Generally speaking, in comparison to large economies, small economies have a relatively limited variety of natural resources. Therefore, they have to import resources that they lack and that are essential to meeting diversified production and consumption needs. Eventually, the increased imports will stimulate exports in order to attain a trade balance.

Besides geographical area, a country's economic size (output) and population also influence its external economic activities. Generally, the larger the GDPs (or GNPs)[3] of trading partners, *ceteris paribus*, the larger the volume of trade between them; by contrast, population is a negative factor in the determination of international trade. This captures the well-known phenomenon that larger countries tend to be relatively less open to trade as a percentage of GDP (or GNP). Therefore, it is easy to understand that Hong Kong, Singapore and Luxembourg are more highly dependent on international trade than the United States, China or India. The former lack not only natural endowments but also room to exploit economies of scale in the domestic market, while the latter, engaging in far more trade in absolute terms (versus less trade as a percentage of GDP, or GNP), can find more business opportunities inside their own territories.

Without considering geographical factors, it could be very difficult to understand the current patterns of both global and regional trade. For instance, bilateral trade flows across the US–Canadian border, between France, Italy, the UK, Germany and the Netherlands, and along the western coast of the Pacific Ocean (including, inter alia, South Korea, Taiwan, Hong Kong and the mainland of China) have risen a great deal more quickly than between more remote and isolated economies. Besides distance, another proxy for geographical factors that influences international trade is adjacency. For example, bilateral trade between France and the United Kingdom will relate to their proximity, but trade between France and Germany will be further boosted by their common border. One of many ways to include 'adjacency' in the international trade model is to treat it as a dummy variable.[4]

During the postwar period technological advances in transportation and communications have been of the greatest importance. The increasing proportion of economic value is weightless – that is, it can be transmitted over fibre-optic cable rather than transported in a container ship. At the same time, improvements in transportation networks and technology are reducing the costs of shipping goods by water, ground and air. More important are the improvements in information technology (IT) that have made it easier to manage the new interconnections worldwide. Among them is the Internet, the fast-growing tool of communication. The Internet has provided a new means of commerce, with clear speed and cost advantages (see Box 6.1). Declining transportation costs should also have contributed increasingly to the growth of global trade.

Past studies on the geographical influence on trade have raised more questions than they answered. For example, among the existing estimated results on the determinants of international trade (in logarithmic form), the statistically significant coefficients on the log of distance have ranged between -0.51 and -1.50, which demonstrates the respective decreases (in percentage) in international trade as a result of a 1 per cent increase in distance.[5] No observable tendency, however, has been found for the effect of geographical proximity to fall over time. Rather, the trend seems to be upward during the courses of, among others, 1950–88 in Boisso and Ferrantino (1997) and 1965–92 in Frankel et al. (1997). In their analyses of the negative correlation between distance and the interdependence of sovereign countries, Frankel et al. (1994) use data from the 1980s and obtain slightly larger coefficients (around 0.5 to 0.6) on distance compared with Eichengreen and Irwin's (1995) interwar estimates (around 0.3 to 0.6) based on data from the 1930s. Similarly, based on panel data from 1970, 1980 and 1990, Rauch's (1999) results show little evidence to support the decreasing tendency for trade with respect to distance from 1970 to 1990.

Box 6.1 Benefits of e-commerce

Electronic commerce involves all sizes of transaction bases. As one would expect, electronic commerce requires the digital transmission of transaction information. While transactions are conducted via electronic devices, they may be transported using either traditional physical shipping channels, such as a ground delivery service, or digital mechanisms, such as the download of a product from the Internet. It is the latter that provides the enabling mechanisms to foster the growth of electronic commerce. The actual and projected growth rates and uses of the Internet indicate that electronic commerce is no passing fad, but rather a fundamental change in the way in which businesses interact with one another and their consumers. The following presents the most obvious potential benefits from engaging in electronic commerce:

(a) Internet and web-based electronic commerce can reach a more geographically dispersed customer base.
(b) Procurement processing costs can be lowered.
(c) Cost of purchasing can be lowered.
(d) Inventories can be reduced.
(e) Cycle times can be lowered.
(f) Customer service can be improved.
(g) Sales and marketing costs can be reduced.

Source: Based on Greenstein and Feinman (2000, pp. 2–3).

Clearly this does not provide any evidence that, as a result of declining transportation costs (see Table 6.1), there should be a decreasingly negative relation between trade and distance. Intuitively, we suspect that some powerful explanatory variables that may either resist or aid international trade must have been missing or simplified, which could in turn reduce to a greater or lesser extent the reliability of the estimated results.[6]

Past theories on the determinants of international trade seem controversial, or at least incomplete. The Heckscher-Ohlin (H-O), or factor-endowment, theory can be expressed in terms of two theorems. According to the H-O theorem, a nation will export the commodity produced by a relatively abundant and cheap factor and import the commodity produced by a relatively scarce and expensive factor (see Heckscher, 1919; and Ohlin, 1933). The factor-price equalization theorem was rigorously proved by P.A. Samuelson and therefore is also known as the Heckscher-Ohlin-Samuelson (H-O-S) theorem (Samuelson, 1948, 1949). According to the H-O-S theorem, international trade will bring about equalization in the relative and absolute returns to homogeneous factors across nations. The first empirical test of the H-O model was conducted by Leontief (1954) using

Table 6.1 Declining costs of transportation and communications

Year	Average ocean freight and port charges per ton	Average revenue per passenger mile	Telephone call (3 minutes, NY/London)	Computers (index, 1990=100)
1920	95	–	–	–
1930	60	0.68	245	–
1940	63	0.46	189	–
1950	34	0.30	53	–
1960	27	0.24	46	12,500
1970	27	0.16	32	1,947
1980	24	0.10	5	362
1990	29	0.11	3	100

Source: IMF (1997a).

1947 US data, which demonstrates that US import substitutes were about 30 per cent more capital-intensive than US exports. Since the United States is the most capital-intensive nation, this result was the opposite of what the H-O model predicted and became known as Leontief paradox. This paradox could be explained by (1) 1947 being a non-representative year, (2) the use of a two-factor (labour and capital) model, (3) the fact that US tariffs gave more protection to labour-intensive industries, and (4) the exclusion of human capital from the calculations. Some empirical studies, however, give conflicting results.[7]

A more uniform size distribution among economies is one explanation for the increase in global trade. Moreover, Helpman (1987) and Krugman (1995) predict that if the distribution of national incomes across countries becomes more equal over time, the volume of trade should increase. According to the Krugman-Helpman theory, the sum of the logs of per capita GNPs of two countries will have a positive effect on the log form of trade between the two countries. One possible explanation for the independent effect of income per capita is that exotic foreign products are perceived as superior consumption goods. Low-income countries meanwhile are dominated by subsistence farming. Other possible explanations come out of the literature relating to endogenous theory on economic growth.[8] Even though more developed countries have more advanced transportation infrastructures, including seaports and airports, which facilitate trade, Frankel et al. (1997) argue that perhaps the most important reason why industrialized countries trade more than the less-developed countries is that countries tend to liberate as they develop. One reason for this is that governments of poor countries depend on tariff revenue for a large portion of their budgets, while more advanced countries can apply other forms of direct and indirect taxes to the domestic economy.

Up to now, it seems that there should have been different hypotheses on the correlation between income level and volume of trade. Markusen (1986) and Deardorff (1998, p. 15), for example, show that if high-income consumers tend to consume larger budget shares of capital-intensive goods, which according to the H-O theory are produced by capital-rich countries, then it follows that (1) capital-rich countries will trade more with other capital-rich countries than with capital-poor countries, and (2) capital-poor countries will trade more with other capital-poor countries than with capital-rich countries. These arguments support the results of Linder (1961), Helpman (1987) and, more recently, Krugman (1995) but not that of the H-O theory.

Classical theory does not offer a satisfactory explanation of why production conditions differ between countries. This is perhaps not surprising, given the nature of production at that time. Resource and cost differences were taken as given and as part of the environment in which the economic system functioned. The underlying cost differences were viewed as being determined outside the economic system for the most part, governed by the natural endowment of a country's resources. The theory does, however, make it clear that even if a country is absolutely more or less efficient in the production of all commodities, a basis for trade still exists if there is a difference in the degree of relative efficiency across commodities. Thus, there is a basis for trade between a developing country and an industrialized country that is more efficient in the production of all commodities. Both can benefit from specialization in production and trade of those commodities in which each has a comparative advantage.

The H-O theory has left a great deal of today's international trade unexplained. To fill this gap, economists have put forward new theories that consider international trade in relation to economies of scale, imperfection, and cross-national differences in technological change, among others. Even if two nations are identical in every respect, there will still be a basis for mutually beneficial trade based on economies of scale. When each nation specializes in the production of one commodity, the combined total world output of both commodities will be greater than without specialization when economies of scale are present. A large portion of international trade today involves the exchange of differentiated products. Such intra-industry trade arises in order to take advantage of important economies of scale in production. Studies show that the more similar nations are in factor endowments, the greater is the importance of intra-industry relative to inter-industry trade.[9] According to the technological gap model, a firm exports a new product until imitators in other countries take its market away. In the meantime, the imitation lag allows delays in the diffusion of technology across national borders. The product cycle theory, which relaxes several assumptions in traditional trade theories, holds that a product goes through five stages, including the introduction of the product, expansion of production for export, standardization and the beginning of production abroad through imitation, foreign imitators underselling the nation in third markets, and foreigners underselling the innovating firms in their home markets as well (Salvatore, 1995, p. 176).

In spite of the theoretical arguments pointing out the net welfare gains that result from specializing and trading on the basis of comparative advantage, the world continues to experience pressures to restrict the movement of goods, services and factors between countries and regions. If free trade is so beneficial to an economy, why are so many groups or individuals trying their best to reduce it? To answer this question, one must pay attention to the political aspect of trade policy. Baldwin (1989, p. 119) summarizes the current situation well: 'International trade seems to be a subject where the advice of economists is routinely disregarded. Economists are nearly unanimous in their general opposition to protectionism ... [T]he increase in US protection in recent years ... demonstrates that economists lack political influence on trade policy.'

As a matter of fact, such policy instruments as, inter alia, import tariffs, export taxes and subsidies and nontariff barriers, have been effectively applied by various countries and regions so as to interface with the free-trade allocation of resources.[10] The political influences on trade policy, however, comprise more than this. Trade policy usually takes place within a political-social milieu and is influenced by some individuals and groups who feel that they will better off with restricted trade, though other individuals and groups and the country as a whole may be worse off. In the last decades, an area of research has emerged which focuses on analysing the actual determinants of trade policy within the political environment in which it is developed (Hillman, 1989). The study of political factors influencing trade policy has proceeded along two major fronts. The first, and perhaps the most usual, focuses on the economic self-interest of the political participants; while the second way in which special interest groups can influence political outcomes is through the funding of political campaigns (Appleyard and Field, 1998).

But the various political influences on international trade are not always clear. Though most existing regional trading blocs have been the outcomes of political influences, the intraregional trade performances of culturally diverse trading blocs have not been very significant. For example, Africa's share of intraregional trade to total trade remained at about 2 per cent from 1965 to 2000; even worse, intraregional trade as a share of total trade in ASEAN declined before 1995, regardless of the supposedly freer trade environment. By contrast, the intraregional trade performances of many culturally homogeneous trading blocs demonstrate considerable achievement. Between 1965 and 2000, for example, intraregional trade as a share of total trade in East Asia – though no trading bloc has been set up the region is primarily characterized by, or to some extent linked with, Chinese culture – rose from 32 per cent to 56 per cent. Even more dramatic was the intra-regional trade between Mercosur (founded in 1991 and including four Latin American states, Argentina, Brazil, Paraguay and Uruguay) and the Andean Community (founded in 1969 and including four Latin American states, Bolivia, Ecuador, Peru and Venezuela), which increased from 12 per cent and 2 per cent in 1965 to 22 per cent and 13 per cent in 2000, respectively (see Table 6.2).

To sum up, current trade theories seem incomplete and, sometimes, controversial, especially when trade partners with different cultural characteristics are taken into account. They cannot be used to explain satisfactorily why world economic activities between partners with the same or similar cultural environments have become increasingly more important, while the opposite is true of partners in cross-cultural environments; neither can they provide a clear and concrete methodology to explain the extraordinary trade performances within the Chinese cultural circle (Taiwan, Hong Kong, Macau, mainland China and other Chinese areas) during the post-Cold War period. The following are still more puzzling for international economic theorists and practitioners. Why has Germany attracted much less foreign direct investment (FDI) than the UK? Why has France achieved a better foreign trade performance than Italy?

Table 6.2 Intraregional trade shares of total trade, selected regions, 1965–2000

Group	1965	1970	1975	1980	1985	1990	1995	2000
East Asia	0.32	0.31	0.33	0.39	0.41	0.46	0.52	0.56
APEC	0.58	0.63	0.61	0.63	0.73	0.72	0.76	0.81
ASEAN-6	0.22	0.18	0.14	0.15	0.18	0.18	0.22	0.22
Europe	0.70	0.73	0.72	0.72	0.72	0.76	0.75	0.78
EU-15	0.62	0.65	0.64	0.64	0.65	0.69	0.67	0.68
EU-12	0.54	0.58	0.58	0.58	0.59	0.64	0.62	0.65
Mercosur	0.12	0.10	0.08	0.13	0.08	0.11	0.20	0.22
Andean Community	0.02	0.03	0.05	0.05	0.05	0.06	0.11	0.13
NAFTA	0.39	0.42	0.40	0.36	0.42	0.39	0.45	0.48
Africa	0.02	0.02	0.01	0.01	0.02	0.02	0.02	0.02

Notes:

(1) ASEAN-6 does not include Vietnam, Laos and Cambodia (as they did not join ASEAN until 1995).

(2) EU-12 does not include Sweden, Austria, and Finland (as they did not join the EU until 1995).

(3) Other groups are as defined in table sources.

Sources: Frankel et al. (1997, p. 281) for 1965–1990 and calculation by the author based on IMF (various years) for 1995 and 2000.

6.2 How culture influences international economic activities

> There was a man who was hawking spears and shields. To advertise the firmness of his shields, he shouted, 'Look, my shields are very strong. Nothing in the world, no matter how hard and sharp, can penetrate my shields.' A moment later, the man put down his shield and picked up a spear. Brandishing the spear, he cried, 'Look, my spears are the best under heaven. They are so hard and sharp that they can penetrate everything, no matter how tough and strong it might be.' 'How about using your own spear to try on your own shield?' someone asked. The man could not make a reply.
>
> (Hanfeizi, *c.* 280–233 BC)

6.2.1 Viewpoint I: culture doesn't influence economic activities

For a long time there has been an argument that there is no correlation between culture and international economic activities. As a result the influences of various cultural factors on economic activities has been all but ignored by mainstream development thinkers and practitioners. For example, on the basis of data from 98 countries from 1960 to 1985, Lian and Oneal (1997) found that ethnic, religious and linguistic differences have no significant influences on growth rates in per capita GDP. They then tried to investigate whether the influence of cultural diversity on economic development might be indirect – through factors such as political instability or political fragmentation – which also shows no correlation.

It seems probable that these conclusions could be correct under certain circumstances. During the Cold War, ideological preferences might have been of greatest significance in decision-making (Huntington, 1996, p. 125). Consequently, the cultural determinants of international economic activities during the Cold War might be different from that of the post-Cold War period.

In a panel study of East Asian economies there are significant differences in the cultural influences on international trade between the Cold War period and the post-Cold War period (Guo, 2006). As shown in Table 6.3, the trade pattern in 1995 is quite different from that in 1985. The estimated coefficients on language and religion are statistically insignificant in 1985. However the influences of both cultural variables (language and religion) on international trade are statistically significant in 1995. Intuitively, the estimated coefficients (that is, 1.737 for LANGUAGE and 1.086 for RELIGION) in Table 6.3 suggest that the volume of trade between economies that are linguistically and religiously similar (that is, LANGUAGE = RELIGION = 1) could have risen to about 13.722 (that is, $\exp(2.619)\approx 13.722$) and 2.835 (that is, $\exp(1.042)\approx 2.835$) times that between economies that are linguistically and religiously different (that is, LANGUAGE = RELIGION = 0).[11]

Table 6.3 Increasing effects of culture on international trade in East Asia, 1985–95

Explanatory variable	1985	1995
Constant	–8.760 (1.288)[a]	–11.309 (0.973)[a]
$\ln(GNP_iGNP_j)$	1.176 (0.027)[a]	1.295 (0.023)[a]
$\ln(GNPPC_iGNPPC_j)$	0.250 (0.039)[a]	–0.087 (0.030)[a]
$\ln(DISTANCE_{ij})$	–1.288 (0.126)[a]	–0.762 (0.098)[a]
$LANGUAGE_{ij}$	–1.670 (1.492)	2.619 (0.890)[a]
$RELIGION_{ij}$	0.327 (0.354)	1.042 (0.286)[a]
R square	0.567	0.617
F-statistic	582.16	940.98
Number of observations	2,226	2,924

Notes:

(1) Dependent variable is the natural log of bilateral trade (in thousand US dollars).
(2) Except LANGUAGE and RELIGION (which, as defined in Equation (7.4), denote each trade partner's linguistic and religious similarities, respectively), all other explanatory variables are measured in the natural log form.
(3) The East Asian economies include Brunei, Cambodia (only for 1995), China (mainland), Hong Kong, Indonesia, Japan, Korea (North), Korea (South), Laos, Malaysia, Myanmar, Philippines, Singapore, Thailand and Vietnam.
(4) Figures within parentheses are standard errors.
a. denotes statistically significant at the 1% level.

Source: Guo (2006).

6.2.2 Viewpoint II: cultural difference retards economic activities

The emphasis on the role of cultural linkage in international economic activities may trace back to a biological basis in which cooperation among animals is importantly influenced by genetic similarity (Wilson, 1980). Although it is not the only tool with which to build trusting relationships, businessmen usually make deals with people they can understand. By contrast, minorities face disadvantages in conducting intercultural economic activities.[12] Trade and economic cooperation are based on cultural commonality, as it is easier and more efficient for people with the same cultural identity (language, religion, or any other cultural element) to trust and communicate with each other than for those with different cultural identities.

Since the adoption of common standards between different cultural groups is unlikely, given that they have markedly differing attitudes as well as different cultural values, the greater the cultural variations in a multicultural society, the higher the managerial risks and costs resulting from it. The problems inherent in intracultural and intercultural behaviours can be summarized as follows (Huntington, 1996, p. 129):

(1) feelings of superiority (and occasionally inferiority) toward people who are perceived as being very different;

(2) fear of and lack of trust in such people;
(3) difficulty of communication with them as a result of differences in language and what is considered civil behaviour;
(4) lack of familiarity with the assumptions and motivations, such as relationships, and social practices of other people.

Since the end of the Cold War, there has been a growing concern that cultural links exhibit a trend towards increasing trade between countries that are similar to each other culturally (see Rauch and Trindade, 2002, among others). Trade within the European Community constituted less than 50 per cent of the community's total trade before the 1980s; by the 1990s this had grown to more than 60 per cent. Trade among the ASEAN, Taiwan, Hong Kong, South Korea and the mainland of China – most of which either fall within or are closely related to the Chinese cultural circle – increased from less than 10 per cent to over 30 per cent of total trade from the 1950s to the 1990s. Similar shifts toward intraregional trade also occurred in Latin America in the 1990s, with trade between Brazil and Argentina tripling and Colombia-Venezuela trade quadrupling between 1990 and 1993. In 1994 Brazil replaced the United States as Argentina's principal trading partner.[13]

Since the 1990s quantitative studies on the cultural influences on international trade have also been conducted. Havrylyshyn and Pritchett (1991), for example, find that three languages – Portuguese, Spanish and English – are significant, in decreasing order of magnitude. In the study of poor countries, Foroutan and Pritchett (1993) find that French, Spanish and English are statistically significant. After supplementing the general language term and allowing each of the major languages to have an independent extra coefficient, Frankel and Wei (1995, table 2) find that two languages, English and Chinese, appear to qualify as especially important.[14]

Frankel et al. (1997) and Rauch (1999) use nine languages (English, Spanish, Chinese, Arabic, French, German, Japanese, Dutch and Portuguese) and treat international linguistic links as a dummy variable to represent when both countries of a pair speak a common language or had colonial links earlier in the twentieth century. Frankel et al.'s results show a highly significant effect when all the languages are constrained to have the same coefficient. The estimate fluctuates over time between 0.33 and 0.77. Pooled time-series estimates of the coefficient (in natural log) cluster around 0.44, which implies that two countries sharing linguistic/colonial links tend to trade roughly 55 per cent (that is, $\exp(0.44) \approx 1.55$) more than they would otherwise (1997, pp. 74–5). However these studies did not consider the influences of such languages as Bengali, Hindi and Russian (the three other major languages in the world) on the international trade of South Asia and Eastern Europe.

The above estimated coefficients on linguistic links are consistently interpreted as exhibiting a trend whereby trade in the postwar period has taken place among countries that are similar to each other linguistically. In other words, they are interpreted as possible evidence of increased cultural barriers to economic activities. However it should be noted that cultural variables have been highly simplified in the above studies, probably due to the fact that they are only treated as complementary variables in the determinants of economic activities. For example, the linguistic links between countries were only treated as a dummy variable. As most countries are linguistically diversified, the international (or interregional) linguistic links should be a much more comprehensive index than being simply expressed by '1' (for countries sharing a common language) or '0' (for other countries).[15] It is worth noting that the existing studies omit another important cultural variable, religion, that plays, at least in some cases, a more important role in economic development than the linguistic variable (see Chapter 5 for details).

6.2.3 Viewpoint III: cultural difference encourages economic activities

By way of contrast to the above, there is a quite different viewpoint, showing that the direction of the correlation between cultural dissimilarity and international economic activities may change under different conditions. In the analysis of bilateral trade and economic cooperation, economists have taken account of resource endowment including quantity of arable land, quality of the soil, presence of natural resources and climate, as well as labour and managerial skills and organizational capacity. But little attention has been paid to cultural differences which could not only decide the characteristics of social resources but also influence trade patterns, either directly or indirectly.

Apart from the fact that intercultural differences generate some management risks and extra costs for bilateral trade, intercultural trade is important not only for the realization of economies of scale but also for the utilization of culturally-based complementary conditions. Although every cultural group runs the risk of being stereotyped because of shared commonalities, no group, culture or person remains static or lives in isolation. Societies have always interacted. History reveals similarities in societal structures, and differences in behaviour and stages of development. Societies benefit from the diversity and plurality of cultures, as cultures discover their own peculiarities and idiosyncrasies.

In order to quantitatively investigate the nonlinear effects of culture on international economic activities, one may build empirical models in which cultural linkage is designed not only as an individual explanatory variable but also as a product with income level. If these explanatory variables are statistically significant when estimated simultaneously, one can further divide the full samples into two groups (that is, one with low-income level trade partners, and one with high-income level trade partners) under which cultural influences on international trade can be estimated.[16] On this basis and using panel data from the USA and China, cultural influences on foreign trade are found to take two different directions during the 1990s: cultural dissimilarity tends to retard trade with poor countries and regions and to encourage trade with richer economies (Guo, 2004). Evidence from a panel of 15 East Asian economies results in a similar finding (especially on the correlation between religious similarity and external trade) for 1995, although such a nonlinear correlation does not exist for 1985 (Guo, 2006).

6.3 A theoretical model

In the previous section, we have discussed different viewpoints on cultural influences on international economic activities. It is therefore worth noting that the changing roles that culture plays in international economic activities are very sensitive to changes in conditions. In order to make the results clearer and more concrete, detailed theoretical analyses are necessary.

The theoretical framework presented here is based on the following. The market structure is one of imperfect competition, with oligopolistic firms producing goods that are perfect substitutes for each other. It is assumed that the markets are segmented in different areas. To facilitate the analysis, we further assume:

1. There are two factors affecting international trade, that is, benefit of economic complementarity and cost of inter-political and intercultural barriers.
2. Technology is identical in all culture areas, that is, trade functions are the same in all culture areas.
3. All commodities are produced under constant returns to scale in all culture areas.
4. There is no intercultural factor mobility.
5. There are no transportation costs, tariffs or other obstructions to the free flow of trade.
6. Trade between the culture areas concerned is balanced.

The meaning of assumption (1) is clear, and it is made to simplify the illustration. Assumption (2) means that all culture areas have access to and use the same general production techniques. Since factor prices usually differ, each culture area will use more of the relatively cheaper factor in the culture area so as to minimize its costs of production and intercultural trade. Assumption (3) means that increasing the amount of labour and capital used in the production of any commodity will increase output of that commodity in the same production. Assumption (4) means that intercultural differences in factor earnings would persist indefinitely in the absence of intercultural trade. Assumption (5) means that specialization in production proceeds until commodity prices are the same in both culture areas with trade. If we allowed for transportation costs and tariffs, specialization would proceed only until commodity prices differed by no more than the costs of transportation and the tariff on each unit of the interculturally traded commodity. Lastly, assumption (6) means that the total value of each culture area's exports equals the total value of the area's imports.

To make the analysis easier, we can further simplify the analytical framework. Assume that in a pair of economically complementary nations, the size of their bilateral trade is jointly determined by only two factors: (1) the cost of intercultural transaction (c) and (2) the benefit of comparative advantage (b). Specifically, trade is supposed throughout this research to be encouraged for $b>c$ and to be retarded for other circumstances.

On this basis, there is always a negative relation between the cost of intercultural transaction and cultural similarity. To make the analytical framework more concrete, we suppose that the function c is monotonously related to cultural similarity (x),[17] that is:

$$c = c(x), \text{ with } c'(x)<0 \text{ and } c''(x) = 0. \tag{6.1}$$

In all circumstances, $b(x)$ is positive for economically complementary nations, that is:

$$b(x)>0 \text{ for all } x. \tag{6.2}$$

However, the marginal benefit of comparative advantage with respect to cultural similarity, denoted by $\partial b/\partial x$, may be positive, negative or zero. Finally, we have Hypothesis 1 for the cultural conditions under which trade is encouraged or retarded:

(1a) When $\partial b/\partial x>0$, trade tends to be retarded for values of cultural similarity to be less than x_1^* and to be encouraged otherwise (see Figure 6.1a).

(1b) When $\partial b/\partial x\leq 0$, trade tends to be retarded for values of cultural similarity to be less than x_1^* and to be encouraged otherwise if $|\partial b/\partial x|<|\partial c/\partial x|$; it tends to be encouraged for values of cultural similarity to be less than x_2^* and to be retarded otherwise if $|\partial b/\partial x|>|\partial c/\partial x|$ (see Figure 6.1b).

(1c) When $\partial b/\partial x = \partial c/\partial x$, trade tends to be retarded if $b<c$ for all values of cultural similarity and to be encouraged if $b>c$ for all values of cultural similarity (see Figure 6.1c).

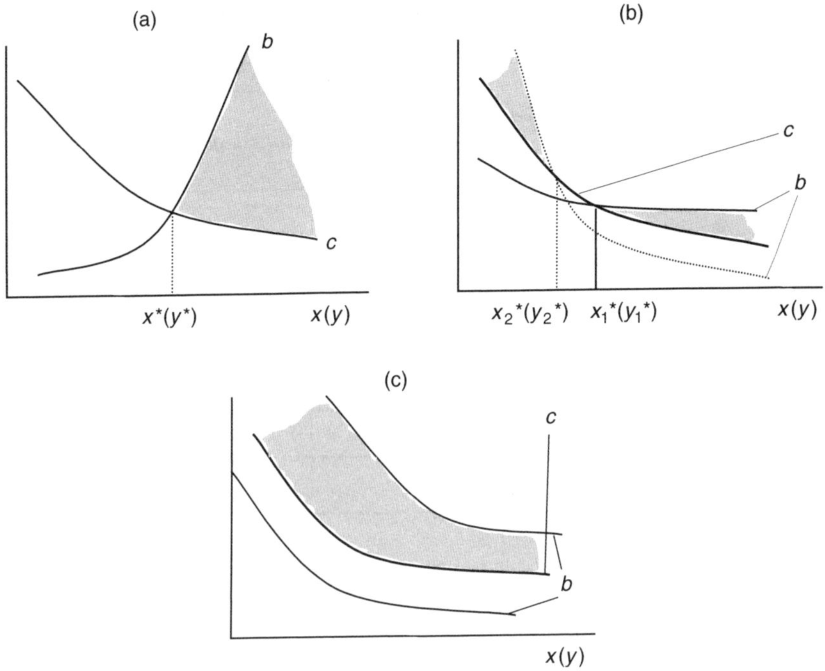

Figure 6.1 Conditions under which trade is encouraged

Next, let us add another explanatory variable, income level (y), into the system in which cultural similarity is fixed at a certain level. It is further assumed that, *ceteris paribus*, the cost of intercultural transaction is negatively related to income level. Perhaps the most obvious evidence to support this view is the decreasing transportation cost as a result of economic development, not to mention that the higher the educational attainment (which is positively related to income level), the easier is it for people from different cultural backgrounds to communicate with and understand each other. The functions of the cost of intercultural transaction and the benefit of comparative advantage now becomes:

$$b = b(x, y);\ c = c(x, y), \text{ with } \partial c/\partial y < 0. \tag{6.3}$$

In a check on the relation between the benefit of comparative advantage and income level, there may be different scenarios. First of all, there is an indication that the benefit of comparative advantage increases with higher income level. This viewpoint has been confirmed by the empirical analyses of, among others, Helpman (1987) and Krugman (1995), in which the sum

Table 6.4 Economic and cultural conditions under which trade is encouraged

Cultural similarity \ Income level			$\partial b/\partial y \geq 0$	$\partial b/\partial y < 0$			
				$\lvert \partial b/\partial y \rvert < \lvert \partial c/\partial y \rvert$	$\lvert \partial b/\partial y \rvert > \lvert \partial c/\partial y \rvert$	$\partial b/\partial y = \partial c/\partial y$	
						$b>c$	$b<c$
$\partial b/\partial x \geq 0$			$(x>x^*)$ $(y>y^*)$	$(x>x^*)$ $(y>y_1^*)$	$(x>x^*)$ $(y<y_2^*)$	$(x>x^*)$	ar
$\partial b/\partial x<0$	$\lvert \partial b/\partial x \rvert < \lvert \partial c/\partial x \rvert$		$(x>x_1^*)$ $(y>y^*)$	$(x>x_1^*)$ $(y>y_1^*)$	$(x>x_1^*)$	$(x>x_1^*)$	AR
	$\lvert \partial b/\partial x \rvert > \lvert \partial c/\partial x \rvert$		$(x<x_2^*)$ $(y>y^*)$	$(x<x_2^*)$ $(y>y_1^*)$	$(x<x_2^*)$	$(x<x_2^*)$	AR
	$\partial b/\partial x = \partial c/\partial x$	$b>c$	$(y>y^*)$	$(y>y_1^*)$	$(y<y_2^*)$	AE	AR
		$b<c$	AR	AR	AR	AR	AR

Notes:
(1) x^*, x_1^* and x_2^* are the values of cultural similarity at which the curves *b* and *c* meet.
(2) y^*, y_1^* and y_2^* are the values of income level at which the curves *b* and *c* meet.
(3) AE denotes that 'trade is always encouraged', and AR denotes that 'trade is always retarded'.

of the logs of per capita GNPs of two countries will have a positive effect on the log form of trade between the two countries. Second, there may be a negative relation between the benefit of comparative advantage and income level, as indicated in some empirical results (Rauch, 1999).[18]

As a result, the marginal benefit of comparative advantage with respect to income level, denoted by $\partial b/\partial y$, may be positive, negative or zero. Finally, Hypothesis 2 includes the following conditions under which trade is encouraged or retarded:

(2a) When $\partial b/\partial y \geq 0$, trade tends to be retarded for values of income level to be less than y* and to be encouraged otherwise (see Figure 6.1a).
(2b) When $\partial b/\partial y<0$, trade tends to be retarded for values of income level to be less than y_1* and to be encouraged otherwise if $\lvert \partial b/\partial y \rvert < \lvert \partial c/\partial y \rvert$; it tends to be encouraged for values of income level to be less than y_2* and to be retarded otherwise if $\lvert \partial b/\partial y \rvert > \lvert \partial c/\partial y \rvert$ (see Figure 6.1b).
(2c) When $\partial b/\partial y=\partial c/\partial y$, trade tends to be retarded if $b<c$ for all values of income level and to be encouraged if $b>c$ for all values of income level (see Figure 6.1c).

After combining Hypotheses 1 and 2, we may have the cultural and economic conditions under which trade is encouraged or retarded (see Table 6.4).

6.4 Summary

Cultural influences on international trade are complex. On the one hand, 'cultural dissimilarity' always generates a cost on intercultural transactions; on the other hand, it also results in 'economic complementarity', an important factor that has direct influences on trade.

Although economists have attempted quantitatively to examine the effect of culture on international trade, few studies have dealt with the positive and negative correlations between the various cultural factors and trade.

This chapter has clarified various economic conditions under which trade may be either encouraged or retarded. The adoption of common standards between different cultural groups is unlikely to be of significance, given that they have markedly differing attitudes as well as different cultural values. As a result, the larger the number of cultural groups involved in a multicultural society, *ceteris paribus*, the higher the managerial risks and costs resulting from it. However, in addition to the cost of intercultural transactions, 'cultural dissimilarity' may also generate more or less 'economic complementarities' that will have direct influences on trade.

In order to present a detailed picture of how culture influences international economic analysis, we need more, empirically-based, evidence.

7
Cultural Influences on International Economic Analysis (II)

> A man from the state of Chu was crossing a river. When the ferry got to the middle of the river, his sword fell into the water. Immediately he took out a knife from his pocket and made a mark on the boat. 'This is where my sword fell off,' he murmured and stepped aside, much relieved. The ferry sailed on and soon got to the dock on the opposite bank. As soon as the boat anchored, the man jumped into the water to look for his sword at the place where he had marked the boat. The boat had moved but the sword had not. Is this not a very foolish way to look for a sword?
>
> (Lü Buwei, (?)–235 BC)

7.1 Framework for empirical analysis

As noted in Chapter 6, a number of quantitative studies have been made on the role that cultural factors play in international trade.[1] These studies minimize the importance of cultural variables, treating linguistics as a dummy variable[2] and omitting altogether the possible inference of religion.

Religion can have a deep impact not only on attitudes but also on values that affect economic matters. As stated in Chapter 5, religion could play a more important role in economic affairs than language. However, studies using different data have produced different results. For example, after examining a large cross-section of conflicts, Fox (1997) finds that in only a small minority do religious issues play more than a marginal role. Similarly, Alesina et al. (2002) find that religious fractionalization does not significantly predict the rent-seeking policy distortions usually associated with other types of ethnic fractionalization.

Among the quantitative studies of international trade and economic cooperation, the gravity model is the tool most commonly used by economists.[3] The classic extensive early application of the model was by Linnemann (1966), who continued work first reported in Tinbergen (1962) and then in Pöyhönen (1963). The most recent work on the application of the gravity model was by Frankel et al. (1997), Deardorff (1998), Rauch (1999) and Rose (2004), among others. Generally, a gravity model assumes that the size of bilateral economic activities between any two countries depends on both the product of the economic sizes of the countries and the distance between them. In addition, income level and whether or not a country-pair shares a common land border have also been considered as standard covariates in the gravity model of international economic trade.

In order to test the effects of the various cultural variables on international trade, we control other political and social variables. Instead, we introduce a set of cultural similarity variables – represented by SIMILARITY. Although the components of culture have been variously defined, we have focused on only two elements – language and religion. Of course, our discussion of these cultural elements is not definitive and perhaps would not satisfy anthropologists. Nevertheless, our consideration is due to the concerns that 'language' is an effective tool of communication and that 'religion' can provide insights into the characteristics of culture. To control for the countries' propensity to foreign economic activities, we use some dummies for the selected countries. Let us first consider a basic form of gravity model:

$$\begin{aligned}\ln(\text{TRADE}_{ij}+1) = {} & \alpha_0 + \alpha_1\ln(\text{GNP}_i\text{GNP}_j) + \alpha_2\ln(\text{GNPPC}_i\text{GNPPC}_j) + \\ & \alpha_3\ln\text{DISTANCE}_{ij} + \alpha_4\text{BORDER}_{ij} + \alpha_5\text{SIMILARITY}_{ij} \\ & + \Sigma\alpha_{6+k}\text{COUNTRY}_k \qquad (7.1)\end{aligned}$$

In Equation (7.1), ln represents natural logarithm; TRADE_{ij} denotes nominal bilateral trade between countries (regions) i and j (in thousand US dollars). In order to make the natural logarithm of TRADE become mathematically meaningful when TRADE = 0,[4] we use ln(TRADE + 1) to approximately denote ln(TRADE). This seems to be reasonable since the size of TRADE (in thousand US dollars) is, if not zero, always far larger than 1.[5] GNP_iGNP_j is the product of nominal GNPs of the ith and jth countries (regions) (all in thousand US dollars). $\text{GNPPC}_i\text{GNPPC}_j$ is the product of nominal per capita GNPs of the ith and jth countries (regions) (all in US dollars). DISTANCE_{ij} represents the distance between the geographical centres of the ith and jth countries (regions) (in kilometres); and BORDER_{ij} is a dummy variable, which takes the value of 1 for countries (regions) i and j to have a common border and 0 otherwise. According to past studies, we expect the estimated coefficients on the above variables to follow: $\alpha_1>0$, $\alpha_3<0$, and $\alpha_4>0$. COUNTRY_k denotes the dummy of the kth country.

Calculation of the distance between trade partners requires some elaboration. Most existing studies use the distance between two major cities to denote the proximity of two trade partners. The cities are either the capitals or economic centres.[6] Another method is to use the geographical centres to measure the distance between the trade partners. According to Boisso and

Ferrantino (1997), there is little difference in whether distance is measured between the most populous cities or the geographical centres. A third method, which has been used by Linnemann (1966), Eichengreen and Irwin (1995) and others, takes the distance measured 'as the crow files' – what is technically called the great-circle distance between the two latitude-longitude combinations.

Studies such as that by Frankel et al. (1995 and 1997) also use dummies for 'membership' in the geographical areas of East Asia, the Western hemisphere and so on. Including these dummy variables could, as stated by Rauch (1999, fn. 6), shrink the estimated coefficients on 'distance'. Dummies for membership in geographical areas are excluded from Equation (7.1) because they could compound the problem of interpretation that will be presented by the cultural variables employed.

Our interest here is in the cultural factors that may resist or aid international trade. To proceed, we use SIMILARITY_{ij} to express the extent to which the *i*th and *j*th trade partners are culturally linked to each other (see Section 7.2 for details of the measurement). Technically, if the cultural variable is statistically insignificant in Equation (7.1), there might exist some possibility for the existence of other form(s) of relationship between international trade and cultural similarity. To investigate the nonlinear relationship, we add a new variable: $\ln(\text{GNPPC}_i\text{GNPPC}_j)$, where $\ln(\text{GNPPC}_i\text{GNPPC}_j)$ is the natural log of the per capita GNP (in nominal US dollars) of the *i*th and *j*th trade partners. The effect of the SIMILARITY index on international trade is now allowed to depend on the level of economic development, measured by per capita GNP. The SIMILARITY variable is now entered into the gravity model of trade linearly and also as a product with the natural log of per capita GNP. Consequently, we have a modified form of gravity model:[7]

$$\begin{aligned}\ln(\text{TRADE}_{ij}+1) = {} & \beta_0 + \beta_1\ln(\text{GNP}_i\text{GNP}_j) + \beta_2\ln(\text{GNPPC}_i\text{GNPPC}_j) + \\ & \beta_3\ln\text{DISTANCE}_{ij} + \beta_4\text{BORDER}_{ij} + \beta_5\text{SIMILARITY}_{ij} \\ & + \beta_6\text{SIMILARITY}_{ij}\ln(\text{GNPPC}_i\text{GNPPC}_j) + \\ & \Sigma\beta_{7+k}\text{COUNTRY}_k \end{aligned} \tag{7.2}$$

In Equation (7.2), if the estimated coefficients on SIMILARITY_{ij} (that is, β_5) and on $\text{SIMILARITY}_{ij}\ln(\text{GNPPC}_i\text{GNPPC}_j)$ (that is, β_6) have different signs (such as $\beta_5>0$ and $\beta_6<0$; or $\beta_5<0$ and $\beta_6>0$) and are statistically significant, we obtain a break-point value ($\text{GNPPC}_i\text{GNPPC}_j^*$) by letting the first-order differentials of the dependent variable ($\ln(\text{TRADE}_{ij}+1)$ with respect to SIMILARITY be zero, that is, $\text{GNPPC}_i\text{GNPPC}_j^* = \exp(-\beta_5/\beta_6)$. Specifically, as for the case $\beta_5>0$ and $\beta_6<0$, we have:

(i) The effect of cultural similarity on international trade is positive if the income level of the *i*th and *j*th trade partners ($\text{GNPPC}_i\text{GNPPC}_j$) is less than $\text{GNPPC}_i\text{GNPPC}_j^*$;

(ii) The effect of cultural similarity on international trade is negative if the income level of the ith and jth trade partners ($GNPPC_iGNPPC_j$) is more than $GNPPC_iGNPPC_j^*$.

7.2 Measures of cultural similarity and data

Cultural similarity as an explanatory variable in Equations (7.1) and (7.2) can be measured differently. The simplest method is to use a dummy index: that is, '1' for countries (regions) to be culturally linked with each other; and '0' otherwise. Although it has been applied in a number of studies (see, for example, Havrylyshyn and Pritchett, 1991; Foroutan and Pritchett, 1993; Frankel and Wei, 1995; and Frankel et al., 1997), this method is highly simplified. Therefore it cannot be used to measure precisely the extent to which countries (regions) are culturally linked, particularly in the case of culturally diverse countries or regions.

In this book, I will use a comprehensive method for the measurement of cultural similarity. Suppose that the population ratios of N cultural groups are expressed by (x_1, x_2,..., and x_N) and (y_1, y_2,..., and y_N) for countries (regions) X and Y, respectively. All i, x_i and y_i (where, $x_i \geq 0$ and $y_i \geq 0$) belong to the same cultural group. Mathematically, the cultural similarity between the two countries (regions) – SIMILARITY (X, Y) – is measured according to the following formula:[8]

$$\text{SIMILARITY } (X, Y) = \Sigma_{i=1}^{N} \min(x_i, y_i) \qquad (7.3)$$

In Equation (7.3), 'min (...)' denotes the minimization of the variables in parentheses. In fact, several other methods can also be used to comprehensively measure cultural similarity.[9] One reason for using Equation (7.3) is that it can prevent the index of SIMILARITY from further reduction when the values of x_i and y_i are very small. Obviously, the value of SIMILARITY ranges between 0 and 1. In the extreme cases, when SIMILARITY =1, the two countries (regions) have the same cultural structure (that is, for all i, $x_i = y_i$); when SIMILARITY = 0, the two countries (regions) do not have any cultural links with each other (that is, for all i, x_i(or y_i) = 0 and $x_i \neq y_i$). In the other cases, the greater the value of SIMILARITY, the more similar the countries (regions) concerned. Appendix 3 presents the linguistic and religious similarity indexes of selected countries with the rest of the world.

Our particular concern is that since the early 1990s, the attitudes of the Cold War era have been displaced by the emergence of a new economic regionalism. Nations have been reshuffling their relations with the rest of the world. Since the end of the Cold War nations have been searching out new groupings, and finding them with countries with similar economic and cultural interests to their own, while discarding groupings with countries with different economic and cultural interests (Huntington, 1996, p. 125). In order to investigate quantitatively the effects of cultural influences on international trade, we use recent data of a panel of nations. Since international trade performance might differ between the Cold War and the post-Cold War periods, we select two years – 1985 (representing the Cold War period) and 1995 (representing the post-Cold War period).[10]

This arrangement also enables us to check that the results are not specific to any particular time period and to allow for changes in coefficients, especially on DISTANCE and SIMILARITY. Such changes might relate to advances in transportation and communication technology. The data come from Brazil, China, the Democratic Republic of Congo (or Zaire for 1985), France, India, Japan, Saudi Arabia and the United States. While they are both economically important and culturally influential nations Germany and Russia are excluded from the analysis since both experienced territorial changes during the 1985–95 period.

These eight countries encompass most of the world economy and population and represent all of the major linguistic and/or religious groups. They have been chosen with the following in mind. First, we intend to present the full trade pictures for the eight nations with *all* their partners (not just with their *major* trade partners). Second, panel data that include only eight country pairs will make it much easier for us to collect the cross-national data on linguistic and religious links. This research design facilitates collection of the cross-national data on the languages and religions of the eight nations. Other languages and religions not represented in the eight nations in the study will be excluded from the calculation of cross-national data of cultural similarity indexes.[11]

Sources for the data on the dependent and explanatory variables in Equations (7.1) and (7.2) are as follows: (1) the International Monetary Fund (2003, *Direction of Trade Statistics*) for TRADE; (2) the World Bank (1986 and 1999) and the United Nations (1986) for GNP and GNPPC; and (3) calculation by the author based on the *World Atlas* (1994) for DISTANCE and BORDER. The data on SIMILARITY indexes, which are based on Equation (7.3) and the *Britannica Book of the Year* (1986 and 1996), include both linguistic and religious aspects. Specifically, the languages to be considered are Amharic, Arabic, Armenian, Bengali, Chinese, Czech, Danish, Dutch, English, Finnish, French, German, Greek, Hebrew, Hindi, Hungarian, Italian, Japanese, Kazak, Korean, Kyrgyz, Miao, Mongol, Norwegian, Polish, Portuguese, Punjabi, Romanian, Russian, Samoan, Serbo-Croatian, Slovak, Spanish, Swedish, Tai, Tajik, Thai, Turkish, Uighur, Ukrainian, Vietnamese, Yao and Yiddish. The religions are Christian, Orthodox, Jewish, Muslim, Buddhist, Chinese folk-religion (a mixture of Confucianism and Taoism), Hindu, Sikh and Bahai.[12]

It is worth noting that, in the selection of religions for the measurement of religious similarity indexes (RELIGION) in Equation (7.3), we do not include such religions as 'folk-religion' (though 'Chinese folk-religion' is an exception), 'traditional religion', 'atheism' and 'non-religion'. This is because these religions cannot be measured as a common religion in the religious similarity index. 'Traditional or folk religionists' from, say, Togo, and 'traditional or folk religionists' from, say, China, do not have a common religious ground.

The descriptive statistics of the eight countries' panel data on selected variables are reported in Table 7.1. Notably, the average size of bilateral trade increased dramatically from 1985 to 1995. While Brazil, the Democratic Republic of Congo, France and the United States had an average value of more than 40 per cent of religious similarities with their trade partners, China, India and Japan had an average value of less than 10 per cent of religious similarities with their trade partners. With regard to the linguistic variable, the mean values of the linguistic similarity indexes with their respective trade partners had increased in Brazil (from 0.006 to 0.019), China (from 0.013 to 0.019), the Democratic Republic of Congo (from 0.000 to 0.008), France (from 0.029 to 0.064), India (from 0.004 to 0.012)

Table 7.1 Descriptive statistics for selected variables

Country	Population (million)	GNP per capita (US$)	Trade (billion US$)		Mean value of	
			Export	Import	LANGUAGE	RELIGION
1985						
Brazil	138.37	1941	24.49	15.64	0.006	0.437
China	1,054.04	298	26.80	41.09	0.013	0.019
Zaire (Congo, Dem.)	31.67	160	0.32	0.53	0.000	0.391
France	31.67	18,738	87.15	96.15	0.029	0.400
India	781.37	291	8.03	15.42	0.004	0.062
Japan	121.49	12,850	169.07	126.32	0.000	0.027
Saudi Arabia	11.98	6,953	24.82	22.46	0.083	0.222
United States	241.60	17,526	201.57	338.33	0.081	0.414
1995						
Brazil	165.16	4,930	51.03	65.86	0.019	0.435
China	1,255.09	745	182.89	139.26	0.019	0.058
Congo, Dem. (Zaire)	49.21	702	1.28	0.98	0.008	0.432
France	58.73	23,843	255.45	238.59	0.064	0.428
India	975.77	402	33.79	40.36	0.012	0.091
Japan	125.92	33,265	392.78	325.96	0.000	0.032
Saudi Arabia	20.21	6,921	59.16	27.94	0.065	0.233
United States	273.75	28,789	665.68	864.13	0.105	0.426

Notes:
(1) GNP per capita and trade are measured at current US dollars.
(2) For trade, only those with the partners included in our panel data are calculated.

and the United States (from 0.081 to 0.105) during the 1985–95 period; while the mean value of the linguistic similarity index of Saudi Arabia with its trade partners had decreased from 0.018 to 0.010 during the same period.

7.3 Estimated results

7.3.1 Regressions with different variables

In tables 7.2a and 7.2b, Reg. (1) indicates no cultural variables, Reg. (2) indicates a linguistic variable, Reg. (3) indicates a religious variable, and both the cultural variables are included in Reg. (4). All regressions yield different statistical evidence for the determinants of trade in both 1985 and 1995, demonstrating that, if one or more cultural variables were ignored, the estimated results would have become less reliable. In all cases, after the cultural variables are included or removed, the estimated coefficients show changes in both magnitude and statistical significance. For example, in 1985 the coefficient on the log of DISTANCE is –1.195 (which is statistically significant at the 1 per cent level) in Reg. (1); however, after the linguistic and religious variables are included, the coefficient becomes –1.124 (which is statistically significant at the 1 per cent level) in Reg. (4) (shown in Table 7.2a).

More significant influences on the determinants of trade can be found in 1995. As shown in Table 7.2b, the coefficient on the log of DISTANCE is –0.788 (which is statistically significant at the 1 per cent level) in Reg. (1); however, after the linguistic and religious variables are included, the coefficient becomes –0.682 (which is statistically significant at the 1 per cent level) in Reg. (4). In other words, if the cultural variables are not included in the gravity model, the estimated result in Reg. (1) suggests 0.788 per cent decrease in international trade as a result of 1 per cent increase of distance. But after the cultural influences are taken into account in Reg. (4), the average decrease of trade would only be 0.682 per cent!

Moreover, the estimated coefficients on the country-specific dummies are also influenced by the inclusion of cultural variables in the gravity model. For example, in 1985 the coefficient on the 'China' dummy is 0.988 (which is statistically significant at the 5 per cent level) in Reg. (4) but it is reduced to only 0.740 (which is statistically insignificant) in Reg. (1); similarly, the coefficient on the 'Saudi Arabia' dummy is –0.835 (which is statistically significant at the 10 per cent level) in Reg. (4) but it is reduced to –1.024 (which is statistically significant at 5 per cent level) in Reg. (1) (see Table 7.2a). In 1995 the coefficient on the 'India' dummy is –1.011 (which is statistically significant at the 1 per cent level) in Reg. (4) but it is reduced to –1.261 (which is statistically significant at 1 per cent level) in Reg. (1) (see Table 7.2b).

Table 7.2a Gravity model regressions on trade, 1985

Explanatory variable	Reg. (1)	Reg. (2)	Reg. (3)	Reg. (4)
(Constant)	–19.690 (2.328)[a]	–19.938 (2.345)[a]	–20.695 (2.389)[a]	–20.777 (2.395)[a]
$\ln(GNP_iGNP_j)$	1.016 (0.043)[a]	1.019 (0.043)[a]	1.026 (0.044)[a]	1.027 (0.044)[a]
$\ln(GNPPC_iGNPPC_j)$	0.198 (0.076)[a]	0.189 (0.076)[a]	0.188 (0.076)[a]	0.184 (0.076)[b]
$\ln(DISTANCE_{ij})$	–1.195 (0.170)[a]	–1.169 (0.172)[a]	–1.135 (0.173)[a]	–1.124 (0.174)[a]
$BORDER_{ij}$	1.316 (0.575)[b]	1.257 (0.579)[b]	1.210 (0.577)[b]	1.182 (0.580)[b]
$LANGUAGE_{ij}$	–	0.649 (0.726)	–	0.376 (0.743)
$RELIGION_{ij}$	–	–	0.641 (0.347)[c]	0.602 (0.355)[c]
Brazil	0.336 (0.411)	0.379 (0.414)	0.340 (0.410)	0.364 (0.413)
China	0.740 (0.470)	0.760 (0.470)[c]	0.992 (0.488)[b]	0.988 (0.489)[b]
Zaire (Congo, Dem.)	–2.013 (0.520)[a]	–1.968 (0.522)[a]	–1.948 (0.521)[a]	–1.925 (0.523)[a]
France	1.497 (0.399)[a]	1.548 (0.403)[a]	1.551 (0.399)[a]	1.578 (0.403)[a]
India	–0.497 (0.472)	–0.468 (0.473)	–0.263 (0.488)	–0.261 (0.488)
Japan	1.248 (0.382)[a]	1.298 (0.386)[a]	1.498 (0.405)[a]	1.511 (0.406)[a]
Saudi Arabia	–1.024 (0.420)[b]	–1.007 (0.420)[b]	–0.833 (0.432)[b]	–0.835 (0.432)[c]
R square	0.600	0.600	0.601	0.601
F-statistical value	171.6	157.3	157.9	145.7
Sig. of the regression	0.000	0.000	0.000	0.000
Number of observations	1,271	1,271	1,271	1,271

Notes:
(1) Empty cells denote that the explanatory variables shown on the left are excluded from regressions.
(2) a., b. and c. denote statistically significant at the 1, 5 and 10 per cent levels, respectively.

7.3.2 Regressions with full variables

We have found that the regressions in which cultural variables are included are statistically more reliable than those in which no cultural variable is

Table 7.2b Gravity model regressions on trade, 1995

Explanatory variable	Reg. (1)	Reg. (2)	Reg. (3)	Reg. (4)
(Constant)	–22.345 (1.903)[a]	–23.005 (1.916)[a]	–23.272 (1.929)[a]	–23.666 (1.936)[a]
$\ln(GNP_iGNP_j)$	1.286 (0.039)[a]	1.296 (0.039)[a]	1.298 (0.039)[a]	1.305 (0.040)[a]
$\ln(GNPPC_iGNPPC_j)$	–0.469 (0.057)[a]	–0.490 (0.057)[a]	–0.503 (0.058)[a]	–0.515 (0.058)[a]
$\ln(DISTANCE_{ij})$	–0.788 (0.143)[a]	–0.738 (0.144)[a]	–0.711 (0.146)[a]	–0.682 (0.146)[a]
$BORDER_{ij}$	0.578 (0.488)	0.453 (0.490)	0.467 (0.489)	0.382 (0.490)
$LANGUAGE_{ij}$	–	1.539 (0.594)[a]	–	1.265 (0.606)[b]
$RELIGION_{ij}$	–	–	0.814 (0.301)[a]	0.684 (0.307)[b]
Brazil	–0.721 (0.337)[b]	–0.589 (0.340)[c]	–0.748 (0.336)[b]	–0.635 (0.340)[c]
China	–0.662 (0.369)[c]	–0.564 (0.370)	–0.437 (0.378)	–0.393 (0.378)
Congo, Dem. (Zaire)	–3.134 (0.391)[a]	–2.973 (0.395)[a]	–3.154 (0.390)[a]	–3.019 (0.395)[a]
France	0.875 (0.342)[a]	0.991 (0.344)[a]	0.944 (0.342)[a]	1.028 (0.344)[a]
India	–1.261 (0.386)[a]	–1.155 (0.387)[a]	–1.067 (0.391)[a]	–1.011 (0.392)[a]
Japan	–0.024 (0.324)	0.145 (0.330)	0.306 (0.346)	0.393 (0.348)
Saudi Arabia	–0.746 (0.363)[c]	–0.633 (0.365)[c]	–0.533 (0.371)	–0.475 (0.371)
R square	0.587	0.589	0.589	0.590
F-statistical value	199.7	184.3	184.4	170.9
Sig. of the regression	0.000	0.000	0.000	0.000
Number of observations	1,558	1,558	1,558	1,558

Notes:

(1) Empty cells denote that the explanatory variables shown on the left are excluded from regressions.

(2) a., b. and c. denote statistically significant at the 1, 5 and 10 per cent levels, respectively.

included. Next, let us look at the economic implications of the estimated coefficients on the full set of explanatory variables.

As shown in tables 7.2a and 7.2b, the estimated coefficient on the natural log of DISTANCE is –1.124 (statistically significant at the 1 per cent confidence level) for 1985 (as shown in Reg. (4) of Table 7.2a) and –0.682 (statistically significant at the 1 per cent confidence level) for 1995 (as shown in Reg. (4) of Table 7.2b). Obviously, this provides evidence to support the contention that geographical influence on trade has been reduced from 1985 to 1995. The estimated coefficient on BORDER is statistically significant at the 5 per cent level for 1985 but not for 1995, showing that the eight countries did not tend to have any extraordinary trade growth with their neighbouring countries and regions in 1995 vis-à-vis 1985. This result seems unlikely to confirm the view that sharing a common land border will contribute to economic cooperation between the countries concerned (for a typical example in this regard, see Box 7.1). In the case of China, the neighbouring countries either were separated by geographical barriers[13] or had not yet set up any efficient cross-border economic and trade relations (such as with Afghanistan and North Korea).

Box 7.1 Maquiladoras

During the Second World War Mexico and the United States signed an agreement that allowed Mexican labourers, principally agricultural workers, to cross the border into the United States to work. The programme continued until 1964 when the United States, largely in response to pressure exerted by organized labour, unilaterally terminated it. Partly as a measure to alleviate this problem, in 1965 the Mexican president, Diaz Ordaz, announced a new programme that would permit US firms to import capital equipment and materials into Mexico for re-export. The Johnson Administration agreed to this proposal. In Mexico, the plants set up under the Border Industrialization Program (BIP) are called *maquiladoras* and the industry is called the *maquila* industry. *Maquila* means measure in Spanish, in the sense that a miller of grain kept a measure or plant of the grain in payment for services.

Most of Mexico's assembly activities are located along the border with the United States, concentrating on six towns from Tijuana, south of San Diego, California, on the Pacific Ocean, to Matamores opposite Brownsville, Texas, near the Gulf of Mexico. The border is fairly accessible and transportation from almost any point in the United States to the border is cheap when compared to overseas trade. Not only geographically but also culturally, the distance between the two countries is not very great. Since the United States has a relatively high real-wage economy in comparison to that of Mexico, its firms have ample incentive to move segmental production processes that are labour intensive to lower real labour cost areas. Real labour cost as a whole is lower in Mexico because labour productivity in general is lower, and because Mexico has abundant supplies of unskilled labour.

With regard to the hypothesis that international relations during the Cold War era were more strongly influenced by ideological similarity than cultural similarity (see, for example, Huntington, 1996), as shown in tables 7.3a and 7.3b, the estimated coefficients on LANGUAGE are statistically significant in 1995 but not in 1985. The estimated coefficients on RELIGION are statistically significant in both 1985 and 1995. Obviously, the above results imply an increasing tendency for cultural influences on international trade during this period.

7.3.3 Patterns for cultural influences on trade

As shown in tables 7.2a and 7.2b, no cultural variables are statistically significant estimated at the 1 per cent level (and the linguistic variable is statistically insignificant even at the 10 per cent level for 1985). This reminds us of a possible nonlinear correlation existing between trade and cultural variables. A glance at the scatter diagrams (Figure 7.1) shows that different patterns of partial correlations exist between trade and cultural variables for the sample of eight nations. These include:

(i) Positive correlations exist for Brazil (language in 1985 and 1995), China (language in 1985 and 1995; religion in 1995), the Democratic Republic of Congo (religion in 1985 and 1995; language in 1995), France (language in 1985), India (religion in 1985 and 1995; language in 1995), Saudi Arabia (in all cases) and the USA (language and religion in 1995).
(ii) Negative correlations exist for France (religion in 1985; language in 1995), India (language in 1985), Japan (language and religion in 1985; religion in 1995), and the USA (language and religion in 1985).
(iii) Neutral or no correlations exist for Brazil (religion in 1995), China (religion in 1985), the Democratic Republic of Congo (language in 1985), France (religion in 1995), and Japan (language in 1995).

In order to investigate the possible nonlinear relationship between cultural similarity and international trade, we employ Equation (7.2). The estimated results (reported in Table 7.3a) show that, in 1995, the estimated coefficients are statistically significant for LANGUAGE and RELIGION and for the products of the natural log of GNPPC with LANGUAGE and RELIGION, respectively; while they are only statistically significant for LANGUAGE and the product of the log of GNPPC with LANGUAGE in 1985. These results suggest that the cultural influences on international trade follow nonlinear patterns. Specifically, the significantly estimated relation implies that the effect of religious influence on trade is positive for the log of per capita GNP below 16.403 and then becomes negative in 1985; and that the effect of religious influence on trade is positive for the log of per capita GNPs below 18.092 and then becomes negative in 1995.[14]

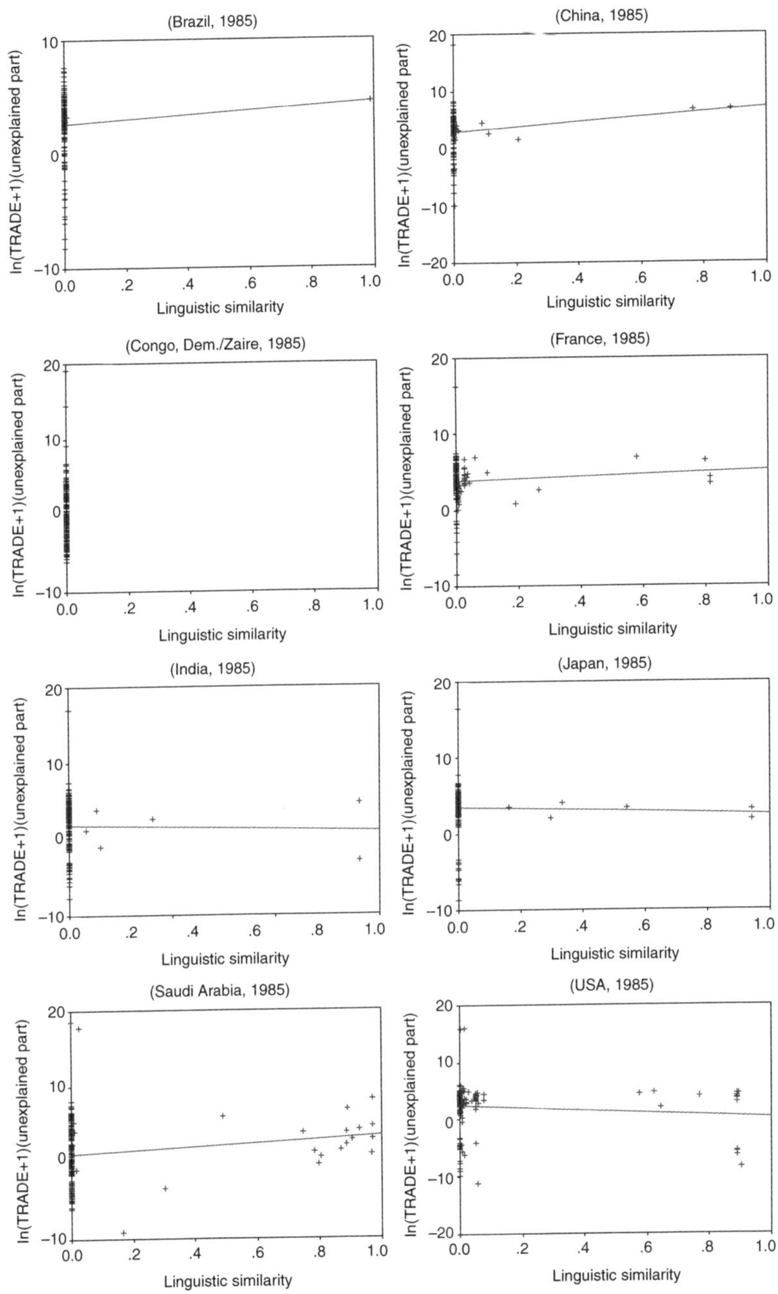

Figure 7.1 Trade versus cultural similarity

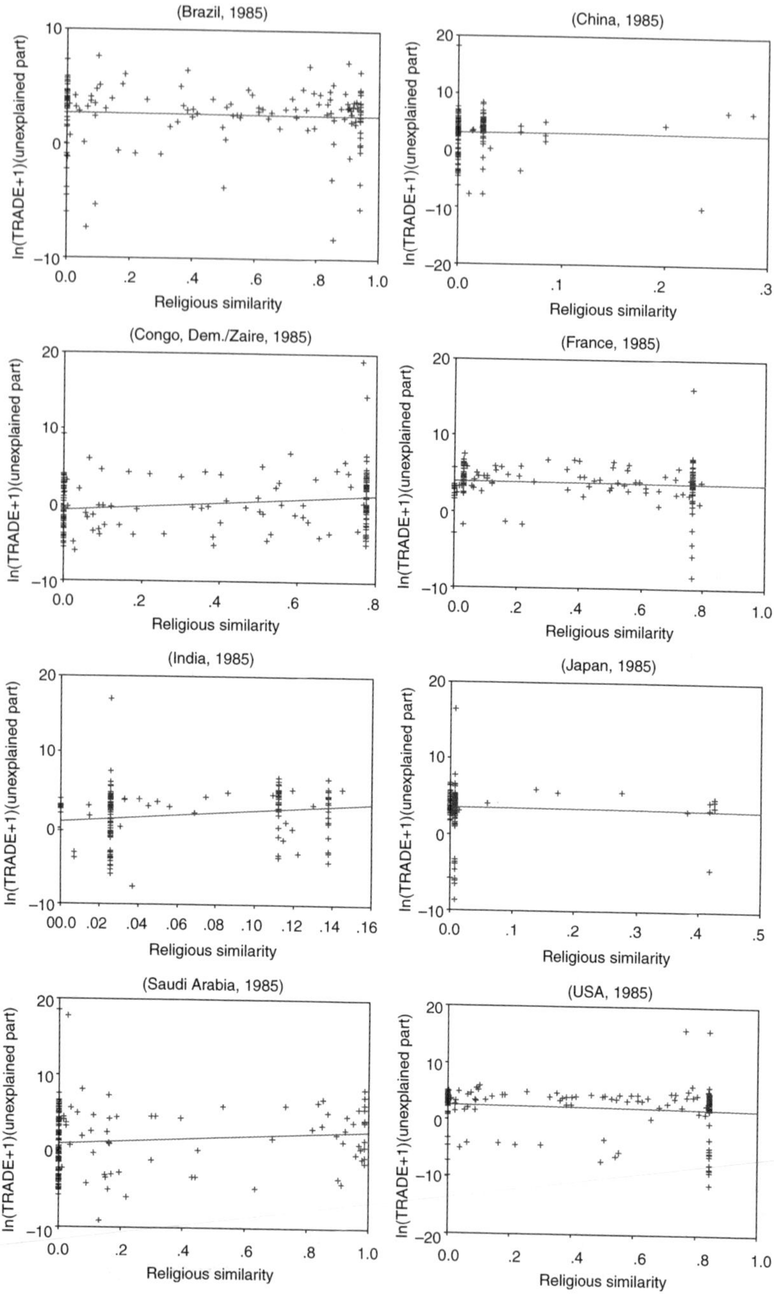

Figure 7.1 Trade versus cultural similarity – *cont'd*

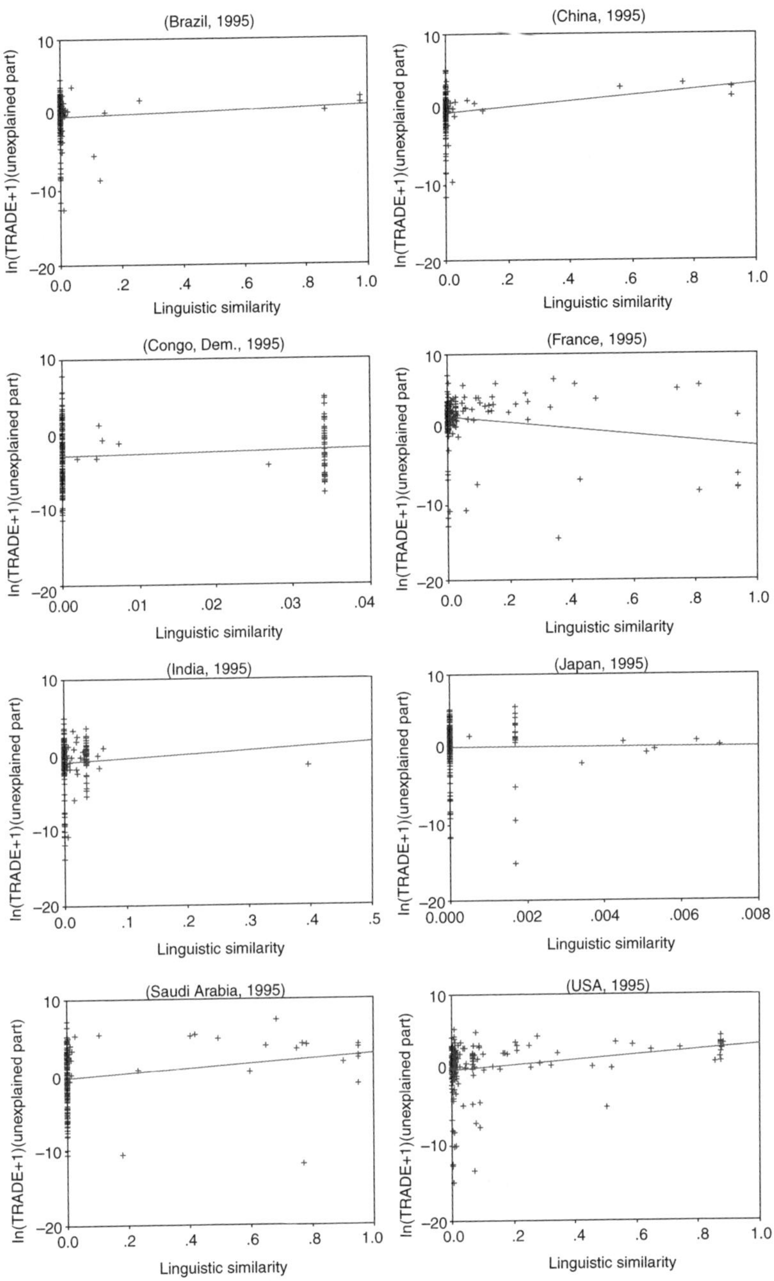

Figure 7.1 Trade versus cultural similarity – *cont'd*

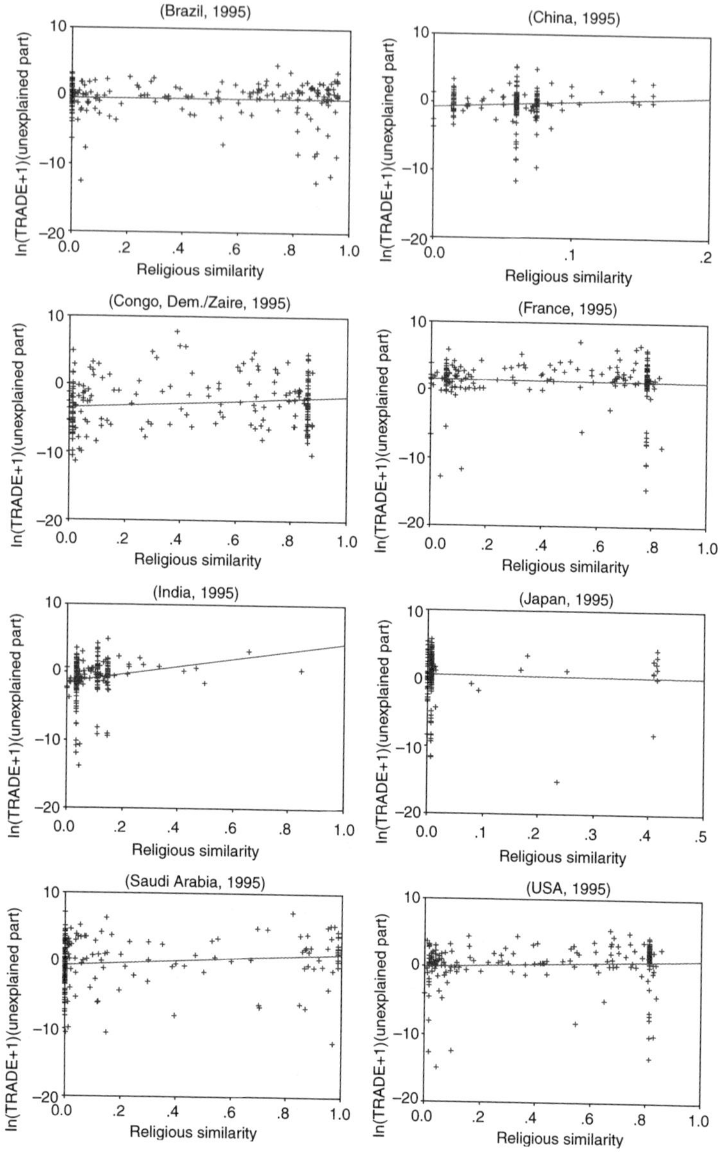

Figure 7.1 Trade versus cultural similarity – *cont'd*

Table 7.3a Modified gravity model regressions on trade

Explanatory variable	1985	1995
(Constant)	–21.898	–25.309
	(2.405)[a]	(1.970)[a]
$\ln(GNP_i GNP_j)$	1.030	1.304
	(0.043)[a]	(0.039)[a]
$\ln(GNPPC_i GNPPC_j)$	0.293	–0.386
	(0.081)[a]	(0.066)[a]
$\ln(DISTANCE_{ij})$	–1.172	–0.708
	(0.174)[a]	(0.146)[a]
$BORDER_{ij}$	1.082	0.341
	(0.578)[c]	(0.488)
$LANGUAGE_{ij}$	9.556	14.606
	(7.661)	(6.072)[a]
$RELIGION_{ij}$	8.579	7.454
	(2.416)[a]	(2.179)[a]
$LANGUAGE_{ij}$*$\ln(GNPPC_i GNPPC_j)$	–0.509	–0.744
	(0.451)	(0.342)[b]
$RELIGION_{ij}$*$\ln(GNPPC_i GNPPC_j)$	–0.523	–0.412
	(0.157)[a]	(0.131)[a]
Brazil	0.121	–0.794
	(0.416)	(0.340)[b]
China	0.987	–0.397
	(0.487)[b]	(0.376)
Congo, Dem. (Zaire)	-2.400	-3.276
	(0.538)[a]	(0.399)[a]
France	1.469	0.959
	(0.404)[a]	(0.343)[a]
India	–0.316	-1.022
	(0.486)	(0.390)a
Japan	1.163	–0.059
	(0.414)[a]	(0.359)
Saudi Arabia	–1.155	–0.830
	(0.438)[a]	(0.378)[b]
R square	0.605	0.595
F-statistical value	128.5	151.2
Sig. of the regression	0.000	0.000
Number of observations	1,271	1,558

Notes:
(1) The variables LANGUAGE*$\ln(GNPPC_i GNPPC_j)$ and RELIGION*$\ln(GNPPC_i GNPPC_j)$ are the products of LANGUAGE and RELIGION indexes and the natural log of per capita GNPs, respectively.
(2) a., b. and c. denote statistically significant at the 1, 5, and 10 per cent levels, respectively.

Table 7.3b Modified gravity model regressions on trade, by export and import

	1985		1995	
Explanatory variable	**Export**	**Import**	**Export**	**Import**
(Constant)	–16.854	–30.106	–24.206	–32.867
	(2.315)[a]	(2.537)[a]	(1.932)[a]	(2.083)[a]
$\ln(GNP_iGNP_j)$	0.934	1.130	1.229	1.440
	(0.042)[a]	(0.046)[a]	(0.039)[a]	(0.042)[a]
$\ln(GNPPC_iGNPPC_j)$	0.198	0.424	–0.363	–0.270
	(0.078)[a]	(0.086)[a]	(0.065)[a]	(0.070)[a]
$\ln(DISTANCE_{ij})$	–1.252	–1.037	–0.651	–0.795
	(0.167)[a]	(0.183)[a]	(0.143)[a]	(0.155)[a]
$BORDER_{ij}$	0.624	1.834	0.670	0.476
	(0.556)	(0.609)[a]	(0.478)	(0.516)
$LANGUAGE_{ij}$	11.861	10.355	15.818	12.698
	(7.376)[c]	(8.084)	(5.954)[a]	(6.422)[b]
$RELIGION_{ij}$	8.459	5.950	8.143	5.483
	(2.326)[a]	(2.549)[b]	(2.137)[a]	(2.305)[a]
$LANGUAGE_{ij}*\ln(GNPPC_iGNPPC_j)$	–0.577	–0.621	–0.781	–0.648
	(0.434)	(0.476)	(0.335)[b]	(0.362)[c]
$RELIGION_{ij}*\ln(GNPPC_iGNPPC_j)$	–0.508	–0.350	–0.435	–0.312
	(0.151)[a]	(0.165)[b]	(0.128)[a]	(0.138)[b]
Brazil	0.294	–1.818	–0.834	–0.955
	(0.401)	(0.439)[a]	(0.334)[a]	(0.360)[a]
China	0.529	0.438	–0.078	–1.257
	(0.469)	(0.514)	(0.369)	(0.398)[a]
Congo, Dem. (Zaire)	–3.616	–0.127	–3.711	–1.563
	(0.518)[a]	(0.568)	(0.392)[a]	(0.422)[a]
France	1.347	1.482	1.053	1.103
	(0.388)[a]	(0.426)[a]	(0.336)[a]	(0.363)[a]
India	–0.976	0.318	–0.754	–1.344
	(0.468)[b]	(0.513)	(0.382)[b]	(0.412)[a]
Japan	1.378	0.623	0.216	–0.200
	(0.399)[a]	(0.437)	(0.352)	(0.379)
Saudi Arabia	–2.752	–0.316	–1.893	–0.400
	(0.422)[a]	(0.462)	(0.371)[a]	(0.400)
R square	0.622	0.590	0.607	0.597
F-statistical value	138.1	120.6	158.9	152.2
Sig. of the regression	0.000	0.000	0.000	0.000
Number of observations	1,271	1,271	1,558	1,558

Notes:
(1) a., b. and c. denote statistically significant at the 1, 5, and 10 per cent levels, respectively.
(2) See notes to Table 7.3a for other information.

One interpretation of the above results involves the idea that, although further theoretical and empirical evidence is still needed, the types of relation between cultural dissimilarity and comparative advantages of industrial production and consumption are determined by income level. Specifically, if other natural and geographical conditions are not considered, (i) comparative advantages can be found in culturally dissimilar economies more often than in culturally homogeneous places; and (ii) the cost of intercultural transaction is usually higher in low-income nations (with low educational attainment and backward technological facilities) than in high-income nations (with high educational attainment and advanced technological facilities). At the same time, the benefit of intercultural transaction is usually higher (or at least not lower) in the high-income nations than in the low-income nations. This tends to retard trade in poor economies and to encourage trade in richer places.

Since current (*not* constant) prices have been used to measure the per capita GNPs of 1985 and 1995, the comparison of the above two break-point values is meaningless. What is more, the quality of the cultural data in 1985 is less reliable than (and not comparable to) that in 1995 (as will be explained later). As a result, we will only analyse the empirical results for 1995.

By letting the first-order differentials of the dependent variable (ln(TRADE+1)) with respect to the explanatory variables (LANGUAGE and RELIGION) in Table 7.3a be zero, we obtain:

$$\text{GNPPC}_i\text{GNPPC}_j = \exp(14.606/0.744) = 335697304 \text{ (for LANGUAGE)}$$
$$\text{GNPPC}_i\text{GNPPC}_j = \exp(7.454/0.412) = 72004056 \text{ (for RELIGION)}$$

On the basis of the above quantitative results, we can divide the existing trade partners into three categories (marked by 'A', 'B' and 'C') for the correlations between trade and cultural similarity indexes: (A) trade is encouraged by both linguistic and religious similarity indexes; (B) trade is encouraged by religious similarity but is retarded by linguistic similarity; and (C) trade is retarded by both religious and linguistic similarity indexes (see Figure 7.2a).

Again, by letting the first-order differentials of the dependent variables (ln(EXPORT+1)) and (ln(IMPORT+1)) with respect to the explanatory variable (RELIGION) in Table 7.3b be zero, we obtain:

$$\text{GNPPC}_i\text{GNPPC}_j = \exp(8.143/0.435) = 134832015 \text{ (for export)}$$
$$\text{GNPPC}_i\text{GNPPC}_j = \exp(5.483/0.312) = 42871505 \text{ (for import)}$$

On the basis of the above quantitative results, we can divide the existing trade partners into three categories (marked by 'A', 'B' and 'C') for the correlations between trade and cultural similarity indexes: (A) import is

(a)

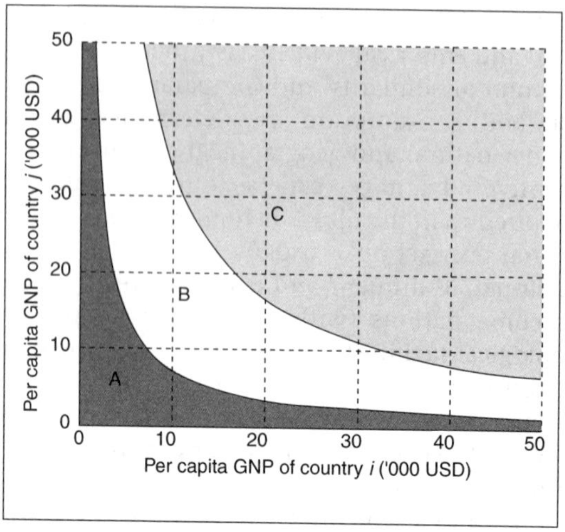

Notes:

(A) Countries between which trade is encouraged by both linguistic and religious similarity indexes.

(B) Countries between which trade is encouraged by religious similarity but is retarded by linguistic similarity.

(C) Countries between which trade is retarded by both religious and linguistic similarity indexes.

(b)

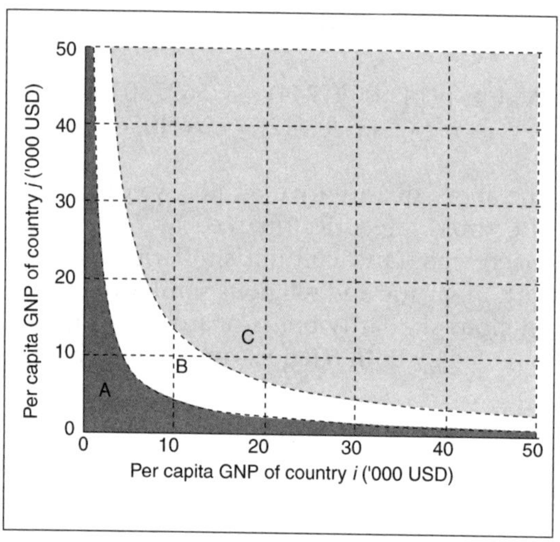

Figure 7.2 Conditions under which cultural similarity encourages (retards) international trade

Notes:

(A) Countries between which import is encouraged by religious similarity index.

(B) Countries between which export is encouraged and import is retarded by religious similarity.

(C) Countries between which import and export are retarded by religious similarity index.

encouraged by religious similarity index; (B) export is encouraged and import is retarded by religious similarity; and (C) import and export are retarded by religious similarity index (see Figure 7.2b).

The economic determinants of trade can be seen as controversial in existing studies. According to the Heckscher-Ohlin theorem (see Heckscher, 1919; Ohlin, 1933), countries with dissimilar levels of per capita income will trade more than countries with similar levels. However, a number of empirical results indicate that if the distribution of national incomes across countries becomes more equal over time, the volume of trade should increase. For example, Linder (1961) predicts that countries with similar levels of per capita income will tend to have similar preferences with somewhat differentiated marketable goods, and thus will trade more with each other. Moreover, Helpman (1987) and Krugman (1995) predict that the sum of the logs of per capita GNPs of two countries will have a positive effect on the log form of trade between the two countries.

The estimated results shown in Figure 7.2 can be used to provide conditions under which the growth of trade is related to income levels:

(i) Trade between countries with dissimilar levels of per capita incomes tends to be encouraged by cultural (especially religious) similarity index.
(ii) Trade between countries with similar levels of per capita incomes tends to be encouraged by cultural (especially religious) similarity index when the income levels are low and tends to be retarded by cultural (especially religious) similarity index when the income levels are high.

7.4 Summary

Although there has been a growing interest in the role of culture in international trade, few studies have dealt quantitatively with the effects of cultural influence. Using a gravity model on trade and the panel data of eight countries, we have found that cultural influences on international trade are more significant for the post-Cold War era than in the Cold War era. Our empirical results provide evidence to support the presumption that high-income trade partners will be less sensitive to the measures of cultural dissimilarity than a developing country in which cultural dissimilarity leads to barriers to international trade. This estimated relation shows that the cultural (especially religious) influence on trade is positive for values of per capita GNP below a break-point and then becomes negative.

If the estimated results are correct, it will be good news for policymakers and managers. The diversity of cultures can enable intercultural trade to become a source of creativity and potential profitability. At best, one could provide 'present and future generations ... tools to meet this challenge, to broaden their knowledge, to discover the world in its imposing diversity, and to allow all individuals to lead a life that is decent, dignified and wise, without losing their identity and sense of community, and without betraying their heritage' (WCCD, 1995). Consequently, native languages are beginning to be re-evaluated, traditional knowledge rediscovered, and local economies revitalized. In fact, a world without the 'other' would be a world of stagnation, for, in culture as in nature, diversity holds the key to innovation and creative, nonlinear solutions (Shanker, 1996).

The treatment of linguistic and religious factors as continuous variables in this research has improved the past quantitative studies in which language was treated as one or more dummies and from which religion was absent. However, restricted by the data collection on cultural variables, this research is only based on the panel data of two years (1985 and 1995) and of eight countries.[15] Moreover, the data on linguistic and religious groups are not as accurate as those on economic and geographical indicators. For example, since some countries collect data on ethnic or 'national' groups only, ethnic distribution often had to be assumed to conform roughly to the distribution of language communications. However this approach should be viewed with caution, because a minority population is not always free to educate its children in its own languages and because better economic opportunities often draw minority group members into the majority-language communities (*Britannica Book of the Year*, 1998, p. 770). It should be noted that data on religious groups are even more unreliable for the year 1985. As pointed out by the *Britannica Book*, until 1989 communist countries had for long consciously attempted to ignore, suppress, or render invisible religious practice within their borders (1998, p. 775).

8
Location, Size and Political Economy of Cultures

> If you understand others you are smart.
> If you understand yourself you are illuminated.
> If you overcome others you are powerful.
> If you overcome yourself you have strength.
>
> (Laozi, *c* 500 BC)

8.1 State-building and culture: narrative

If everything goes according to plan, South Korea will build a new capital, with work beginning in 2007. The South Korean government has announced that, by 2014, it will move its seat of government out of Seoul to the rural area between Yeongi and Kongju, about 160 kilometres to the south, at a cost of US$52 billion. Why has South Korea decided to move its capital away from Seoul? Before answering this question, let us have a brief review of the history of the Korean peninsula.

The Korean peninsula protrudes southward from the north-eastern corner of the Asian continent and is surrounded on three sides by sea. As is true of all countries, the geography of Korea and the external environment have shaped its particular history, including the political, economic and cultural legacy.

During the first millennium BC, a gradual flow of cultural influences from China encouraged the formation of Korean states. Towards the end of the bronze culture of the Karasuk affinity, rising Chinese power brought the impact of the iron culture to ancient Koreans. The rise of Puyo was seen in Manchuria along with China's developing centralized power. In the southern part of the Korean peninsula, tribal leagues of the Three Han gradually developed to the stage of state-building. (Here, Han is written with a different Chinese character from that used for the like-sounding 'Han' dynasty and 'Han' people of China.) Paekche (with its capitals first at Hansong, in modern Seoul, and later at Ungjin, in current Kwangju) and Shilla (with its capital located in current Kyongju) were prominent in the south, with

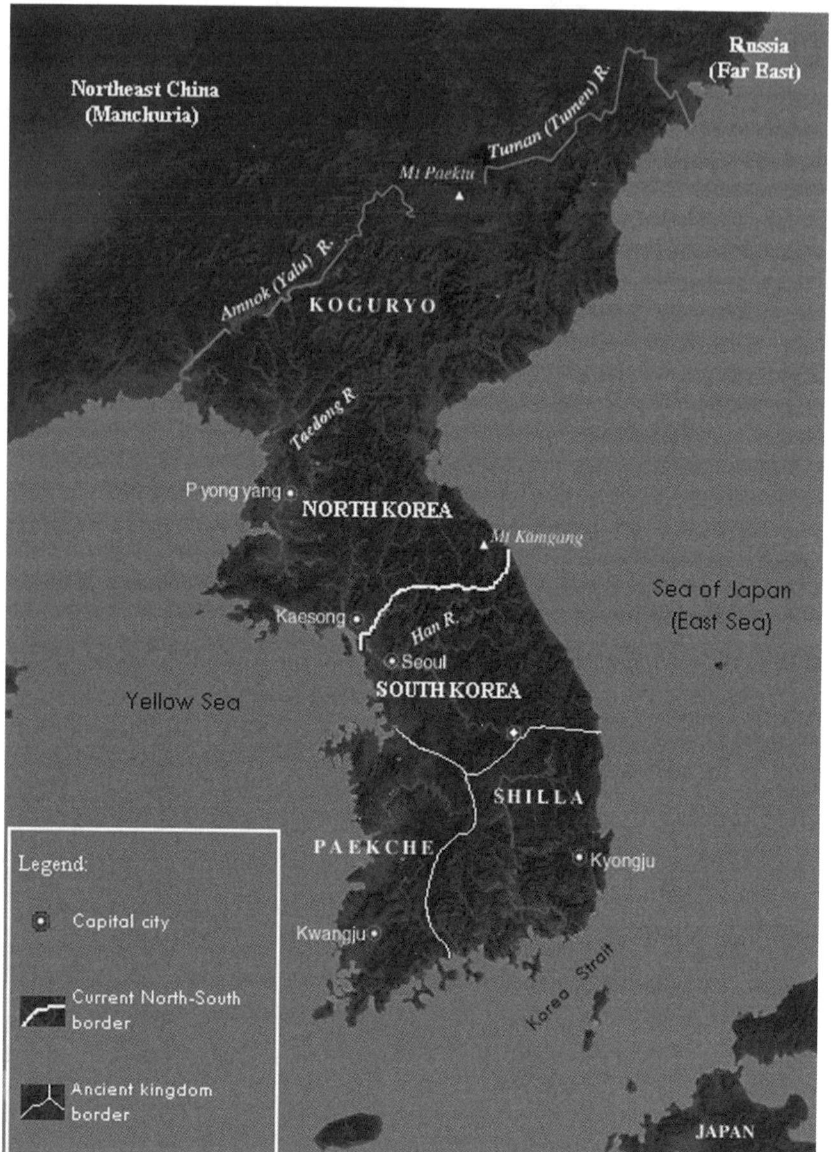

Figure 8.1 Geo-political evolutions of the Korean peninsula

Koguryo (with its capital located in current Pyongyang) in the north (see Figure 8.1).[1]

By the first century, Koguryo was firmly established as a state power and destroyed the Chinese colony Lolang (Nangnang) in AD 313. Paekche amassed power while Koguryo was fighting against the Chinese, and came into conflict with Koguryo in the late fourth century. Then came the growth of Shilla with a more fully organized state power.

Buddhism was introduced to Korea from China, transmitted first to the northern kingdom of Koguryo in AD 372, and then to the south-western kingdom of Paekche in AD 384. Shilla kingdom, however, didn't officially sanction the practice of Buddhism until AD 528. Obviously, Shilla's geographically isolated position on Korea's south-eastern coast slowed the penetration of Sinitic culture.

The Three Kingdoms developed highly sophisticated state organizations on the Korean peninsula, adopting Confucian and Buddhist hierarchical structures with the king at the pinnacle. State codes were promulgated to initiate a legal system to rule the people. The Three Kingdoms competed with each other, strengthening their Buddhist-Confucian state power in an attempt at serious territorial expansion. In this process, Koguryo annexed Puyo in the north, and Shilla conquered Kaya (a political entity comprised of a group of small city-states) in the south.

At the same time, China's Sui dynasty (AD 589–618) sent major expeditions to conquer the Koguryo kingdom but failed. For example, in AD 612, Koguryo General Ulchi Mundok held the fortresses against the Chinese army and navy for several months and destroyed the Sui troops in retreat. An ambush at Salsu (Choongchdon-gang) river allowed only 2700 Sui troops, out of a force of 300,000 men, to escape. Sui fell from power partly as a result of the defeat by Koguryo. The subsequent dynasty, Tang (AD 618–907), dispatched three unsuccessful expeditions against Koguryo in AD 644, 648 and 655.

With assistance from the Chinese Tang dynasty, Shilla was able to defeat the other two kingdoms in AD 668. However reliance on China's Tang dynasty was the price for the unification. Eventually, Shilla had to resist by force the imposition of Chinese rule over the peninsula. This it did, but its strength never again extended beyond the Daedong river. Much of the former Koguryo territory was given up to the Chinese and other tribal states. In AD 671, Shilla started its own operations against Chinese rule and took the Chinese administrative headquarters, thereby retaking all of the Paekche territory. In the following years, the Chinese army persistently claimed the territories of Paekche and Koguryo until AD 676 when they gave in to Shilla's claim of territory south of the Taedong river. Shilla became a unique state, covering most of the Korean peninsula and the majority of the people of the former Three Kingdoms.

The Shilla unification marks the beginning of a unified Korean language and ethnic identity. Many new political, legal, and educational institutions were introduced during the unified Shilla period (AD 668–935). Domestic and foreign trade with both China and Japan prospered. Scholarship in Confucian learning, mathematics, astronomy and medicine flourished. Buddhism, which first came to the peninsula in AD 372, was later accompanied by cultural refinements such as literacy in Chinese characters.

During the early period Shilla maintained its kingdom with a strong hand. Military commanders were stationed throughout the country, and a system of hostage-holding learned from the Chinese was established, whereby prominent tribal chiefs throughout the conquered territories had to send their eldest sons to Kyongju (the capital of Shilla kingdom) to guarantee that the tribes would not instigate rebellions against the central government. In the latter part of the eighth century, however, Shilla started to decline. By the second half of the ninth century local and regional uprisings were no longer under the capital's control. The rebels in the former Paekche area declared the later Paekche kingdom, and later Koguryo was also declared. Tax revenues fell off, leading to a further weakening of the state. The chaotic situation eventually resulted in the emergence of a new dynasty – Koryo – in AD 915.[2]

The founder of Koryo and his heirs consolidated control over the Korean peninsula and strengthened political and economic foundations by closely following the bureaucratic and land grant systems of China. The Koryo dynasty witnessed nearly a century of thriving commercial, intellectual and artistic activities parallel to those of China's Song dynasty (AD 960–1279). Kaesong, Koryo's capital, became a trade centre in the Korean peninsula.

While early Koryo was a glorious period, with flourishing cultural innovations, later Koryo experienced growing external threats. In 1231, when the Mongols dominated all mainland Asia, they launched a massive invasion on Koryo. Eventually, the Korean peninsula came under the control of the Mongol Empire through the intermarriage of the royal families. In the early fourteenth century, when China's new Ming dynasty (1368–1644) was founded, Koryo was split between pro-Ming and pro-Mongol factions. In 1392, the pro-Ming forces, led by General Yi Song-gye, took the throne and founded a new dynasty, which was named Chosen (calm land of the morning).

The Chosen (Yi) (1392–1910) dynasty introduced the Confucian social norms and moral values which were to govern Korea for the next five centuries. In 1394 the capital was moved from Kaesong to Seoul (also known as Hanyang and later as Hanseong), located on the lower reach of the Han river with easy access to water transportation.

The most productive period of the Yi dynasty came under its fourth king, Sejong (r. 1418–50), who was noted for his mastery of Confucian learning. One of King Sejong's most celebrated achievements was the creation of the

Korean alphabet, *han-gul*, which became the official way of expressing the language of the Korean people from that time onwards. After Sejong, however, the dynasty saw many ups and downs. During the late nineteenth and twentieth centuries, the Yi dynasty was subject to the battles for hegemony and expansion in East Asia between Japan and China, and later between Japan and Russia. The Chosen court pursued at that period a completely isolationist policy against the Western world. With endless conflicts, rebellions and quarrels from within and as a result of international political games between the superpowers of Great Britain, Russia and the United States, Chosen was annexed by Japan as a colony in 1910.[3]

The Japanese colonization of the Korean peninsula lasted for 36 years. In 1945 Japan surrendered unconditionally to the US and Soviet-led allied forces. The two superpowers agreed to divide Korea into areas north and south of the 38th Parallel for the purpose of military operations relating to the surrender of Japanese troops. The border, originally a temporary expedient, eventually divided the country into Russian-occupied North Korea and American-occupied South Korea. North Korea, officially the Democratic People's Republic of Korea (DPRK), was established on 9 September 1948, with Pyongyang as its capital. South Korea, or the Republic of Korea (ROK), was established on 10 May 1948, with Seoul as its capital.

The two countries have technically been at war since the Korean War (1951–53) ended in a truce, and relations have been uncertain (and sometimes tense) since then. The division of the country extends through all areas of Korean life – political, economic and social. The artificial division at the 38th Parallel destroyed national unity, and severed the mutual complementarities between the northern and southern parts of the economy. As noted by Choy (1984, p. 14):

> Before the division of the country, northern Korea had almost 70 to 80 per cent of the heavy industry including most sources of hydroelectric power supply, while southern Korea dominated most of the light industry as well as rice production. The consumer-goods industry of the south depended upon northern supply of both electrical power and raw and semi-finished materials. The south depended on the chemical fertilizer produced in the north, while the north needed the rice from the south.[4]

The move of South Korea's capital is designed to relieve development pressure on Seoul, which has a population of 10 million, while shifting government operations farther away from the border with North Korea. The current capital, Seoul, located in the northwestern part of South Korea on the Han river, is about 42 kilometres from the North Korean border, within the range of rocket attack should hostilities break out.

The spatial distribution of socioeconomic activities within Seoul Special Municipality has been significantly affected by its geographical proximity to the border. Seoul's economic activity used to be concentrated on Chung-gu (central district), on the northern side of the Han river. Since the Korean War, the Municipality's urbanization has expanded, via the construction of 18 bridges across the Han river, into the far southern suburbs instead of the northern fringes, simply because the southern areas are further from the demilitarized zone (DMZ). The distribution of economic activities has been particularly uneven within Seoul's urban area. For example, the value of real estate in the southern Han river area increased hundreds of times from the 1950s to the 1990s. Gangnam-gu (south Han river district), which was Seoul's urban fringe, has become one of the most prosperous districts, with many economic, trade, educational and research centres, and modern buildings (such as the 1988 Olympic Complex and the KOEX Exhibition Centre). However few South Koreans have been willing to set up their businesses or to live in the northern suburban fringe.

The South Korean government has eventually decided to construct a new capital so as to move most government agencies from Seoul to a geographically central area (around the Yeongi-Kongju area). Is military concern the only reason to explain the above decision? Might other factors also play a role? Further, why did the unified Shilla dynasty sustain a much shorter period than both the Koryo and Chosen dynasties? And after the reunification of North and South Korea in the future, what will the spatial structure of Korea be – politically, economically and culturally?

8.2 Spatial efficiency of authoritarianism: theory

8.2.1 Some basic concepts

The term 'authoritarian' refers to an organization or an independent state which enforces strong and sometimes oppressive measures against the population, generally without attempting to gain the consent of the population. In an authoritarian state, citizens are subject to state authority in many aspects of their lives, including many that other political philosophies would see as matters of personal choice.

Authoritarianism often arises from the governing bodies' presumption that they know what is right or wrong for the country and from intolerance of dissent. The government then enforces what it thinks is right, often with use of considerable force. Dissenting voices are ignored, or, more strikingly, are considered to be plotting against the best interests of the country. Such was, for instance, the case during the Reign of Terror in France or in Spain under Franco. In most cases, the leadership (government) of an authoritarian regime comprises an elite group that uses repressive means to stay in power. However, unlike totalitarian regimes, there is no desire or ideological justification for the state to control all aspects of a person's life, and the state will generally ignore the actions of an individual unless they are perceived to constitute a direct challenge to the state. Totalitarian governments tend to be revolutionary, intent on changing the basic structure of society, while authoritarian ones tend to be conservative.[5]

Many independent countries have more than one culture. The former Soviet Union, for example, was composed of Eastern Orthodox, Islamic and Western (Christian) cultures. But in a single culture area there may exist more than one political unit. The ethnic Chinese area, for example, includes four independent or internationally independent political systems (Taiwan, Hong Kong, Macau and mainland China). In order to simplify our spatial analysis, we use in what follows a new phrase 'authoritarian area'. In brief, 'authoritarian area' refers to 'a recognizable cultural area that is under the jurisdiction of an authoritarian government'.

Historical events have provided an ample and valuable narrative; and the narrative matters because from the historical point of view some specific events can yield a multiplicity of equilibria. But narrative alone cannot answer the above questions sufficiently since they relate to events that did *not* take place (or have not yet taken place) and the motivation for *not* behaving in a particular way. This is especially true when data and infor-

Box 8.1 Analytic narrative approach

There are various methodological problems that are common to all analyses of cultural influences on economic activities. First, the studies of the relations between culture and economy embrace a wide diversity of substantive backgrounds. Second, the specific context is particularly relevant to each of the research questions, which means that each economic process or each culture has unique characteristics. While some of the problems can be handled with methodological tools that are pretty standard, others are more difficult to address and call for relatively new methodologies.

A priori, the most relevant advantage of the analytic narrative method is that it would allow us to model historical 'one-off' processes and events that have unique characteristics. Likewise, the method would render some problems of empirical testing of hypotheses manageable. Some political and cultural events can pose insurmountable difficulties to traditional panel data or time-series methods. According to Bates et al. (1998, pp. 14–18), there are five steps to evaluate a narrative:

(i) Do the assumptions fit the facts, as they are known?
(ii) Do conclusions follow from premises?
(iii) Do its implications find confirmation in data?
(iv) How well does the theory stand up to comparison with other explanations?
(v) How general is the explanation? Does it apply to other cases?

mation on which the narrative is based are not full and accurate. Addressing these questions requires an appropriate model for linking what we observe with what we do not observe. The phrase 'analytic narrative' captures our conviction that theory linked to data is more powerful than either data or theory alone (see Box 8.1).

8.2.2 A spatial model

All established theories are based on a number of unrealistic assumptions. The art to successfully setting up theoretical models lies in the fact that the simplifying assumptions are made only whenever it is unavoidable, and only where final results will not be sensitive. In order to model culture formulation as a result of a specific trade-off between the benefits of large cultural jurisdictions and the costs and risks of cultural diversity resulting from large populations, let us first consider an isolated authoritarian area and make the following assumptions:

1. There is mobility of socioeconomic factors within the authoritarian area, but not with the outside world.
2. All these socioeconomic factors are uniformly distributed throughout the authoritarian area.
3. There exists an isotropic communication and transport network in the authoritarian area.
4. The size of the authoritarian area can change freely, which means that it can be as small as zero, or as large as is necessary in the analysis.
5. The aim of the authoritarian area is to be seeking to maximize its well-being through the behaviour of its economic agents.

Obviously, assumption (1) is characteristic of all kinds of isolated authoritarian areas. Assumptions (2) and (3) are very common in most spatial economic analyses. In assumption (4), there are different ways to measure the size of authoritarian areas: (i) land area reflects the size of natural resources on which a culture is necessarily based; (ii) population size usually reflects the size of social resources on which a culture is necessarily based; and (iii) economic output reflects all the final products and services generated within the authoritarian area or all the income items produced by and distributed to the population of the authoritarian area. But since the authoritarian area defined here is spatially uniform, the use of all these approaches will not affect the consistency of our analysis. Finally, assumption (5) simplifies our topic to a pure economic issue, in which consumers seek to maximize satisfaction and firms seek to maximize their return from productive activity.

There is a series of challenges to the study of the economic mechanisms within as well as between authoritarian areas differing in size. Why have some small economies that are culturally different from each other voluntarily formed a large economic zone, while large economies that are culturally similar to each other have not? Why are the political and economic agreements between culturally heterogeneous economies less stable than those of culturally homogeneous economies that are politically different? In order to explore the above dilemmas, we will define below our ways of creating a new authoritarian regime or eliminating an existing one.

Rule A. *If the net benefit of governing a defined area is larger than zero, then the existing authoritarian regime will survive or a new authoritarian regime will be born.*

Rule B. *If the net benefit of governing a defined area is less than zero, then the existing authoritarian regime will disappear or a new authoritarian regime will not be born.*

On the basis of the above assumptions and rules, we can build a spatial model of authoritarian areas (see Appendix 1).

8.2.3 Spatial optimality

For a given set of sizes for the authoritarian area (as defined in assumption (4) above), there is an expansion that defines the least-cost combinations of culture size inputs and thus specifies the lowest total variable cost attainable at each rate of administered size. Generally, the sources of benefit from economies of scale for the authoritarian area may be grouped into three categories:

(1) *Technical economies.* The large authoritarian areas can make relatively efficient uses of their fixed costs and hence gain considerable advantages over small authoritarian areas.
(2) *Marketing economies.* Marketing in a larger economy has many benefits, but the main economies of scale from marketing include bulk purchases and distribution potentialities.
(3) *Risk-bearing economies.* A number of advantages can lead to larger authoritarian areas experiencing risk-bearing economies. The underlying factor is that large authoritarian areas frequently engage in a range of diverse activities, so that a fall in the return from any one unit of economy does not threaten the stability of the whole economy.

While increases in size frequently confer advantages on an authoritarian area, there is a limit to the gains from growth in many cases. In other words, there is an optimal level of spatial capacity, and increases in size beyond this level will lead to a loss of economies of scale and manifest themselves in rising average costs. Without doubt, the increasing complexity of managing a large authoritarian area is the major source of administrative inefficiencies when the area grows beyond a certain size, and control and management of diverse socioeconomic affairs and risks become increasingly difficult. Diseconomies of scale mainly result from managerial difficulties, which are, under certain circumstances, positively related to cultural diversity. Since a large population is likely to be less homogeneous, the average cultural distance between individuals is likely to be positively correlated with the size of the authoritarian area.[6]

After solving the spatial model as defined in Appendix 1, we can derive the following results.

Proposition 1. *Given the homogeneous natural and social conditions, the transaction cost (benefit) of an isolated authoritarian area can be minimized (maximized) at the geographical centre of, and be maximized (minimized) at the geographical periphery of the area.*

Proposition 2. *Given the homogeneous natural and social conditions, the optimal size of an open authoritarian area is larger than that of an isolated one; and that the optimal size of a developed authoritarian area is larger than that of a less developed one.*

Proposition 3. *In a world of two or more authoritarian areas, economic centres will move close to each other, if the inter-political and intercultural barriers are removed or reduced.*

Proposition 4. *Different authoritarian areas that are open to each other may be integrated, under conditions that the actual size of each authoritarian area is smaller than its optimal size and that the actual size of the integrated authoritarian area is not larger than its optimal size.*

8.3 Analytic narrative results

Most anthropologists would agree that the earliest human societies must have been small and simple in social organization, and poor in technological equipment. As a result cultures must have been highly diversified. Since these characteristics contrast greatly with modern industrial societies, we must assume that the world has experienced some forms of cultural integration.[7] How about the Korean peninsula?

During the early stage of the Three Kingdoms (Koguryo, Paekche and Shilla), China underwent a period of political upheaval following the collapse of the Han dynasty (206 BC–AD 220). Vying for power on the peninsula, the rulers of Koguryo, Paekche and Shilla sought to strengthen their positions through alliances with the contending states on the Chinese mainland. International connections maintained by diplomatic missions served as important conduits for the transmission of Chinese culture to the Korean peninsula. Each of the Three Kingdoms eventually adopted elements of Chinese statecraft and Confucianism. In the fourth century AD Chinese writing, which had been introduced to Korea between the first century BC and the second century AD, was adapted to the Korean language using a system known as *idu*.

Other notable evidence for cultural integration throughout the Korean peninsula during the late stage of the Three Kingdoms is the earliest known extant Buddhist sculpture. The small gilt-bronze image of a seated Buddha was discovered at Ttuksom, near the Han river in modern-day Seoul, part of the ancient territory of the Paekche kingdom. The Ttuksom statue may be a copy of a Chinese figure from the late fourth or early fifth century. If it is indeed a Korean statue, it could be a Paekche piece, based on its provenance, or a Koguryo piece, based on its stylistic affinities with northern Chinese models resulting from Koguryo's frequent contacts with the northern nomadic states.[8]

This cultural integration provided a foundation for Shilla to unify the Three Kingdoms into a single authoritarian area (nation-state) in AD 668. However Shilla was unable to control the whole territory of Koguryo which extended to Manchuria (now north-east China). The geographical scope did not extend beyond the Daedong river. Much of the former Koguryo territory was given up to the Chinese and other tribal states. It remained for later dynasties to push the border northward to the Yalu and Tumen rivers.

It is reasonable to think that the decreasing geographical size of the unified Shilla dynasty (compared to those of its predecessors – Koguryo, Paekche and Shilla kingdoms as a whole) resulted from the rise of China during the prosperous Tang dynasty (AD 618–907). But this is not the only and perhaps not the vital reason why the unified Shilla lost control of its far northern peripheries. This can be witnessed by the various unsuccessful wars waged by China on Korea (see Section 8.1). Another key factor was the disadvantageous location of Shilla's capital. Even though Shilla maintained its kingdom with a strong hand (as already stated in Section 8.1), it was very difficult, if not impossible, for the Shilla court in Kyongju (on the far south-east coast) to maintain efficient control of its far northern frontier areas, especially after the latter part of the eighth century when the Shilla dynasty started to decline. By the second half of the ninth century, local and regional uprisings were no longer under the capital's control. The rebels in the former Paekche area declared the later Paekche kingdom, and later Koguryo was also declared. Tax revenues that had bankrolled state survival fell off, leading to a further weakening of the state. The chaotic situation eventually resulted in the emergence of a new dynasty – Koryo – in AD 915.[9]

After Koryo replaced Shilla, there were several locations in which the new ruler could have built its capital: Pyongyang in the central north and Kyongju in the south-east were prime candidates. Pyongyang had been the capital of the Koguryo kingdom (from the first century AD to 668). The

Koryo dynasty derived its name from the later Koguryo kingdom. Clearly, according to Proposition 1 (*transaction cost (benefit) of an isolated authoritarian area can be minimized (maximized) at the geographical centre of, and be maximized (minimized) at the geographical periphery of the area*), Pyongyang was an ideal (even if not the best) location for the Koguryo and the later Koguryo kingdoms to build their capital cities. But after much of the northern area fell to Chinese rule and the rest of the Korean peninsula was unified as a single state, Pyongyang – as a northern city with close proximity to China – lost its geographic advantages as an optimal capital. Neither could Kyongju (capital of the Shilla kingdom, located on the south-east coast of the peninsula) become the capital of the new dynasty, positioned as it was on the periphery of the new state. The Koryo ruler eventually chose Kaesong – a city almost equidistant from the northern and southern frontiers – as the capital of the newly unified country.

The relocation of its capital from the geographical periphery (Kyongju) to the central area (Kaesong) has had far reaching implications for Korea. The Koryo dynasty (915–1392) and the Chosen dynasty (1392–1910) survived for 477 and 518 years, respectively, and could have ruled even longer had the country not been invaded by external forces. By contrast, the unified Shilla dynasty (668–935) survived for 267 years. Taking into account only the length of reign over the whole territory (that is, from 668 to 915), the unified Shilla dynasty lasted only 247 years, less than the Koryo, and less than half that of the Chosen. It is reasonable to believe that it was the disadvantageous location of the capital that caused the court gradually to lose efficient control over the northern peripheries and eventually the whole country as well (see Table 8.1 for a brief comparison of the three unified dynasties).

So why was Korea's capital transferred from Kaesong to Seoul during the Chosen (Yi) dynasty (1392–1910)? The first possible driving force for the southward move of the capital might be the change in territorial size. As a result of the fall of the Koryo, the land area on the northern sides of Mount Paektu and the Yalu (or Amnok) and Tumen (or Tuman) rivers, formerly part of the Koryo dynasty, had been under Chinese control. If Kaesong is a geographically optimal location as the capital of the Koryo dynasty, *ceteris paribus*, the optimal location for the capital of the new Chosen (Yi) dynasty, according to Proposition 1, should move more or less to the south.

Moreover, the Chosen dynasty's move of the capital from Kaesong to Hansong (modern Seoul) provides evidence to support, and can be further explained by, Proposition 3: *In a world of two or more authoritarian areas, economic centres will move close to each other if the inter-political and intercultural barriers are removed or reduced.* As soon as the Chosen dynasty was established, it created closer political, economic and cultural relations with China's Ming dynasty (with its capital in Beijing) than its predecessor.[10] It

Table 8.1 A brief comparison of Korea's three unified dynasties

Item	**Unified Shilla (668–935)**	**Koryo (915–1392)**	**Chosen[a] (1392–1910)**
Major force for emergence	Exogenous (reliance on China's Tang dynasty)	Endogenous (domestic uprisings)	Endogenous (domestic factions)
Geographical location of central government	Periphery (Kyongju)	Centre (Kaesong)	Centre (Hansong/Seoul)[b]
Spatial cost of territorial administration by central government[c]	High	Low	Low
Spatial benefit of territorial administration by central government[d]	Low	High	High
Length of existence (years)	267[e]	477[e]	518
Major force(s) for collapse	Endogenous (domestic uprisings)	Exogenous (controlled by the Mongols) and endogenous	Exogenous (annexed by Japan)

Notes

a. Renamed Daehan (great Korea) from 1897 to 1910.

b. Kaesong as capital from 1392 to 1394.

c. Judged by the author based on Proposition 1. Spatial cost is expressed by Equation (A1.8) of Appendix 1.

d. Judged by the author based on Proposition 1. Spatial benefit is expressed by Equation (A1.9) of Appendix 1.

e. Twenty years should be subtracted from the total if whole territorial reigns are taken into account for Unified Shilla (668–915) and Koryo (935–1392), respectively.

is even plausible that General Yi Song-gye (r. 1392–98), founder of the Chosen dynasty, chose such names as 'Chosen' and 'Hansong' in order to please the Ming emperors. In fact, Chosen (calm land of the morning) was intended to refer to an eastern land, contrasting to the Chinese mainland in the west and Hansong (Han city) sounds like a Chinese city rather than a Korean capital. Economically, even though both Seoul and Kaesong are proximate to the Yellow Sea, which gave the Korean government more efficient connections with China than any land routes, Seoul has advantages over Kaesong. There are no suitable places to establish coastal ports for large-vessel transportation close to Kaesong, while Seoul, though also an inland city, can get easy access to the Yellow Sea via the port of Incheon. It also has access to the inland transportation network via the Han River.

During the nineteenth and early twentieth centuries, the Chosen court pursued a completely isolationist policy against the Western world. With endless conflicts, rebellions and quarrels from within and as a result of international political games between the superpowers of Great Britain, Russia and the United States, the Korean peninsula was annexed by Japan as a colony in 1910. Since the end of the Second World War, Korea has been divided by external forces into two rivals, with Pyongyang and Seoul as the capitals of North and South Korea, respectively. Geographically, Pyongyang, as North Korea's capital city, is supported by Proposition 1, but Seoul, as South Korea's, is not. The current capital, Seoul, located in the northwestern part of South Korea, has a population of 10 million and is about 65 kilometres from the North Korean border, within the range of rocket attack should hostilities break out. According to Proposition 1, the capital should move from the geographical border in the north to a more geographically central area (around the Yeongi-Kongju area as was suggested at the beginning of this chapter).

The two Koreas have technically been at war since the Korean War (1951–53) ended in a truce, and their relations still remain uncertain. The Korean peninsula belongs to a single culture in terms of ethnicity, language and history. If our analytic narrative result is correct, it could be suggested that, as a result of rising income levels throughout the Korean peninsula and after political and ideological barriers are removed or significantly reduced, North and South Korea will be reunified under conditions that *the actual size of each authoritarian area is smaller than its optimal size and that the actual size of the integrated authoritarian area is not larger than its optimal size* (Proposition 4).

Of course, it is impossible to precisely calculate the optimal sizes for both North and South Korea. However, it seems clear that, compared to any average-sized European country (not to mention China or Russia), both North and South Korea can only be defined as small economies in terms of land area and population.[11] If the DMZ (North–South border) were to be torn down, the Korean peninsula could not only achieve the benefit of the comparative advantages from both sides of the border (as mentioned by Choy's (1984, p. 14) note cited in Section 8.1), it would also demonstrate the 'economies-of-scale' principle: *the optimal size of an open authoritarian area is larger than that of an isolated one; and that the optimal size of a developed authoritarian area is larger than that of a less developed one* (Proposition 2).

A summary of the analytic narrative results is shown in Table 8.2.

8.4 Broader implications

Throughout history one can see that the world economic and cultural structures have been changing constantly. On the one hand, some

Table 8.2 How the Korean narrative fits with the analytical model

Period	Major events	Supported by Proposition
Last stages of bronze culture	Various tribal leagues developed to the initial stage of state-building.	2
4th–7th centuries AD	Koguryo annexed Puyo; Shilla conquered Kaya and eventually unified three kingdoms; Buddhism and Confucian culture were completely adopted throughout the Korean peninsula.	2 and 4
915–935	Koryo replaced Shilla; the capital was moved from Kyongju in the southeast to Kaesong, on the northern side of the 38th Parallel.	1 and 3
1392–1910	After defeating pro-Mongol factions in the north, Yi Song-gye founded Chosen (Yi) dynasty in Seoul; political, economic and cultural relations developed between Korea and China.	1 and 3
1946–1953	North and South Korea were established by external superpowers with capitals in Pyongyang and Seoul, respectively.	1 (for North Korea)
2007–2014	South Korea is to move its capital from Seoul to the south, near the Yeongi-Kongju area.	1

countries with the same or similar cultures have formed into single economic communities, or emerged as new and larger political unions (such as the European Union), in the hope of achieving increased returns from economies of scale. On the other hand, artificial barriers still separate neighbouring communities so as to protect individual countries' political and economic interests, as between North and South Korea, within the Chinese area (including Hong Kong, Macau, Taiwan and the Chinese mainland) and in the Islamic world.[12]

Why have small, culturally different economies formed economic unions, while large, culturally similar economies have not? Why is the operation of the culturally heterogeneous unions less stable and economically efficient even than that of the culturally homogeneous economies that are politically and economically different from each other?

To be sure, our analytic narrative result has been developed in regard to the specific conditions of the Korean peninsula, which is both culturally homogeneous and politically authoritarian. Another intriguing and understudied context for the modern Korean narrative is the Japanese colonization and the interventions by the superpowers (the USA and the former USSR). However, this is not to say that the analytic narrative result may not afford some general tests that may be applicable to other economies that are either culturally diverse or politically democratized. The analytic narrative result may still be more or less generalizable to other economies, given that the latter are shaped by some (if not all) conditions similar to those of the Korean case.

Like Korea, many other East Asian nations were under some form of authoritarian rule, at least till the end of the twentieth century. Authoritarianism may take different forms. Specifically, absolute monarchies are almost always authoritarian, and dictatorships are always so. Democracies are normally not authoritarian, but may exhibit authoritarian behaviour in some respects. Modern democracies once enforced laws that would be nowadays considered abusive and authoritarian: for instance, countries such as the United States and the United Kingdom, until recently, enforced sodomy laws which imposed the moral and religious values of the majority over matters of private life.[13]

Rooted in a single culture, the Chinese economic area is politically separated. Hong Kong (until 1997) and Macau (until 1999) were colonial territories ruled by the UK and Portugal. Long before their return to China under the principle of 'one country, two systems', these two capitalist economies had set up close and efficient economic links with their communist rival on the mainland. Mainland China traditionally supplied most of Hong Kong's food and fresh water, and Hong Kong traditionally served as China's main port. After 1978 the links between the two economies were extended to production, investment, provision of services and financial relations (Dodsworth and Mihaljek, 1997). Regardless of the political and military tensions between Taiwan and the mainland of China, bilateral trade and economic exchanges across the Taiwan Strait have grown dramatically, as have tourism, and technological and labour cooperation. It seems extraordinary that economic ties of this kind could have been sustained between two such politically distrustful and hostile economies.

However the great size of the Chinese nation does impose some negative influences on the Chinese economy, especially in its huge and backward inland areas. Since the advent of the administrative decentralization in the early 1980s, China's national economy has become effectively 'cellularized' into a plethora of semi-autarkic regional enclaves. Public finance, as an important component of the Chinese economic system, has undergone a series of reforms on central–local relations. The main goals of these reforms were to decentralize the fiscal structure and to strengthen the incentives for local governments to collect more revenue for themselves. Obviously, the economic decentralization has been a major factor in China's current economic success.[14] However these reforms have also had negative impacts on interprovincial relations. For example, in order to protect local market and revenue sources, it became common in China for some provinces to restrict import (export) from (to) other provinces by levying high, if informal, taxes and by creating non-tariff barriers on commodities whose production is seen as important to their provincially 'domestic' economies.[15] Moreover, this unfair competition between provinces has created fierce economic 'battlegrounds' in border areas and there have been numerous examples of 'trade embargoes' or 'commodity wars' between provinces over, amongst other items, rice, wool, tobacco, soy beans and mineral products.[16]

Most of China's provinces, autonomous regions and municipalities directly under the central government are on a size and scale equivalent to a European country in population and land area. They are considerable political and economic systems in their own right. The differences between these provinces have long been a defining characteristic of China's politics. In most cases their boundaries were created over two thousand years ago (Gottmann, 1973). In addition, Chinese culture is not homogeneous across provinces. There is a broad range of ethnic and linguistic groups as well as religious adherents in the nation. The holding of markedly differing religious beliefs and values implies that the chances of the adoption of a common standard between different groups of people are unlikely to be enhanced. Consequently, China's great diversity in physical geography, resource endowment, political economy and ethnic identity has given rise to many difficulties in interprovincial administration.

Of China's 66 interprovincial borderlines, 65 are disputed and have even been published, according to their own preferences, by the provincial level authorities in their official maps and documents (Zhang, 1990, p. 8). According to statistics released by the Ministry of Civil Affairs, of the 52,000 km of interprovincial borders in the Peoples Republic of China, only 5 per cent are legally fixed; 77 per cent are regarded as informal (or customary borderlines) and about 18 per cent (about 9500 km) remain the subject of active dispute.[17] According to the various sources, there were over 800 cross-border disputes in 333 of the 849 interprovincial border counties of almost all provinces. The total disputed areas (about 140,000 square kilometres) include grassland (about 95,000 square kilometres), mining field (about 4000 square kilometres), arable land (about 3000 square kilometres), forestry (about 2000 square kilometres), areas of water (about 1000 square kilometres) and mixed grass-mining-forestry area (about 30,000 square kilometres) (Guo, 1993, p. 176). In defiance of the State Council (1981 and 1988) regulations concerning the resolution of interprovincial border disputes, many disputes were the subject of armed fights between different groups of people. This has seriously affected the social security and sustainability of economic development in those cross-border areas.[18]

By way of contrast to the culturally homogeneous Chinese economic area, ASEAN is based to a large extent on cultural heterogeneity (whose cultural complex includes, among others, Buddhism, Islam, Christianity, Confucianism and atheism, as well as non-religion). In fact, from its foundation, the ASEAN was designed to achieve 'economic cooperation rather than economic integration'. As a result a free trade area has not been contemplated. In 1978, the ASEAN put into force a preferential trade arrangement (PTA) granting 10 to 15 per cent margins of preference on 71 commodities and industrial projects. A stronger free trade proposal had been rejected during negotiations. Between 1985 and 1987 the ASEAN leaders agreed to expand the list of sectors in the PTA and to increase the margin of preferences. Until 1989, however, the fraction of goods eligible for regional preferences was still only in the order of 3 per cent.[19] A series of talks beginning in the early 1990s led to the decision to create the ASEAN Free Trade Area (AFTA). Furthermore, the treatment of non-tariff barriers is vague. Even if fully implemented, the AFTA will still allow intra-bloc tariffs.

The European Union (EU) is another case in point. In 1986 the West European nations amended the Treaty of Rome with the Single European Act. This Act provided for the removal of all remaining restrictions to the free flow of goods, services, capital and labour among member nations, so that the member nations became a single unified market at the beginning of 1993. This was intended to produce substantial efficiency gains and other benefits for the EU. The static welfare benefits resulting from the formation of the EU are estimated to be 1 to 2 per cent of GDP, while the dynamic benefits were estimated to be much larger. Specifically, the GDP of the EU was expected to increase by 0.2 per cent from the removal of non-tariff trade barriers, 2.2 per cent from the removal of production barriers, 1.65 per cent from economies of scale, and 1.25 per cent from intensified competition, for an overall total (one-time) gain of 5.3 per cent of the EU's GDP in 1988. In addition, the overall rate of inflation was expected to fall by 6.1 per cent and the average unemployment rate to fall by 1.5 per cent (Cecchini, 1988). The programme also induced large amounts of foreign direct investment (FDI) from other nations, especially the United States and Japan, in anticipation of a new increase in EU protectionism against outsiders.

However, the greatest benefit has been the birth of a new political power, in which once bitter enemies (such as France and Germany) are members of a single unified community. The efforts to unify independent economies, however, have not been successful in Europe. The Organization for Security and Cooperation in Europe (OSCE), including countries from at least three cultures (Eastern Orthodox, Islam, and the West) with quite different values and interests, has posed major obstacles to its developing a significant institutional identity and to a wide range of important activities.

The overall benefits of multicultural economic integration are subject to different conditions. First of all, the higher the level of pre-union tariffs and the lower the common external tariff, the more likely it is that the net effects will be positive. Along this same line, the more elastic supply and demand in the member economies are, the more likely the net results will be positive. Also, the greater the ease of switching from a higher-cost domestic source to a lower-cost member source, the greater the pre-union per-unit cost differences between the two sources; and the greater the scope for experiencing economies of scale and attracting foreign investment, the larger the potential gains from cooperation. Second, since the adoption of a common standard and the socioeconomic cooperation between different cultural groups of people are likely to be difficult, given that they have markedly differing attitudes as well as different cultural values, the larger the number of cultural groups involved in a multicultural society, *ceteris paribus*, the higher the consequent managerial risks and costs. Lastly, the formulation of multicultural economic cooperation may differ in different cultural and economic environments.

Generally, from the least to the most integrated, six levels of multicultural economic integration can be established:

- sectoral cooperation,
- preferential trade arrangement,
- free trade area,
- customs union,
- common market, and
- economic union.

Among the six types of multicultural economic cooperation, 'sectoral cooperation' (SC) is the loosest form, involving straightforward cooperation in one or more selected sectors. As the advanced form of economic cooperation, 'economic union' goes further by harmonizing or even unifying the monetary and fiscal policies of members. While separate political entities are still present, an economic union generally establishes supranational institutions whose decisions are binding upon all members. Going beyond the free movement of goods, services and factors, economic union involves harmonizing national economic policies, typically including taxes and a common currency. For example, the decision of the European Community to change its name to the European Union in 1994 represented a determination to proceed to this higher stage of integration. The full unification of economic policies typically would in turn require political federalization.

8.5 Summary

Since the end of the Cold War the map of the world has been redrawn to an extent that is exceptional in modern peacetime history. On the one hand, several culturally or ethnically heterogeneous countries (such as the Soviet Union, Yugoslavia and Czechoslovakia) have disintegrated. On the other hand, Germany has reunited, and the linguistically diverse European Union (EU) is moving toward political integration. The issues of separation, unification, and the redrawing of borders are at the forefront of the world's concerns. While many of the issues raised by this process are primarily political, there are also economic and cultural considerations that bear on this problem. To try and answer these questions, we have constructed a simple analytic narrative model for the geo-political evolution of the Korean peninsula.

The Korean peninsula provides an ample narrative of events reflecting on the interactions between the location, size and political economy of cultures. Besides, our analytic narrative also has broader implications for the interactions between cultures differing in size. There is an indication that the increasing complexity of managing a large authoritarian area is the major source of administrative inefficiencies when the authoritarian area grows beyond a certain size.

When countries with different cultural identities form an economic union, their efforts represent a partial movement to free trade and an attempt by each participating country or region to obtain some of the benefits of a more open economy without sacrificing control over the goods and services that cross its borders and hence over its production and consumption structure. The participating countries and regions will soon realize that the more they remove restrictions on the movement of goods and services between members of the group, the more domestic control of the economy is lost.

9

Globalization, Conflict Management and Culture

Yea! Whoso, shaking off the yoke of flesh
Lives lord, not servant, of his lusts; set free
From pride, from passion, from the sin of 'Self'
Toucheth tranquility! O Pritha's Son!
That is the state of Brahma! There rests no dread
When that last step is reached! Live where he will,
Die when he may, such passeth from all planning,
To blest Nirvana, with the Gods, attaining.

(Bhagavad-Gita, ch. ii)

9.1 Is the clash of civilizations inevitable?

Globalization, as an increasingly dominant force since the last decades of the twentieth century, is shaping a new era of interaction between various economies throughout the world. It is increasing the contacts between people across various boundaries – geographical, political and cultural. Today, the interactions between people with different national and cultural identities are deeper than ever before. Some obvious evidence can be found in the following statistics:[1]

(1) Foreign direct investment (FDI) topped US$500 billion in the late 1990s, more than seven times the level in real terms in the 1970s.
(2) The daily turnover in foreign exchange markets increased from around US$10–20 billion in the 1970s to US$1.5 trillion in 1998.
(3) International bank lending grew from US$265 billion in 1975 to over US$6 trillion in 1999.
(4) People travel more around the world, with tourism more than doubling between 1980 and 1996, from 260 million to 590 million travellers a year.
(5) International migration, despite the tight restrictions, continues to grow, with the workers' remittances reaching US$58 billion in 1996.

There is no doubt about the increasing awareness of the importance of international and intercultural transactions in our daily life. When people say that 'the world is becoming smaller every day', they are referring not only to the increased speed and ease of transportation and communications but also to the increased use of international and intercultural markets to buy and sell goods. The overall heightened presence of foreign goods, foreign producers and even foreign-owned assets causes many to question the impact and desirability of all international and intercultural economic transactions. An increasing number of companies rely on production chains that straddle many politically and culturally distinctive areas. Raw materials and components may come from different linguistic or religious areas and be assembled in another, while marketing and distribution are managed in still other venues. Consumers' decisions in, for example, New York or Tokyo may become information that has an almost immediate impact on products that are being made – and the styles that influence them – all over the world.

According to Huntington (1993), cultural communities are replacing Cold War blocs. Specifically, since the end of the Cold War countries with similar cultures are coming together; countries with different cultures are coming apart. He argues that world politics is entering a new phase, in which the great divisions between humankind and the dominating source of international conflict will be cultural. Civilizations – the highest cultural groupings of people – are differentiated by religion, history, language and tradition (see Table 9.1). These divisions are deep and increasing in importance. The fault lines of civilizations may become the battle lines of the

Table 9.1 Huntington's hypothesis on intercultural relations

	Sinic	**Japanese**	**Hindu**	**Islamic**	**West**	**Orthodox**	**Latin American**	**African**
Sinic	–	♣	♣♣♣	♣	♣♣♣	♣	–	–
Japanese	♣	–	–	–	♣♣	♣♣♣	–	–
Hindu	♣♣♣	–	–	♣♣♣	♣♣	♣	–	–
Islamic	♣	♣	♣♣♣	–	♣♣♣	♣♣♣	–	♣♣♣
West	♣♣♣	♣♣	♣♣	♣♣♣	–	♣	♣	♣
Orthodox	♣	♣♣♣	♣	♣♣♣	♣		–	–
Latin American	–	–	–	–	♣	–	–	–
African	–	–	–	♣♣♣	♣	–	–	–

Notes: ♣♣♣ denotes an extremely serious conflict; ♣ denotes a moderately serious conflict; and – denotes data not available.

Source: Huntington (1996, figure 9.1).

future. In this emerging era of cultural conflict the United States must, he argues, forge alliances with similar cultures and spread its values wherever possible. With alien civilizations the West must be accommodating if possible, but confrontational if necessary. In the final analysis, as he suggests, all civilizations will have to learn to tolerate each other.

There has been serious concern about the critical role of culture in the formation of intercultural conflicts. Each culture not only provides the basis of identity (ethnicity, religion) and the mode of communication (language, ideas), but also distinguishes the motives for human behaviour and the criteria of evaluation (good or bad, ugly or beautiful). For example, the comparatively smooth creation of the European Union (EU) is the product of a common European culture or sub-European cultures that have been to some extent integrated. By contrast, the South Asian Association for Regional Cooperation (SARC), formed in 1985 and including seven Hindu, Muslim and Buddhist states has been ineffectual, even to the point of not being able to hold meetings. A similar example is Israel and Palestine, which share a narrow territory along the eastern coast of the Mediterranean Sea, west of the Jordan River and the Dead Sea. Cultural and religious conflicts between the two different groups of peoples (the Israelis and Palestinians) have not stopped since the founding of the state of Israel.

In short, cultural differences underlie many conflicts, both international and domestic. The conflicts in the Middle East, the Congo, Nigeria, Northern Ireland and Sri Lanka, to name but a few, all are framed in cultural terms, as ethnic or religious. Some argue that the major cause of violent conflict in the post-Cold War era will be clashes between cultures or culturally-defined civilizations. In this scenario, cultural difference itself is the cause of violence. But conflicts can also be found in culturally homogeneous areas. According to the *New York Times* (7 February 1993, p. 14), in 1992 there were 59 ethnic conflicts in 48 places throughout the world, of which 31 (about 52.4 per cent) were between ethnic groups and 28 (about 47.5 per cent) were within ethnic groups. Moreover, among the 50 ethnic and political conflicts for the period from 1993 and 1994, 30 (60 per cent) were intraculturally based, whereas only 20 (40 per cent) were interculturally based.[2] By way of contrast to these examples of internal strife and dissent, there is another landscape in the heart of Westem Europe where one may find a special Alpine country: in Switzerland different language groups live peacefully in cantons allocated to speakers of Swiss German, French, Italian and Rhaeto-Romanic.

To check whether there is any correlation between intercultural conflict and cultural dissimilarity, let us calculate the cultural linkages for each pair of the culture areas defined in Section 2.3 of Chapter 2. The results of the linguistic and religious similarity indexes between the seven contemporary culture areas are shown in tables 9.2a and 9.2b. According to the linguistic similarity indexes (shown in Table 9.2a), the most serious tensions should occur between the Eastern Orthodox and Indian areas, and the least serious tensions should occur between the African and Western areas. According to the religious similarity indexes (shown in Table 9.2b), the most serious tensions should occur between the Islamic and Latin American areas, and the least serious tensions should occur between the Latin American and Western areas. A comparison of tables 9.1 and 9.2a and b reveals some conflicting information.[3] For example, Table 9.2b does not support the view that there are low potentials for intercultural conflict between the Indian and Latin American and Western areas as demonstrated in Table 9.1; neither does it support the view that there is high potential for intercultural conflict between the African and Islamic areas, as Huntington (1996) suggests.

Table 9.2a Linguistic similarity matrices by culture areas

Culture area	African	East Asian	Eastern Orthodox	Indian	Islamic	Latin American	Western
African	1.000	0.019	0.001	0.053	0.071	0.032	0.555
East Asian	0.019	1.000	0.000	0.030	0.020	0.013	0.025
Eastern Orthodox	0.001	0.000	1.000	0.000	0.004	0.020	0.002
Indian	0.053	0.030	0.000	1.000	0.051	0.037	0.074
Islamic	0.071	0.020	0.004	0.051	1.000	0.039	0.077
Latin American	0.032	0.013	0.020	0.037	0.039	1.000	0.050
Western	0.555	0.025	0.002	0.074	0.077	0.050	1.000

Source: Calculated by the author based on Equation (7.3) and *Britannica Book of the Year 2001*.

Table 9.2b Religious similarity matrices by culture areas

Culture area	African	East Asian	Eastern Orthodox	Indian	Islamic	Latin American	Western
African	1.000	0.148	0.110	0.132	0.271	0.373	0.422
East Asian	0.148	1.000	0.396	0.103	0.094	0.077	0.149
Eastern Orthodox	0.110	0.396	1.000	0.069	0.073	0.041	0.105
Indian	0.132	0.103	0.069	1.000	0.123	0.023	0.029
Islamic	0.271	0.094	0.073	0.123	1.000	0.020	0.030
Latin American	0.373	0.077	0.041	0.023	0.020	1.000	0.689
Western	0.422	0.149	0.105	0.029	0.030	0.689	1.000

Source: Calculated by the author based on Equation (7.3) and *Britannica Book of the Year 2001*.

Intercultural conflict is usually attributed to cultural dissimilarity, since the latter implies a degree of difficulty that the disparate groups concerned have in communicating or cooperating with one another. Precisely, each culture possesses a common system of signifying and normative values, some shared basis (such as common history, language, race or ethnicity or religion) through which people identify themselves as members of a single group, and the will or decision to be primarily self-identified as a member of a given community. Ultimately, this may to some extent be traceable to a biological basis, since, in human societies, ascriptive ties are said to dampen coalition building and to inhibit compromise across groups (which cross-cutting cleavages promote), thus increasing chances for social conflict (Bollen and Jackman, 1985).

However, it is too arbitrary to say that cultural dissimilarity will inevitably result in intercultural conflicts. Where diverse groups have learned to live with each other and pursue their differences within a stable political system cultural difference is likely to have a very small effect on intercultural conflict. This leads at once to the presumption that the so-called industrial democracies will be less sensitive to the measures of cultural diversity than developing countries in which cultural diversity leads to barriers to intranational contacts or, worse, to violence. Furthermore, as Shanker (1996) argues, since the cultural raw material for any civilization allows for various options, different patterns will emerge as people combine modern rationality with cultural heritage, economic progress with national identity. Through this process peoples and countries will come to share experience, to walk parallel rather than converging paths.

In sum, it is reasonable to believe that culture plays different roles in the formation of intercultural conflicts. On the one hand, cultural dissimilarity brings about political distrust or instability. On the other hand, it generates 'differentiation of production' or complementarity in economic terms, which in turn induces cooperation between distinctive groups of people.[4] As a result cultural dissimilarity is not only a determining source for intercultural conflicts, but also the source for intercultural dependence and intercultural cooperation.

9.2 Hypotheses

International land boundaries separate independent states and dependencies, areas of special sovereignty, and other miscellaneous entities. Ethnicity, culture, race, religion and language have affected the division of states into separate political entities as much as history, physical terrain, political fiat or conquest, resulting in sometimes arbitrary and imposed boundaries. Boundary, borderland resource and territorial disputes vary in intensity from managed or dormant to violent or militarized. Most disputes over the alignment of political boundaries concern short segments and are

Box 9.1 Culture as economic goods and economics of culture

The rise of culture as economic goods has added to the identification of culture with commodities that can be sold and traded – crafts, tourism, music, books and films. A UNESCO study (UNDP, 1999, p. 33) shows that world trade in goods with cultural content – printed matter, literature, music, visual arts, cinema and photographic, radio and television equipment – almost tripled between 1980 and 1991, from US$67 billion to US$200 billion. The vehicles for this trade in cultural goods are the new technologies. Satellite communications technology from the mid-1980s gave rise to a powerful new medium with global reach and to such global media networks as CNN. The number of TV sets per 1000 people worldwide doubled between 1980 and 2000. The development of the Internet is spreading culture around the world, over an expanded telecommunications infrastructure of fibre optics and parabolic antennas.

At the same time, academics initiated the study of the 'Economics of Art and Culture' as an independent sub-discipline within the field of economics. Before the 1970s, such a subject area would have come as a surprise even to the majority of economists. Up to that time, few economists, mainly those personally interested in the arts, had provided contributions in this area. One of them is Alan Peacock, who in 1969 had already been involved in analysing the public promotion of arts and culture. Along with broadly-based study of the performing arts in the US, the *Journal of Cultural Economics*, a specialized scholarly journal, was published in 1980s. Since then, biennial congresses have been held under the auspices of the Association for Cultural Economics.

today less common and less hostile than borderland resource and territorial disputes. Undemarcated, indefinite, porous and unmanaged boundaries, however, encourage illegal cross-border activities, uncontrolled migration and confrontation. Territorial disputes may evolve from historical and/or cultural claims, or they may be brought on by resource competition. Ethnic clashes continue to be responsible for much of the territorial fragmentation around the world. Sources of contention include disputes over islands at sea or in rivers as well as access to water and mineral (especially petroleum) resources, fisheries and arable land. Regional discord directly affects the sustenance and welfare of local populations, often leaving the world community to cope with the consequent problems: refugees, hunger, disease, impoverishment, deforestation and desertification.

A host of factors, including, inter alia, immigration, increased diplomatic and cultural contacts, the diffusion of science and technology, the mass media and international travel and trade, are dramatically transforming contemporary international political and economic relations. As a result interactions between different cultures are becoming more and more important in our changing world. However conflicts and misunderstanding may also result from the increasing interactions between the cultures. Ethnic, linguistic and religious differences (as discussed in the previous chapters) influence the ways in which intercultural relations have been formed, in patterns of either détente or confrontation. Thus, the need to understand differences in basic values, norms and beliefs and their influence on resolution of these conflicts is greater than ever before.

Early theoretical works such as Choucri and North (1975 and 1989) contend that internal demands on resources push states toward outward expansion, increasing the possibility for conflicts to arise through hostile lateral pressure. Resource-poor regions will create environments that are highly competitive, where the creation of institutions to manage conflict will be lacking and/or ineffective. Resource-rich regions, on the other hand, will be faced with fewer potential conflicts overall, which will enhance the prospects for the creation of institutions to manage conflicts that do arise (Hensel et al., 2004). Gleditsch (2001, p. 253) provides a nice summary for these Malthusian type arguments. Population growth and high resource consumption per capita (demand-induced scarcity) lead to deteriorated environmental conditions (supply-induced scarcity), which increase resource scarcity further and create harsher resource competition. This process, when combined with inequality with respect to resource access (structural scarcity), increases the chances for violence. As a result, we have Hypothesis 1.

Hypothesis 1. *Conflicts grow with respect to resource scarcity and population growth.*

Resource scarcity and environmental damage involve real threats to public health, agricultural and industrial production and to national security. Clearly, as populations increase the demand for resources increases as well. The lack of alternatives for resources increases dependency on both sides of a border. Critchley and Terriff (1993, pp. 332–3) argue that resources directly result in conflict when (i) they are becoming increasingly scarce in a region, (ii) they are essential for human survival, and (iii) the resource can be physically seized or controlled. They assert that direct conflict over renewable resources will be rare, but competition over scarce resources will have a strong indirect effect on the propensity for conflict. Limited availability of resources places stress on society, which makes the society less stable and more conflict-prone.

Like Critchley and Terriff (1993), Homer-Dixon (1999) believes that the probability of conflict rises due to disruption of legitimate institutions and social relations, among others. As a result, we have Hypothesis 2.

Hypothesis 2. *Conflicts occur more frequently in areas with less developed political and legal systems.*

Difficulties in cross-border management of natural and environmental resources have proved a major obstacle for developing and transition nations differing in economic, political and cultural systems to implement sustainable development strategies (Guo, 2005). In certain circumstances, conflicts may arise because national interests differ and nations develop diverging policies and plans which are not compatible (Kirmani, 1990; Frey, 1993; Wolf, 1998; and Savenije and van der Zaag, 2000). As a result, we have Hypothesis 3.

Hypothesis 3. *Conflicts occur more frequently in areas with different political systems and development strategies.*

Economic factors, such as economic stagnation and income inequality, serve critical roles in the creation of political instability in some nations (see, for example, Londregan and Poole, 1989). It has long been considered that inequality of wealth and income motivates the poor to engage in crime, riots and other disruptive activities (see, for example, Hibbs, 1973; Venieris and Gupta, 1986; Gupta, 1990; and Alesina and Perotti, 1996). As a result, we have Hypothesis 4.

Hypothesis 4. *Conflicts occur less frequently in areas with higher average income levels and in areas with lower income inequalities.*

There has been a concern that border conflict is usually attributed to cultural dissimilarity (Huntington, 1993). Ultimately, this may to some extent be traceable to a biological basis, since in most circumstances cooperation among animals is importantly influenced by genetic similarity (Wilson, 1980). In human societies, ascriptive ties are said to dampen coalition building and to inhibit compromise across groups (which cross-cutting cleavages promote), thus increasing chances for social conflict (Bollen and Jackman, 1985). Consequently, we have Hypothesis 5.

Hypothesis 5. *Conflicts tend to be less serious between culturally homogeneous areas than between culturally heterogeneous areas.*

There has been also a concern that people with some cultural identities prefer to employ confrontational strategies in handling conflict situations, whereas other people generally utilize more passive strategies and conflict-avoidance (Chua and Gudykunst, 1987; Leung, 1987; and Ting-Toomey, 1988). As a result, we have Hypothesis 6.

Hypothesis 6. *Conflicts tend to be less tensional between cultures which prefer passive strategies than between those which prefer confrontational strategies.*

Various problems are common to the studies of conflict management and culture. First, both embrace a wide range of elements including ethnicity, language, religion and so on. Second, specific context is extremely important in studying incidents of conflict, which means that each conflict process has unique characteristics. While some of the problems can be overcome using methodological tools that are pretty standard, others are more difficult to address.

Scholarship on international conflicts worldwide employs various approaches. Much fruitful work has developed through large-scale statistical studies. Our analysis is based on an analytic narrative, rather than a large-scale statistical approach. We intend to choose cases where disputes or conflicts are either still fairly active or have been peacefully settled, in order to learn from both kinds. A case-based, time-limited approach helps to explain patterns of conflict resolution.[5]

In the remainder of this chapter, six case studies will be described, in an attempt to provide empirical evidence to support the hypotheses listed above.

9.3 Empirical evidence

Case 1

The genocide in Rwanda was unleashed on 6 April 1994, immediately following the shooting down of a plane carrying Rwandan President Habyarimana and Burundian President Cyprien near Kigali Airport. On the following day the Prime Minister, a moderate Hutu, was assassinated and ten Belgian soldiers tortured and executed by Rwandan militiamen. The Belgian contingent (the best-equipped in the United Nations Assistance Mission for Rwanda – UNAMIR – founded on 5 October 1993, following UN resolution 872) decided to withdraw unilaterally from the UNAMIR. The situation continued to deteriorate and the killing of Tutsi civilians escalated. Nonetheless, the discussion in the UN Security Council on Rwanda in April 1994 had little to do with civilian massacres, but focused on a ceasefire between the government and the Rwanda Patriotic Front (RPF) – formed in 1988 by Tutsi refugees and dissident Hutus in Uganda. Furthermore, on 21 April 1994, the UN Security Council unanimously decided to reduce the size of UNAMIR from 2539 to 270 troops. Resolution 918 (which set a maximum of 5500 troops) was adopted on 17 May, too late to prevent the massacre since most of the killings took place between early April and mid-May. In total, the genocide lasted for about 100 days, and ended with the Tutsi-dominated RPF defeating the Hutu-led government and declaring a unilateral ceasefire on 18 July. At least 800,000

Rwandans were killed, mostly by *interahamwe* (those who stand together) militias – gangs of youths armed with machetes, guns and other weapons supplied by officials loyal to President Habyarimana.

It has been widely believed that colonial authorities were largely responsible for creating tribal identities among the Tutsis and the Hutus.[6] Before colonization the terms 'Hutu' and 'Tutsi' did not bear the same political meaning as they do today. In order to affirm their authority, colonial rulers redistributed power and privilege between the two groups. Belgium governed the region through Tutsis who, with more European features, were considered to be born to rule (Lee, 2002, p. 83). Even during the struggle to regain independence from Belgium, Hutu-Tutsi divisions in Rwanda were apparent. Following the death of Mwami (king) Matara III in 1959, farm workers organized by the Party of the Hutu Emancipation Movement (Parmehutu) revolted against Tutsi rule and seized power in 1961. Independence was granted in July 1962, resulting in the empowerment of the Hutu majority and ending the dominance of the Tutsi minority. In the wake of bloody inter-ethnic conflicts between 1963 and 1967, thousands of Tutsis were killed and tens of thousands fled into neighbouring countries, the majority to Uganda. On 1 October 1990 the RPF invaded the northern parts of Rwanda. In August 1993, the Government of Rwanda and the RPF signed a peace accord in Arusha, Tanzania, and agreed to establish a transitional power-sharing government in order to end a 30-year refugee crisis in Uganda.

To follow up the Arusha Peace Agreement (APA), and in response to serious concerns at the state of human rights in Rwanda, the UN Secretary-General sent a delegation to reassess the possible functions of the Neutral International Force (NIF) which was established to supervise the implementation of the APA. The delegation recommended a rapid deployment of the international force to avoid a collapse of the peace process. However, because of financial constraints, the UN was not able to implement all the delegation's recommendations. On 11 January 1994, Romeo Dallaire, UNAMIR's Force Commander, informed UN Headquarters of plans for ethnic attacks on Tutsis and the accumulation of arms caches. Apparently the UN did not take the information seriously. As the security situation continued to deteriorate in early 1994, including violent demonstrations, nightly grenade attacks, and assassination attempts, the UNAMIR sought the guidance and approval of the UN to commence deterrent operations. However some key members of the UN Security Council, especially the United States, were reluctant to label the situation as 'genocide' in Rwanda (Gambari, 1999; Lee, 2002).

Case 2

Within Africa there are two river-basin organizations which provide comparative examples of water management and conflict resolution. The Senegal River Authority (Organization pour La Mise en valeur de Fleuve

Sénégal, or OMVS), which was founded in 1963 by Guinea, Mali, Mauritania and Senegal, is a genuine active joint-management organization (OMVS, 1988). The functions of the OMVS are navigation, promotion of irrigation and hydropower production and the authority has the power to construct and operate joint projects. The OMVS not only plans and formulates policies, it also implements them. The structure of the OMVS enables effective project implementation. The political layer, made up of government ministers, is the upper and decisive level. The OMVS successfully conciliated between Senegal and Mauritania on the sharing of the resources of the Senegal after the 1988 conflict in which farmers and herders on both sides of the river fought over the same land and water resources (Green Cross, 2000, p. 84). The two dams constructed by the OMVS are owned jointly by the member states, as are the seaports at the river mouth that the OMVS has developed and maintained.

However, as the case of the nearby river basin, the Niger, shows, good organization is not always sufficient for successful functioning. The Niger River is the principal river of western Africa, extending over about 4000 km. It runs in a crescent through Guinea, Mali, Niger, Benin and Nigeria, discharging through a massive delta, known as the Oil Rivers, into the Gulf of Guinea. The Niger takes one of the most unusual routes of any major river. Its source is just 240 km inland from the Atlantic Ocean, but the river runs away from the sea into the Sahara Desert, and then takes a sharp right turn and heads southeast to the Gulf of Guinea. This unusual geography makes the northern part of the river, known as the 'Niger bend', an important area. The bend is the closest source of water to the Sahara desert and it thus became the focal point of trade across the Western Sahara.

Cooperation in the Niger basin started in 1963 when seven of the nine riparian states (Nigeria, Niger, Benin, Burkina Faso, Mali, Guinea, Sierra Leone, Algeria and Côte D'Ivoire) signed the Act of Niamey. The structure of the Niger Basin Authority (NBA) is similar to the OMVS: secretariat, technical committee of experts and the Council of Ministers. However, unlike the OMVS, the NBA's performance has been poor (Rangeley et al., 1994, pp. 43–8). The failure of the earlier multinational management organization, the Niger Commission, and its replacement, the NBA, could be the result of the heterogeneous composition of their seven member states. In 1980 the structure was reformed and an upper level of the Summit of Heads of State was added in order to improve performance, but this did not prove effective. The main reason was the fact that only a few of the nine states really shared a common interest in the joint development of the basin (Ofosu-Amaah, 1990, pp. 246–8).

Case 3

The Jordan River originates in the mountains of eastern Lebanon. As the Jordan flows south through the entrance to the Great Syrian Rift Valley, it is fed from underground sources and small streams at various points in Jordan, Israel, Syria and Lebanon. The Jordan's main sources are the Hasbani River, which flows from Lebanon to Israel, the Banyas River, which flows from Syria to Israel, the Dan River, which begins and flows inside Israel, and the Yarmouk River, which begins near the Golan Heights and flows to the Jordan River. Following its flow into Lake Galilee, the Jordan River continues southward into the centre of the Jordan Valley, forming the border between the western edge of Jordan and the eastern side of Israel including part of the Palestinian Autonomy. The Jordan River continues into the Dead Sea, and as a smaller stream makes its way eventually into the Red Sea.

The Jordan River is the largest and longest river in Israel and Jordan. Moreover, it is the only river within Israel that has a permanent year-round flow. The Jordan River supplies Israel and Jordan with the vast majority of their water. Over 50 per cent of Israel's water sources rely on rain which falls outside the Israeli border. Israel is dependent for water on rivers that originate outside the border, or from disputed lands. For the State of Jordan, the Jordan River supplies about 75 per cent of its needs. In contrast to Israel, only 36 per cent of the total river flow originates outside the Jordanian border. However in 1990 Jordan had only 260 m^3 per capita of water, which is almost a quarter less than the minimum water requirement for an industrial nation (Grunfeld, 1997).

The struggle for fresh water in the Middle East has been a primary cause of military disputes in the region. The Syrian government, inside its borders, attempted to divert the Banyas River which is one of the Jordan River's tributaries. This was followed by three Israeli army and air force attacks on the site of the diversion. These incidents led up to the outbreak of the Six-Day War in June 1967 between Israel and Syria, Jordan and Egypt. During that war, Israel captured the Golan Heights and the site of the Banyas headwaters, which enabled it to prevent the diversion of the Banyas by the Syrians. Israel also gained control of the West Bank of the Jordan River as well as the northern bank of the Yarmouk (Cooley, 1984, p. 16). Like other conflicts that revolve around scarce resources, there are ways to determine the likelihood of water issues escalating into a large-scale multinational conflict. The degree of scarcity of water in a region, the need of several nations to share one freshwater source, the military or economic power of the state that controls the water, and the existence of other freshwater sources aids the ability to predict the causes and possible solutions for these conflicts.

The Middle East is locked into a multistate dispute, since not only Israel and Jordan but other parties, such as Syria and the Palestinians, have attempted to control the river. Israeli and Jordanian attempts are represented by constructions such as the King Talal dam, built by the Jordanians, and the National Water Carrier, built by the Israelis. These led to reactions that were often followed by military attacks. The Israeli War of Independence in 1948 and the Six-Day War in 1967 highlight this dispute as a 'war threat' conflict, in which the need for water encouraged actual war between states.[7] Control over cross-border resources by one party usually indicates a decrease in the amount of the resources available to the other party, which can be described as a zero-sum game. For example, in the year following the Six-Day War, Israel increased its water use from the Jordan River by 33 per cent (Grunfeld, 1997). As a result of the war, Jordan not only lost the significant access to the water from the Jordan River, it also had to terminate plans to expand usage of the river and its canal system. In addition, Palestinians took control of large sectors of the Jordan Valley that held these source waters.

The scarcity of fresh water in the Middle East is connected not only to meteorological and geographic but also to demographic factors. Throughout most of the region rainfall is irregular. The rainy season is short, between 6–8 months a year, and rainfall varies between 250–400 mm annually. This is insufficient for basic agriculture which requires at least 400 mm of regular rainfall. Irrigated agriculture is further restricted because there are few major rivers (Grunfeld, 1997). Furthermore, there is the issue of the vastly expanding population. This population growth stems from two sources. In Jordan the population increase is due to natural birth rate but in Israel waves of immigrants in the years following the Second World War increased the population. The prospect of substantial increases in water demand in the coming years renders it imperative that a solution be found to Palestine's water shortage. Both the Israeli and Palestinian populations are expected to increase dramatically, which will heighten demand on water resources.

The Middle East is a region of ideological, religious and geo-political differences. In the past decades, Israel and Jordan have searched for alternative means to maximize the use of fresh water from the Jordan River. However each country has developed expensive independent solutions, and both have come to realize that water resources need protection (Abu-Taleb, 1994, p. 37). Nevertheless, the two countries possess different standards of living which suggest different approaches: Israel, a first world country, concerns itself with environmental issues and sustainable solutions, while Jordan, a developing country, lacks the capacity to deal with such problems (Copaken, 1996, p. 86).

The Palestinian people believe that the West Bank ought to be a part of their sovereign nation, and that the presence of Israeli military control is a violation of their right to self-determination. By contrast, Israel argues that its presence is justified because the disputed territories have not been part of any state since the time of the Ottoman Empire and that Israel's eastern border has never been defined by anyone. According to the 1995 Israeli-Palestinian Agreement, the Israeli army should redeploy from the seven largest Palestinian towns on the West Bank, including a partial withdrawal from Hebron; and tentatively, from 450 smaller towns and villages. Together, these two areas contain the great bulk of the West Bank Palestinians – but less than 30 per cent of the territory (Israel-PLO, 1995). The rest of the West Bank, which includes the Israeli settlements and so-called state land, is still under Israeli army control. The future status of the West Bank, together with the Gaza Strip on the Mediterranean shore, has been the subject of negotiation between the Palestinians and Israelis, although the current Road Map for Peace, proposed by the 'Quartet' comprising the United States, Russia, the European Union, and the United Nations, envisions an independent Palestinian state in these territories living side by side with Israel.

Case 4

With a total area of 222,236 square kilometres, Jammu and Kashmir comprises three major ethnic areas: Ladakh in the north-west, which is majority Buddhist; the Kashmir Valley (controlled largely by India, and partly by Pakistan), which is majority Muslim; and Jammu in the south, which is majority Hindu. Pakistan, India and China each claim all, or part of, the former princely state of Jammu and Kashmir. A ceasefire agreement in 1949 divided the region into two sectors: the eastern part administered by India as the state of Jammu and Kashmir, and the western part administered by Pakistan and known as Azad (free) Kashmir and the Northern Areas.

In 1950 China occupied the north-east portion of Kashmir, a region known as Aksai Chin, which is located at the conjunction of the borders of the People's Republic of China, Pakistan and India. It is administered by China and claimed by India. It accounts for about 16.9 per cent of the land area of Jammu and Kashmir and is very sparsely populated. In 1963 Pakistan ceded to China another 2.33 per cent of land claimed by India. Currently India controls 45.62 per cent of the former princely state of Jammu and Kashmir, Pakistan controls 35.15 per cent, and China 19.23 per cent.[8]

In 1947, as part of the decolonization process, British India was divided into India and Pakistan. At the time of partition the rulers of nearly five hundred princely states which were directly under British rule were advised to join either India or Pakistan, bearing in mind proximity, demographic profiles and other factors. Most states were integrated into either India or Pakistan. However, integration was problematic for Jammu and Kashmir, which had a Hindu Maharajah and a majority Muslim population. It had borders with both India and Pakistan. From 1947 to 1948 the state of Jammu and Kashmir was attacked by a large number of tribesmen supported by regular Pakistani troops. When Pakistani regulars and tribesmen were within gunshot of Srinagar (the capital of Jammu and Kashmir), the Maharajah sought India's assistance in exchange for acceding to India.

Aksai Chin, under the administration of the People's Republic of China, is subsumed mainly into Hetian county, in the Xinjiang Uygur autonomous region. India claims the area as a part of the Ladakh district of the state of Jammu and Kashmir. Aksai Chin is of strategic importance to China because it contains National Highway 219, a major road connecting Tibet and Xinjiang Uygur autonomous regions. From 20 October to 22 November 1962 there was a short border war between China and India. Costing 1853 lives, the war ended with a Chinese victory and the birth of the Line of Actual Control (LAC). Since 1962 the LAC has been the current, though disputed, boundary between Chinese and Indian occupied zones in the contested territories.

India has repeatedly claimed the whole of Jammu and Kashmir as an integral part of India. India's stand is based on the historical fact that the state of Jammu and Kashmir, represented by the Maharajah, acceded to India. Pakistan has its own security concerns with India's claim. If the whole area of Kashmir were to go to India then it would pose a direct threat to Pakistan's North West Frontier and Pakistani Punjab. On the other hand if Pakistan had the whole of Kashmir it could threaten Indian Punjab. From the resource point of view all the three great rivers – Chenab Jhelun, Indus and Sutlei – flowing into Pakistan originate from Jammu and Kashmir. Many attempts have been made to devise a formula for peace in Jammu and Kashmir between the two warring nations, although little progress has been made.

Chinese-Indian relations are overshadowed by territorial disputes. India lays claim to vast territories currently in the possession of China. These territories are of interest to India because of their water resources. However, the Aksai Chin region, called the 'White Desert', is almost uninhabited and is considered of more importance for China than for India. In spite of many unresolved differences, both sides have instituted enough co-operative mechanisms since the 1990s to ensure peace and tranquillity in the region. Hence the China-India border dispute, though important, is not urgent.

Case 5

The Beagle Channel is located in extreme southern South America. It separates the Tierra del Fuego archipelago's main island to the north from Navarino, Hoste, and other smaller islands to the south. From east to west, the Beagle Channel is about 240 km long and 5–13 km wide. At its western end the channel splits into two branches that encircle Gordon Island. The eastern portion of the channel forms part of the Chile-Argentina border. However, the western portion lies entirely within Chile.

Chile and Argentina attempted definitively to resolve their territorial disputes through a comprehensive agreement known as the Boundary Treaty of 1881. To the south of the Magellan Strait, the 1881 treaty stipulated that the border would run to the south from Cape Espiritu Santo, on the northern shore of Tierra del Fuego to the Beagle Channel. Tierra del Fuego was thus to be divided into an eastern portion belonging to Argentina and a western portion belonging to Chile.

With respect to the Beagle Channel and the islands south to Cape Horn, the key problem was the treaty's failure to specify the eastern terminus of the channel. Since the Boundary Treaty granted Chile possession of all the islands south of the Beagle Channel, the channel effectively defined the longitudinal scope of Chilean sovereignty to the south of Tierra del Fuego. It was therefore impossible definitively to separate Chilean and Argentine claims in this region without determining where the channel ends. The Chilean view was that the Beagle Channel extended well to the east of Navarino Island, and beyond the three smaller islands – Picton, Nueva and Lennox – which were the focus of the dispute. Under this interpretation, all three islands are south of the channel, and thus Chilean. Argentina, on the other hand, argued that the Beagle Channel veered sharply to the south along the east side of Navarino Island, making everything to the east of that island Atlantic, and thus, under the terms of the Boundary Treaty, Argentine.

In the course of attempting to resolve this initial problem, however, the parties confronted several collateral issues of great importance, including navigation rights, sovereignty over other islands in the Fuegian archipelago, delimitation of the Straits of Magellan, and maritime boundaries south to Cape Horn and beyond. The three islands at the channel's eastern end, Lennox, Picton and Nueva, were the subject of a territorial dispute between Argentina and Chile. The dispute began in the 1840s and almost led to war between the two nations in 1978. In 1979 the two countries agreed – via the Act of Montevideo – to allow the Vatican to mediate the dispute through the good offices of Antonio Cardinal Samoré, the Pope's special envoy.

On 12 December 1980, the Pope received the two delegations and presented to them his proposal for resolving the conflict. Under the papal proposal, Chile would retain all of the islands, but Argentina would be entitled to maintain certain limited facilities there and would receive important navigation rights. The Pope's ruling resulted in the ratification of a treaty to settle the dispute in Rome. The dispute officially ended after the treaty came into effect between the two countries on 2 May 1985.

The key element to this proposal was the creation of a vast ocean area known as the Sea of Peace. In this area, extending to the east and southeast of the disputed chain of islands, Chile would be limited to a narrow territorial sea, in which it would be obliged to afford Argentina equal participation in resource exploitation, scientific investigation and environmental management. Beyond the Chilean territorial waters would be a much broader band of ocean subject to Argentine jurisdiction, but also subject to the same joint provisions that applied in Chilean waters.

The resolution of the Beagle Channel conflict has had a number of implications. It brought the parties to an agreement that stopped the immediate military crisis, allowing the mediator time to craft a process which would allow all parties concerned to grapple with increasingly difficult issues. The process was remarkable because it was flexible enough to accommodate the changing political environments in all parties concerned. Thus, the resolution serves to protect a fragile peace between the parties and ultimately allows them to create an agreement. It is also significant that regional and legal institutions (such as the Organization of American States and the International Court of Justice in the case of Beagle Channel conflict resolution) played a role. Last but not least, a vital factor in the peaceful resolution of the Beagle Channel conflict was that the mediator was the Vatican, whose supreme moral authority and influence over the large Catholic populations in each country made it a mediating body that the parties could not ignore (Laudy, 2004).

9.4 Summary

Since the end of the Cold War, the study of intercultural relations has become a popular topic in the field of global politics and economics. But support has been found for views emphasizing both intercultural conflict and cooperation. With all the positive ways of gaining from intercultural cooperation, it seems logical to inquire why economic cooperation has failed. Regions are a basis for cooperation among states only to the extent that geography coincides with culture. Divorced from culture, propinquity does not yield commonality and may foster just the reverse. The overall effectiveness of multicultural organizations generally varies inversely with the cultural diversity of their members. As a result single cultural organizations are more stable and successful than multicultural organizations. This is true for both political and economic organizations.

In this chapter, we argue that cultural dissimilarity may result in either intercultural conflict or intercultural cooperation, depending on the socioeconomic conditions of all the culture areas concerned. Specifically, intercultural cooperation will be sensitive to the measures of cultural difference in countries where cultural difference leads to serious intranational and international barriers. However, cultural dissimilarity would have a very small effect on conflict if the diverse groups have learned to live with each other in a stable political system. Rather, it even encourages cooperation for the groups intending to pursue their difference through the utilization of intercultural comparative advantages.

Finally and for those who are interested in a further study of intercultural relations, a neutral methodology should be applied to the investigation of the characteristics and mechanisms of intercultural conflicts and cooperation. Any attempts to illustrate correlation between the peculiarity of a specific culture and the extent of intercultural conflict would be both unwise and potentially risky. It would provoke the possibility of reductionism, elitism and ethnocentrism. We hope such studies will not be themselves a part of conflict-making.

Epilogue

> I will not instruct my disciples until they have really tried hard but still failed to understand. If I give them one instance and they cannot draw inferences from it, I would not teach them any longer.
>
> (Confucius, 551–479 BC)

The world is changing so rapidly that any rational forecast of future events is simply not feasible. We know from the records of prehistory and history that the patterns of culture of every human society change constantly.[1] The rate and type of culture change may be slow and gradual, as it was during the Paleolithic, or fast and drastic, as it has been in contemporary societies. Generally, the factors influencing culture change are diversified – both internal and external. Internal factors, such as socioeconomic evolution and technical inventions, may lead to changes in people's lifestyle; external factors, such as conquest by another culture, may bring about culture change. The roles of internal and external factors in culture change may be different, depending on different space and time conditions.[2]

Among the external factors by which culture change is influenced are intercultural contacts and exchanges. Cultural diffusion is generally taken to mean the spread of a culture from one area or ethnic group to another area or ethnic group. Diffusion has always had a catalytic function in cultural development, as the comparatively rapid growth of human culture as a whole has arisen from the ability of all societies to borrow elements from other cultures and to incorporate them into their own. Moreover, the necessity of integrating newly acquired elements into one's cultural heritage creates new problems, which require new solutions and thereby engender new ideas. It was the opportunity for relatively rapid interchange of inventions and ideas between local cultures that made possible the birth of the newest civilizations.

During the prehistoric period human civilization did not exist or, at least, only appeared in a preliminary stage. Thus, some cultural elements –

language and religion – were at only a primitive level. As a result the intercultural differences were very small.[3] During most of the civilizational period, and as a result of cultural evolution, intercultural difference increased. Witness to this are the newly-born languages as well as diverse religions. Since the start of the post-industrial era there have been signs of interculturalization in the world economy. Thanks to technological progress and the division of social labour, intercultural trade, immigration and so on, the speed of cultural diffusion throughout the world has been much faster than in any period in the past centuries.

Technology has been the most fundamental element in promoting economic interculturalization. In pre-modern times the spread of ideas and technology could take centuries.[4] Intercontinental journeys, which now only need a few hours via air, would have taken several months before the twentieth century. Mobile telephones, computer networks and other technological inventions, which were considered to be either impossible or useless, are now becoming the necessities of our daily life. Technological advances in communication have made it possible to know in an instant what is happening in a household or factory or on a stock market half a world away. The growing importance of services and information in the world economy means that an increasing proportion of economic value is weightless – that is, it can be transmitted over fibre-optic cable rather than transported in a container ship. At the same time improvements in transportation networks and technology are reducing the costs of shipping goods by water, ground and air, and improvements in information technology have made it easier to raise productivity, as well as to increase intercultural specialization of labour.

There are two divergent views on the future development of cultural diversity. On the one hand, there is a concern that cultural differences could vanish under the onslaught of modernization. To this end, some pessimists simply assume that cultural beliefs and practices are incompatible with modern rationality, which demands not only secularization but also secularism. On the other hand, globalization has also been accompanied by a resurgence of local culture. As a result, optimists believe that there is or will be a growing realization that local cultures play an important part in guiding human action and holding the fabric of society together. Development, through inappropriate policies, could destroy some cultural values. However, appropriate policies, programmes and projects, could help cultural and economic development to benefit from each other.

At its twenty-sixth session, in 1991, the General Conference of UNESCO adopted a resolution requesting the Director-General, in cooperation with the Secretary-General of the United Nations, to 'establish an independent World Commission on Culture and Development comprising women and men drawn from all regions and eminent in diverse disciplines, to prepare a World Report on Culture and Development and proposals for both urgent and long-term action to meet cultural needs in the context of development'. This request was endorsed by a resolution adopted by the General Assembly of the United Nations a few weeks later. The Commission began its work in the spring of 1993, focusing its international agenda on achieving a clearly defined set of goals. Foremost among them is to provide a permanent vehicle through which some of the key issues of culture and development can be explored and clarified. *Our Creative Diversity*, the Commission's first report on culture and development, was designed to address a diversified audience across the world, ranging from community activists, field workers, artists and scholars to government officials and politicians. Its aim is to show them how culture shapes all our thinking, imagining and behaviour. It is the transmission of behaviour as well as a dynamic source of change, creativity, freedom and the awakening of innovative opportunities.

The central argument advanced in *Our Creative Diversity* is that development embraces not only access to goods and services, but also the opportunity to choose a full, satisfying, valuable and valued way of living together, thus encouraging the flourishing of human existence in all its forms and as a whole (WCCD, 1995). Even the goods and services stressed by the narrower, conventional view are valued because of what they contribute to our freedom to live in the manner to which we aspire. Culture, therefore, however important it may be as an instrument of development (or an obstacle to development), cannot ultimately be reduced to a subsidiary position as a mere promoter of (or an impediment to) economic growth. The role of culture is not exhausted as a servant of ends – though in a narrower sense of the concept this is one of its roles – but is the social basis of the ends themselves.

No culture is not influenced by, or in turn influences, other cultures. Nor is any culture changeless, invariant or static. All cultures are in a state of constant flux, driven by both internal and external forces. Pearson (1955, pp. 83–4) warns that humans are moving into 'an age when different civilizations will have to learn to live side by side in peaceful interchange, learning from each other, studying each other's history and ideas and arts and culture, mutually enriching each other's lives. The alternative, in this overcrowded little world, is misunderstanding, tension, clash, and catastrophe.'

By now, pluralism is an all-pervasive and enduring characteristic of almost all of the more than 200 nations and regions that make up the world community. However, ethnic, religious and other forms of group identification can trigger violent conflict when mobilized and manipulated to do so. Hence 'nation-building' that seeks to make all groups homogeneous, or allow one to dominate the others, is neither desirable nor feasible. A nation that depends on cultural diversity needs to create a sense of itself as a civic community, freed from any connotations of ethnic exclusivity. All its policy approaches should be grounded in this awareness. Defining and applying an effective cultural policy implies finding new ways of holding together multicultural societies based on pluralism.

The principle of pluralism, in the sense of tolerance and respect and rejoicing over the plurality of cultures, is vital in dealings between countries, but it also applies within countries, in the relations between different ethnic groups. These relations have become problematic in the course of development. In general, intercultural harmonization must follow at least two courses: (i) intercultural exchange, and (ii) mutual understanding. The intercultural contacts and exchanges are the basis for intercultural harmonization. But without mutual understanding, these contacts and exchanges would only result in intercultural conflicts. Furthermore, more respect should be paid to the millions of indigenous peoples all over the world: it is imperative that their rights be protected, that more appropriate models be developed to promote their education, and that they have greater access to the tools of modern communication.

Where there is willingness to compromise, there is hope. The hope emerges when peoples from all civilizations find themselves not so fundamentally different from one another after all. Both sides will come to understand this 'sameness' and their basic heterogeneity if they can make further progress in the worldwide dialogue and mutual understanding. It should be noted that although the various cultural groups in the world have some commonalties, it is unlikely that cultural universalism would become a possibility in the foreseeable future. Surely, it is time to learn how to let cultural diversity lead not to the clash of cultures, but to peaceful coexistence and creativity!

Appendix 1 Mathematical Proofs

A1.1 Proof of Proposition 3 in Chapter 5

On the basis of the assumptions given in Section 5.3.1 of Chapter 5, we can develop a multicultural economic optimization model.

To begin with the analysis, let us first assume that there is only a single culture in the target economy (S) (that is, $N = 1$). For the sake of expositional ease, m policy variables are used here to denote the production factors (such as labour force, capital, technology, natural resource and information), that is, $X^1 = (X_{111}, X_{112}, \ldots, X_{11m})$. In addition, the constraints for the m policy variables are noted as $g_1\ (X^1) \in g_1$, and the objective of the regime is defined as a function of the policy variable set X^1, that is, $f_1(X^1)$. According to Assumption 5, $f_1(X^1)$ can be optimized via the following formula:

$$\max f_1(X^1) \tag{A1.1}$$

$$\text{subject to} \begin{cases} g_1 \in (X^1)\ g_1 \\ X^1 \in (0, \infty). \end{cases}$$

On the basis of the assumptions in Section 5.3.1 of Chapter 5, we can obtain an optimal solution for the 1-dimension (1–d) cultural system from Model (A1.1), that is:

$$F_1^* = f_1(X^{1*}), \text{ where } X^{1*} = (X_{111}^*, X_{112}^*, \ldots, X_{11m}^*).$$

Assume that the economy (S) is now divided into two different culture areas (S_1 and S_2), the policy variables of which are defined as $X^{21} = (X_{211}, X_{212}, \ldots, X_{21m})$ and $X^{22} = (X_{221}, X_{222}, \ldots, X_{22m})$, respectively. The technical implications of X^{21} and X^{22} follow that of X^1. The constraints for the two sub-areas are noted as $g_{21}(X^{21})$ and $g_{22}(X^{22})$, respectively. S_1 and S_2 are now politically separated, the constraints for each culture area become tighter than that for the 1-d cultural system, that is, $g_{21}(X^{21}) \subset g_1$, $g_{22}(X^{22}) \subset g_1$ and $g_{21}(X^{21}) \cup g_{22}(X^{22}) = g_1$. $f_{21}\ (X^{21})$ and $f_{22}(X^{22})$ are defined as two independent objective functions for the culture areas S_1 and S_2, respectively. According to assumption 5 (see Section 5.3.1 of Chapter 5), $f_{21}(X^{21})$ and $f_{22}(X^{22})$ can be optimized via the following formula:

$$\max P^{21}\ f_{21}(X^{21}) + P^{22}\ f_{222}(X^{22}) \tag{A1.2}$$

$$\text{subject to} \begin{cases} g_{21}\ (X^{21}) \in g_{21} \\ g_{22}\ (X^{21}) \in g_{22} \\ X^{21} \in (0, \infty) \\ X^{22} \in (0, \infty) \\ P^{21} \in (0, \infty) \\ P^{22} \in (0, \infty) \end{cases}$$

In Model (A1.2), P^{21} and P^{22} are set to identify the priorities under which the first and second cultural systems (S_1 and S_2) are optimized. Obviously, when $P^{21} > P^{22}$, the optimization of S_1 is given a higher priority than that of S_2; when $P^{21} = P^{22}$, S_1 and S_2 are equally treated. As a result the optimal solutions for S_1 and S_2 can be obtained from Model (A1.2):

$$F_{21}^* = f_{21}(X^{21*}), \text{ where } X^{21*} = (X_{211}^*, X_{212}^*, \ldots, X_{21m}^*);$$

$$F_{22}^* = f_{22}(X^{22*}), \text{ where } X^{22*} = (X_{221}^*, X_{222}^*, \ldots, X_{22m}^*).$$

The total output value of the 2-dimension (2-d) cultural system is $F_2^* = F_{21}^* + F_{22}^* = f_{21}(X^{21*}) + f_{22}(X^{22*})$. On the basis of assumptions 1–5 from Section 5.3.1, we may prove that the optimized output of the 2-d cultural system expressed by Model (A1.1) will not in any case exceed that of the 1-d system expressed by Model (A1.1), that is:

$$F_2^* \leq F_1^*.$$

Suppose that the two culture areas (S_1 and S_2) in Model (A1.2) are merged into a single culture area. As a result the constraints of the two culture areas become:

$$g_{21}(X^{21}) \cup g_{22}(X^{22}) = g_2(X^{21}, X^{22}) \text{ and}$$

$$g_{21} \cup g_{22} = g_2.$$

Now, Model (A1.2) becomes:

$$\max P^{21} f_{21}(X^{21}) + P^{22} f_{22}(X^{22}) \qquad \text{(A1.2a)}$$

$$\text{subject to} \begin{cases} g_2\,(X^{21}, (X^{22}) \in g_2 \\ X^{21} \in (0, \infty) \\ X^{22} \in (0, \infty) \\ P^{21} \in (0, \infty) \\ P^{22} \in (0, \infty) \end{cases}$$

The optimal output for S_1 and S_2 as a whole can be obtained from Model (A1.2a): $C_2^* = C_{21}^* + C_{22}^*$, where $C_{21}^* = f_{21}(X^{21*})$, and $C_{22}^* = f_{22}(X^{22*})$.

Since the constraints of Model (A1.2a) (that is, g_{21} and g_{22}) are more relaxed than those of Model (A1.2) (that is, $g_2 = g_{21} \cup g_{22}$), we have:

$$C_2^* \geq F_2^*.$$

Let us compare Models (A1.2a) and (A1.1). Since the inter-political and intercultural barriers have been removed, the objective functions of the two culture areas (S_1 and S_2) can be merged as $F_2(X^2) = f_{21}(X^{21}) \cup f_{22}(X^{22})$.

Therefore, Model (A1.2a) now becomes:

$$\max f_2(X^2) \qquad \text{(A1.2b)}$$

$$\text{subject to} \begin{cases} g_{21}\,(X^{21}) + g_{22}\,(X^{22}) \in g_1 \\ X^{21} \in (0, \infty) \\ X^{22} \in (0, \infty) \end{cases}$$

After having compared Models (A1.2b) and (A1.2), we can find that the optimal output of Model (A1.2b) (C_2^*) will not in any case exceed that of Model (A1.1) (F_1^*), that is:

$$C_2^* \le F_1^*.$$

As a result, we have $F_2^* \le C_2^* \ge F_1^*$.

Next, let us assume that the economy (S) is now composed of N culture areas (S_1, S_2..., and S_N). The policy variable set of the ith culture area (S_i) is defined as $X^{ni} = (X_{ni1}, X_{ni2}, ..., X_{nim})$ (i = 1, 2, ..., N). The technical implications of X^{ni} follow that of X^1. The constraints for the ith culture area are noted as $g_{ni}(X^{ni})$ (i = 1, 2, ..., N). In addition, as all sub-areas are now separated from each other, the constraints for all sub-areas may be expressed as $g_{ni}(X^{ni}) \subset g_1$ and $g_{n1}(X^{n1}) \cup g_{n2}(X^{n2}) \cup ... \cup g_{nN}(X^{nN}) = g_1$. $f_{ni}(X^{ni})$ (i = 1, 2, ..., N) stands for the objective function of the ith culture area. If $f_{n1}(X^{n1})$, $f_{n2}(X^{n2})$, ..., and $f_{nN}(X^{nN})$ are set to be optimized, the optimization of the N-dimension (N-d) cultural system is written as

$$\max \sum_{i=1}^{N} P^{ni} f_{ni}(X^{ni}) \tag{A1.3}$$

$$\text{subject to} \begin{cases} g_{ni}(X^{ni}) \in g_{ni} \\ X^{ni} \in (0, \infty) \\ P^{ni} \in (0, \infty) \\ (i = 1, 2, ..., N) \end{cases}$$

In Model (A1.3), P^{ni} is set to identify the priority under which the ith culture area (i = 1, 2, ..., N) is optimized. Obviously, when $P^{ni} \neq P^{nj}$ (i = 1, 2, ..., N; j = 1, 2, ..., N; and $i \neq j$) it implies that the ith and jth culture areas (S_i and S_j) are unequally treated and that the larger the parameter of P^{ni} (i = 1, 2, ..., N), the higher priority is given for the optimization of S_i, (i = 1, 2, ..., N); when $P^{ni} = P^{nj}$, S_i and S_j are equally treated. Similarly, Model (A1.3) yields an optimal solution for S_i, that is:

$$F_{ni}^* = f_{ni}(X^{ni*}), \text{ where } X^{ni*} = (X_{ni1}^*, X_{ni2}^*, ..., X_{nim}^*).$$

The total output of the N-d cultural system is summed to $F_N^* = F_{n1}^* + F_{n2}^* + ... + F_{nN}^*$. Obviously, $F_N^* \le F_{N-1}^*$, that is, the largest output of an i-d cultural system (F_i) decreases with respect to i.

A1.2 Proof of propositions in Chapter 8

On the basis of the assumptions made in Section 8.2 of Chapter 8, we can further define that the cost (c) and benefit (r) resulting form the transactions between a given site (x, y) and any other site (x', y') of the isolated authoritarian area (denoted by Ω) are related to the distance (l) between the two sites. Here, l ranges between 0 and L (L is the longest distance within the given authoritarian area). The total cost and benefit of the given site (x, y) within the authoritarian area can be expressed by different integral calculus functions with respect to distance. As for the total cost function ($C(l)$), we have:

$$C(x, y) = \oint_{\Omega} c(l)dl, \text{ with } l \in (0, L) \text{ and } (x, y) \in \Omega \tag{A1.4}$$

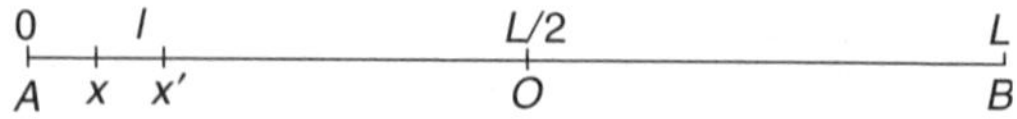

Figure A1.1 A simplified culture area

For simplicity of exposition, we only analyse the one-dimension case.[1] Consider Figure A1.1 in which A and B (with the coordinates of 0 and L, respectively) symbolize the borders of the authoritarian area and O (with the coordinate of $L/2$) is the geographical centre of the area. According to assumptions 2 and 3 in Section 8.2, the transaction cost (c) and benefit (r) between any two sites in the authoritarian area can be expressed respectively by the monotonously increasing and monotonously decreasing functions of the distance (l) between the two sites. In the simplest case, we use two linear functions:

$$c(l) = a + bl, \text{ with } a \geq 0 \text{ and } b \geq 0. \tag{A1.5}$$

$$r(l) = e - fl, \text{ with } e \geq \text{ and } f \geq 0. \tag{A1.6}$$

In Equations (A1.5) and (A1.6), we define that there exist two parts for the cost and benefit, respectively: (1) fixed cost (a) and the fixed benefit (e) are constant and have nothing to do with distance (l); and (2) variable cost (bl) and variable benefit ($-fl$) are related to distance (l). Obviously, the longer the distance (l), the larger (smaller) the variable cost (benefit). Literally, 'b' is defined as 'marginal cost on distance', and '$-f$' is defined as 'marginal benefit on distance'. So far, we can have the following definitions:

Definition A. The fixed cost (benefit) between any two sites of the authoritarian area is *not* related to the distance between the two sites.

Definition B. The variable cost (benefit) between any two sites of the authoritarian area is *positively* (*negatively*) related to the distance between the two sites.

According to assumptions 2 and 3 in Section 8.2, the total cost of the authoritarian area can be further expressed as a function of the geographical location (that is, x in the one-dimensional case). Inserting Equation (A1.5) into Equation (A1.4), we have:

$$C(x) = \int_0^x (a + bl)\,dl + \int_0^{L-x} (a + bl)\,dl, \text{ with } x \in (0, L) \tag{A1.7}$$

Finally, after solving Equation (A1.7), we obtain a nonlinear function of the total cost (C) with respect to the geographical location (x):

$$C(x) = bx^2 - bLx + aL + bL^2/2 \tag{A1.8}$$

Let the differential of C with respect to x be zero, that is, $\partial C/\partial x = 2bx - bL = 0$, we can find that when $x = L/2$, the function of the total cost (C) goes to an extremity site. Apparently, since $C = aL + bL^2/2$ is maximized when $x = 0$ and L (that is, the given site is at the periphery), it can be seen that $C = aL + bL^2/4$ is minimized when $x = L/2$ (that is, the given site is at the core). Obviously, the above results show that the lowest cost should be found in the geographical core while the highest cost should be found in the geographical periphery of the isolated authoritarian area.

The assumptions of Section 8.2 can also help us to build up a function of the total benefit with respect to the geographical location in the authoritarian area. Let Equation (A1.6) denote the benefit function with respect to the distance between x and $x'1$ (shown in Figure A1.1). The function of the total benefit ($R(x)$) now becomes:

$$R(x) = \int_0^x (e - fl)\,\mathrm{d}l + \int_0^{L-x} (e - fl)\,\mathrm{d}l = -fx^2 + fLx + eL - fL^2/2, \text{ with } x \in (0, L). \quad \text{(A1.9)}$$

Like Equation (A1.8), Equation (A1.9) also has three kinds of marginal properties for $R(x)$ with respect to x. Let $\partial R/\partial x = -2fx + fl = 0$, then $x = L/2$. Specifically, (1) when $0 \le x < L/2$, $\partial R/\partial x > 0$, that is, R is an increasing function of x; (2) when $L/2 < x \le L$, $\partial R/\partial x < 0$, that is, R is a decreasing function of x; and (3) when $x = L/2$, $\partial R/\partial x = 0$. As a result, we can conclude that when $x = 0$ and $x = L$, $R(0) = R(L) = eL - fL^2/2$; when $x = L/2$, $R(L/2) = eL - fL^2/4$. In other words, $R(x)$ is maximized in the geographical centre ($x = L/2$) and is minimized in the boundaries ($x = 0$ and $x = L$) of the authoritarian area. Obviously, the benefit expressed by Equation (A1.9) yields an inverted-U shaped curve, that is, the authoritarian area's total benefit of intracultural exchanges always decreases from the centre (that is, O in Figure A1.1) to the peripheries (that is, A and B in Figure A1.1). Finally, we have the following: *Given the homogeneous natural and social conditions, the transaction cost (benefit) of an isolated authoritarian area can be minimized (maximized) at the geographical centre of, and be maximized (minimized) at the geographical periphery of the area.*

QED of Proposition 1.

Before providing evidence in support of Proposition 2, let us first apply the model built in Section 8.2 to investigate if there is any optimal size for an authoritarian area. Economically, for a given set of sizes for the authoritarian area (as defined in assumption 4), there is an expansion that defines the least-cost combinations of culture size inputs and thus specifies the lowest total variable cost attainable at each rate of administered size. In the simplest case, we may derive the total transaction cost for the authoritarian area by the integral calculus of Equation (A1.8), that is:

$$TC(L) = aL^2 + bL^3/3 \quad \text{(A1.10)}$$

Again, we may derive the total benefit for the authoritarian area by the integral calculus of Equation (A1.9), that is:

$$TR(L) = eL^2 - fL^3/3 \quad \text{(A1.11)}$$

Subtracting TC from TR, we obtain the net benefit for the isolated authoritarian area $Y = TR - TC$, where TR and TR are defined in Equations (A1.10) and (A1.11), respectively. By deriving the first order differential of the net benefit (Y) with respect to culture size (here, it refers to L) and let it be zero, we obtain:

$$\partial Y/\partial L = TR'(L) - TC'(L) = 2(e - a)L - (b + f)L^2 = 0 \quad \text{(A1.12)}$$

Solving Equation (A1.12), we have:

$$L^* = 2\frac{e - a}{b + f} \quad \text{(A1.13)}$$

Equation (A1.13) indicates that an optimal size can be found for an isolated authoritarian area if $e > a$, $b \neq 0$ and $f \neq 0$. On the basis of the above results, we may conclude that (1) the net benefit (Y) increases with respect to the size of the authoritarian area

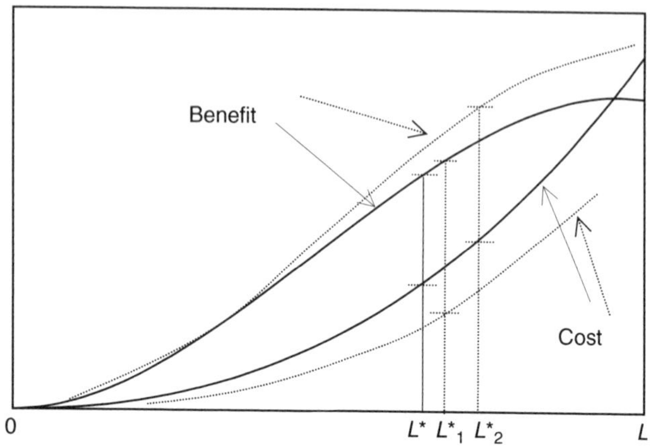

Figure A1.2 Seeking the optimal size of the culture area

(L) when $L<L^*$; (2) the net benefit (Y) decreases with respect to the size of the authoritarian area (L) when $L>L^*$; and (3) the net benefit (Y) is maximized when $L=L^*$ (see Figure A1.2). Finally, we have the following: *Given the homogeneous natural and social conditions, the size of an isolated authoritarian area can be optimized at a certain level, if $e>a$ in Equation (A1.13).*

The total cost and the total benefit grow at different rates when the authoritarian area grows in size (here, it refers to L), as demonstrated in Figure A1.2. When the culture size administered is small, the increased total cost will decrease with respect to the increase of culture size because the fixed cost remains as a constant. However, when the culture size exceeds a certain quantity, socioeconomic affairs will no longer be efficiently managed. As a result of the management difficulties of the additional quantity of culture size, there will eventually be a relatively higher increased rate of administrative expenditure (cost) with respect to the increase of culture size. If the functions of the total cost and benefit with respect to culture size are known, we can derive the most efficient level of culture size by maximizing the net benefit Y (that is, benefit minus cost).

Next, let us suppose that the isolated authoritarian area has now transformed from a backward transportation and communication network to a well-developed one. Along with the reduced transaction cost throughout the whole area, the coefficients a and b (in Equation (A1.5)) will be reduced accordingly. Under the condition that $e>a$, the optimal level of the culture size (as illustrated by L_1^* in Figure A1.2) will be, *ceteris paribus*, larger than L^*, that is: *Given the same natural and social conditions, the optimal size of an isolated authoritarian area is positively related to the stage of economic development, if $e>a$ in Equation (A1.13).*

Finally, let us suppose that the authoritarian area has now transformed from the isolated status to an open one. The major consequence is that the latter can benefit not only from internal but also from external trade and other economic activities. As a result Equation (A1.6) will bear the following changes: the coefficient of e will increase and that of f will decrease accordingly. At last, we may find that, if $e>a$, the optimal level of the culture size (as illustrated by L_2^* in Figure A1.2) will be, *ceteris paribus*, larger than L^*, that is: *Given the same natural and social conditions, the optimal* *size of an open authoritarian area is larger than that of an isolated one, if $e>a$ in Equation (A1.13).*

QED of Proposition 2

Generally, the sources of benefit from economies of scale for the authoritarian area may be grouped into three categories. (1) *Technical economies*. The authoritarian areas with large sizes can make relatively efficient uses of their fixed cost and hence give themselves considerable advantages over small authoritarian areas. (2) *Marketing economies*. Marketing in a larger size of economy gains many benefits, but the main economies of scale from marketing include bulk purchases and distribution potentialities. (3) *Risk-bearing economies*. A number of advantages can lead to larger authoritarian areas experiencing risk-bearing economies. The underlying factor is that large authoritarian areas frequently engage in a range of diverse activities, so that a fall in the return from any one unit of economy does not threaten the stability of the whole economy.

While increases in size frequently confer advantages on an authoritarian area, there is a limit to the gains from growth in many cases. In other words, there is an optimal level of spatial capacity and increases in size beyond this level will lead to a loss of economies of size and manifest themselves in rising average costs. Without doubt, the increasing complexity of managing a large authoritarian area is the major source of administrative inefficiencies when the authoritarian area grows beyond a certain size. It becomes increasingly difficult to control and manage the various socioeconomic affairs and risks as the authoritarian area grows in size. Diseconomies of scale mainly result from managerial difficulties, while the latter are, under certain circumstances, positively related to cultural diversity. Since a large population is likely to be less homogeneous, the average cultural distance between individuals is likely to be positively correlated with the size of the authoritarian area.[2]

Next, let us discuss another issue: in a world of two or more cultures how will the geographical pattern of intercultural actions be after culture-related barriers are removed or reduced?

To make composition easier, we analyse two adjacent authoritarian areas (that is, AB and BC, as shown in Figure A1.3), both of which are characterized by assumptions 2–5 of Section 8.2, except that they are open to each other. Thus we can assume that the total cost and benefit of site x (here $0 \le x \le L$) within Areas AB and BC are expressed by Equations (A1.10) and (A1.11), respectively. The total cost $C_{ABC}(x)$ and benefit $R_{ABC}(x)$ of the given site x within Areas AB and BC may then be expressed by:

$$C_{ABC}(x) = C_{AB}(x) + \alpha C_{BC}(x) = \int_0^x (a + bl)\mathrm{d}l + \int_0^{L-x} (a + bl)\mathrm{d}l + \alpha\int_{L-x}^{2L-x} (a + bl)\mathrm{d}l \qquad \text{(A1.14)}$$
$$= bx^2 - (1 + \alpha)bLx + (1 + 3\alpha)bL^2/2 + (1 + \alpha)aL, \text{ with } \alpha \ge 1.$$

$$R_{ABC}(x) = R_{AB}(x) + \beta R_{BC}(x) = \int_0^x (e - fl)\mathrm{d}l + \int_x^{L-x} (e - fl)\mathrm{d}l + \beta\int_{L-x}^{2L-x} (e - fl)\mathrm{d}l \qquad \text{(A1.15)}$$
$$= -fx^2 + (1 + \beta)fLx - (1 + 3\beta)fL^2/2 + (1 + \beta)eL, \text{ with } \beta \in (0, 1).$$

In Equation (A1.14) α is defined as an intercultural cost multiplier. Usually, when the inter-political and intercultural barriers change from the maximum to the minimum level, α will decrease to 1 accordingly. In Equation (A1.15), β is used as an intercultural benefit reducer. Usually, when the inter-political and intercultural barriers change from the maximum level to zero, β will increase from 0 to 1 accordingly. In the extreme case when $\alpha = \beta = 1$, no inter-political and intercultural barriers exist.[3]

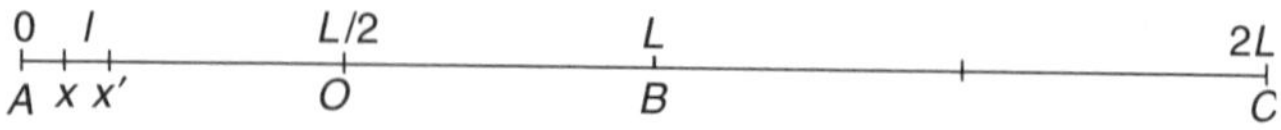

Figure A1.3 Two simplified culture areas

Let $dC_{ABC}/dx = 2bx - (1 + \alpha)bL = 0$, then $x_1^* = (1 + \alpha)L/2$ is the value at which the total cost is minimized; $dR_{ABC}/dx = -2fx + (1 + \beta)fL = 0$, then $x_2^* = (1 + \beta)L/2$ is the value at which the total benefit is maximized. Obviously, only when $\alpha = \beta$, x_1^* equals to x_2^*. In most cases, however, x_1^* does not equal to x_2^*, which means that the minimization of total cost and the maximization of total benefit cannot always occur at the same site. In order to solve this dilemma, let us look at the optimization of the net benefit which is expressed by the total benefit less total cost, that is, $Y_{ABC} = R_{ABC}(x) - C_{ABC}(x)$. Let $dY_{ABC}/dx = -2fx + (1 + \beta)fL - 2bx + (1 + \alpha)bL = 0$, we obtain a value:

$$x^* = \frac{(1 + \alpha)b + (1 + \beta)f}{2(b + f)}L = \frac{L}{2} + \frac{\alpha b + \beta f}{2(b + f)}L \qquad \text{(A1.16)}$$

at which the net benefit is maximized. Obviously, as $b>0$, $f>0$, $L\geq 0$, $\alpha\geq 1$, and $\beta\geq 0$, then we have $x^*\geq L/2$. This result implies that the optimized economic centre of Area *AB* will move away from its geographical core (*O*), as a result of the removal of inter-political and intercultural barriers. In the extreme case, when $\alpha = \beta = 1$, (that is, all inter-political and intercultural barriers are removed), Equation (A1.16) becomes $x^* = L/2 + L/2 = L$, indicating that the optimized economic centre of Area *AB* will be located at the peripheral area (*B*). The above result is also applicable to Area *BC* when its inter-political and intercultural barriers are removed or reduced, as demonstrated in Figure A1.4. Finally, we have the following: *In a world of two or more authoritarian areas, economic centres will move close to each other, if the inter-political and intercultural barriers are removed or reduced.*

QED of Proposition 3

In order to analyse the conditions for cultural integration, we analyse two adjacent authoritarian areas as shown in Figure A1.3. According to Proposition 3, after the inter-political and intercultural barriers are reduced, the optimized economic centres of Areas *AB* and *BC* will move close to each other. Using Equation (A1.16), we can find the optimized economic centres of Areas *AB* and *BC*:

$$x^*_{AB} = \frac{L}{2} + \frac{\alpha_{AB}b + \beta_{AB}f}{2(b + f)} \qquad \text{(A1.17)}$$

$$x^*_{BC} = \frac{L}{2} + \frac{\alpha_{BC}b + \beta_{BC}f}{2(b + f)} \qquad \text{(A1.18)}$$

In Equations (A1.17) and (A1.18), α_{AB} and β_{AB} are the intercultural cost multiplier and benefit subtractor of Area *AB*, respectively; α_{BC} and β_{BC} are the intercultural cost multiplier and benefit subtractor of Area *BC*, respectively. As Areas *AB* and *BC* are open to each other, there do not exist any inter-political and intercultural barriers between Areas *AB* and *BC*, that is, $\alpha_{AB} = \alpha_{BC} = 1$ and $\beta_{AB} = \beta_{BC} = 1$. As a result Equations (A1.17) and (A1.18) become $x^*_{AB} = x^*_{BC} = L$. In other words, the optimized economic centres of Areas *AB* and *BC* have now moved simultaneously to their joint border *B*, as a result of the

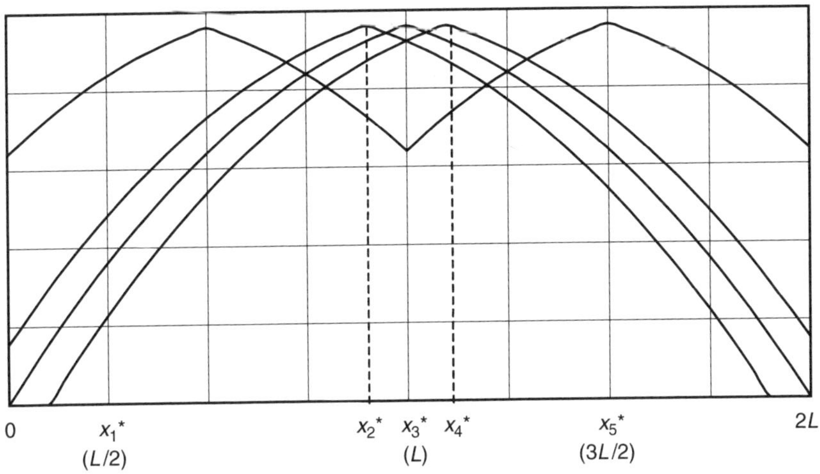

Figure A1.4 Optimal locations of economic centres under different conditions

Notes:

(1) x_1^* and x_5^* denote the optimal centres of areas *AB* and *BC*, respectively when the two areas are isolated;

(2) x_2^* and x_4^* denote the optimal centres of areas *AB* and *BC*, respectively when the barriers between areas *AB* and *BC* are reduced; and

(3) x_3^* denotes the optimal centre of areas *AB* and *BC* when the barriers between areas *AB* and *BC* are removed.

removal of all inter-political and intercultural barriers. Due to the fact that the actual size is less than its optimal size for each culture, Areas *AB* and *BC* will each additionally benefit from their cultural enlargement, as suggested in Proposition 2. Under Rule A (see Section 8.2 of Chapter 8), the two authoritarian areas may be integrated. The pole of the enlarged authoritarian area should be at the border of Areas *BC* and *AB*, as only this way can the cost minimization and benefit maximization for the new authoritarian area (that is, *AC*) be realized.

There will exist three cases for the newly integrated culture if it is characterized by Proposition 2: (i) its actual size is larger than the optimal level; (ii) its actual size is smaller than the optimal level; and (iii) its actual size is equal to the optimal. In Case (i), the integrated authoritarian area is unstable, as any reduction in culture size will lead to increase in net benefit, the incentives for cultural disintegration will exist, till the actual size of the new authoritarian area reaches the optimal level at which the net benefit is maximized. Therefore, in both Case (ii) and Case (iii), as any reduction in culture size will lead to decrease in net benefit, the incentives for cultural disintegration will disappear. Finally, we can conclude that the integrated culture is stable when the actual size is not larger than the optimal size. Finally we have: *Different authoritarian areas that are open to each other may be integrated, under conditions that the actual size of each authoritarian area is smaller than its optimal size and that the actual size of the integrated authoritarian area is not larger than its optimal size.*

QED of Proposition 4

Appendix 2 Cultural Diversity Indexes of Existing Countries and Regions

	Language			Religion		
Country or region	NUM	POP	DIVERSITY	NUM	POP	DIVERSITY
Afghanistan	11	52.425	2.129	3	83.993	0.192
Albania	4	97.965	0.029	4	70.213	0.511
Algeria	3	59.675	0.557	3	99.559	0.005
American Samoa	5	49.593	1.251	3	57.377	0.597
Andorra	6	46.875	1.591	2	92.188	0.056
Angola	14	27.603	5.757	3	72.740	0.349
Antigua and Barbuda	2	95.313	0.033	4	41.538	1.249
Argentina	4	96.837	0.045	5	87.715	0.219
Armenia	3	93.369	0.076	2	64.456	0.279
Aruba	5	76.190	0.467	2	71.429	0.219
Australia	22	81.319	0.781	8	27.337	3.531
Austria	9	92.000	0.192	4	77.998	0.357
Azerbaijan	5	88.976	0.194	4	93.307	0.097
Bahamas, The	2	89.655	0.074	4	55.052	0.865
Bahrain	2	68.333	0.245	3	61.290	0.530
Bangladesh	10	95.219	0.116	3	88.304	0.137
Barbados	2	95.094	0.035	4	32.830	1.537
Belarus	5	65.637	0.739	3	50.676	0.719
Belgium	8	59.274	1.332	2	87.929	0.087
Belize	5	50.661	1.212	4	93.220	0.099
Benin	11	34.407	3.820	4	62.034	0.693
Bermuda	1	100.000	0.000	4	37.097	1.392
Bhutan	3	50.000	0.732	2	74.713	0.192
Bolivia	8	42.193	2.327	3	88.417	0.136
Bosnia and Herzegovina	2	99.042	0.007	4	40.064	1.295
Botswana	7	53.952	1.450	4	56.000	0.840
Brazil	6	97.545	0.045	3	72.323	0.355
Brunei	8	45.752	2.090	2	67.208	0.255
Bulgaria	6	80.863	0.409	3	50.420	0.724
Burkina Faso	24	47.400	4.321	3	50.000	0.732
Burundi	5	75.492	0.484	3	65.124	0.467
Cambodia	5	88.632	0.201	3	94.995	0.057
Cameroon	26	14.858	15.023	4	34.963	1.464

Country or region	Language			Religion		
	NUM	POP	DIVERSITY	NUM	POP	DIVERSITY
Canada	28	60.808	2.691	11	45.196	2.722
Cape Verde	1	100.000	0.000	2	99.579	0.003
Central African Republic	11	44.709	2.765	4	31.250	1.594
Chad	14	27.014	5.863	5	53.986	1.097
Chile	4	89.687	0.154	3	76.749	0.291
China	49	65.783	2.787	7	51.915	1.549
Colombia	7	98.165	0.036	2	91.906	0.058
Comoros	8	71.337	0.815	2	99.322	0.005
Congo, Dem. Rep. of the	15	30.401	5.585	6	41.011	1.878
Congo, Rep. of the	12	30.992	4.556	4	40.927	1.268
Costa Rica	6	97.240	0.051	2	81.268	0.139
Côte d'lvoire	7	25.768	3.240	6	41.458	1.855
Croatia	2	96.017	0.028	5	72.117	0.566
Cuba	1	100.000	0.000	2	60.500	0.315
Cyprus	3	74.118	0.329	3	73.256	0.342
Czech Republic	15	81.186	0.664	7	39.961	2.217
Denmark	10	94.456	0.136	2	87.121	0.093
Djibouti	4	50.746	0.979	2	97.267	0.019
Dominica	2	52.482	0.390	3	70.270	0.386
Dominican Republic	2	97.951	0.014	3	81.795	0.221
Ecuador	2	92.965	0.050	2	92.462	0.054
Egypt	3	98.349	0.018	3	89.003	0.128
El Salvador	1	100.000	0.000	3	78.269	0.270
Equatorial Guinea	3	84.091	0.191	2	93.182	0.048
Eritrea	9	49.025	2.065	2	69.359	0.237
Estonia	6	64.138	0.901	3	66.438	0.446
Ethiopia	8	31.012	3.198	5	34.156	1.886
Faroe Islands	1	100.000	0.000	2	79.545	0.152
Fiji	4	42.431	1.221	4	52.956	0.920
Finland	6	92.847	0.137	2	85.825	0.103
France	15	87.870	0.389	7	76.220	0.588
French Guiana	3	94.079	0.067	2	54.605	0.370
French Polynesia	4	46.309	1.105	3	50.220	0.728
Gabon	8	26.415	3.619	4	50.420	0.988
Gambia, The	11	34.054	3.861	2	95.200	0.034
Gaza Strip	2	99.514	0.003	2	98.735	0.009
Georgia	7	71.642	0.736	5	44.238	1.453
Germany	8	90.816	0.210	4	42.805	1.210
Ghana	8	37.599	2.660	6	29.337	2.547
Gibraltar	3	88.889	0.130	2	77.778	0.167
Greece	3	98.575	0.016	3	91.746	0.095
Greenland	2	87.500	0.091	2	98.214	0.012
Grenada	1	100.000	0.000	3	53.061	0.675
Guadeloupe	2	95.150	0.034	2	81.395	0.138
Guam	9	37.179	2.976	3	74.359	0.325
Guatemala	7	41.354	2.131	3	75.979	0.302
Guernsey	1	100.000	0.000	2	64.516	0.279
Guinea	12	35.661	3.947	4	86.775	0.201
Guinea-Bissau	10	29.881	4.026	3	65.254	0.465

Country or region	Language			Religion		
	NUM	POP	DIVERSITY	NUM	POP	DIVERSITY
Guyana	3	96.382	0.041	6	34.023	2.261
Haiti	2	83.565	0.121	3	68.533	0.413
Honduras	5	98.214	0.029	3	86.770	0.156
Hong Kong	12	59.279	1.751	4	73.806	0.438
Hungary	7	98.524	0.029	3	63.091	0.500
Iceland	2	95.941	0.029	2	90.406	0.069
India	72	10.704	44.554	10	80.257	0.576
Indonesia	10	39.431	3.034	6	87.211	0.258
Iran	20	45.259	4.155	3	93.420	0.075
Iraq	6	77.127	0.507	3	62.483	0.510
Ireland	3	74.120	0.329	2	91.758	0.059
Isle of Man	1	100.000	0.000	2	62.500	0.297
Israel	4	62.898	0.673	3	80.389	0.240
Italy	12	94.070	0.159	3	81.739	0.222
Jamaica	3	94.071	0.067	4	47.244	1.078
Japan	7	99.092	0.018	4	53.393	0.908
Jersey	2	93.407	0.047	3	61.628	0.524
Jordan	3	97.792	0.025	2	96.460	0.025
Kazakstan	11	45.954	2.655	4	47.009	1.085
Kenya	31	37.992	7.409	7	29.529	2.940
Kiribati	3	98.908	0.012	3	53.659	0.664
Korea, North	2	99.836	0.001	4	68.298	0.552
Korea, South	2	99.890	0.001	8	50.099	1.823
Kuwait	2	78.082	0.164	4	45.000	1.144
Kyrgyzstan	10	59.565	1.537	3	70.000	0.390
Lao PDR	5	66.992	0.701	3	57.813	0.590
Latvia	7	55.061	1.398	4	62.864	0.673
Lebanon	4	74.948	0.415	8	33.938	2.950
Lesotho	3	70.954	0.376	5	39.000	1.669
Liberia	19	42.428	4.448	3	67.692	0.426
Libya	3	95.929	0.046	2	96.991	0.021
Liechtenstein	4	87.859	0.183	2	80.645	0.144
Lithuania	6	81.183	0.401	3	71.968	0.361
Luxembourg	12	67.381	1.249	2	95.238	0.034
Macau	6	85.308	0.301	3	60.808	0.538
Macedonia (FYP of)	7	66.532	0.918	3	53.769	0.662
Madagascar	3	89.974	0.116	4	52.028	0.945
Malawi	6	55.556	1.217	6	23.771	2.919
Malaysia	14	33.053	4.852	6	52.920	1.325
Maldives	1	100.000	0.000	1	100.000	0.000
Mali	17	42.689	4.072	3	89.950	0.117
Malta	3	95.733	0.048	2	93.333	0.047
Marshall Islands	3	50.000	0.732	3	63.333	0.496
Martinique	2	96.742	0.023	2	87.500	0.091
Mauritania	8	76.953	0.615	2	99.585	0.003
Mauritius	13	61.734	1.668	4	50.877	0.976
Mayotte	5	42.105	1.539	2	96.875	0.022
Mexico	38	86.580	0.629	4	90.390	0.142
Micronesia	9	41.628	2.606	3	41.121	0.910

	Language			Religion		
Country or region	NUM	POP	DIVERSITY	NUM	POP	DIVERSITY
Moldova	6	62.069	0.973	3	55.505	0.630
Monaco	5	41.935	1.546	2	81.250	0.139
Mongolia	12	78.819	0.693	2	96.203	0.027
Morocco	3	65.026	0.468	2	99.816	0.001
Mozambique	26	27.793	9.513	5	47.771	1.318
Myanmar	9	68.952	0.978	6	89.449	0.208
Namibia	12	46.816	2.749	5	51.445	1.185
Nauru	6	49.758	1.460	3	50.962	0.714
Nepal	22	50.327	3.643	4	86.468	0.206
Netherlands, The	5	91.845	0.140	6	40.013	1.929
Netherlands Antilles	3	85.981	0.167	2	73.832	0.199
New Caledonia	6	45.274	1.666	3	61.194	0.532
New Zealand	4	90.912	0.134	9	21.644	4.594
Nicaragua	4	94.848	0.074	3	76.674	0.292
Niger	10	46.019	2.466	3	87.007	0.153
Nigeria	16	25.060	6.987	7	42.995	2.032
Northern Mariana	11	47.502	2.521	2	79.630	0.152
Norway	5	96.549	0.057	2	88.209	0.085
Oman	2	76.652	0.176	5	73.451	0.533
Pakistan	10	43.107	2.706	5	75.004	0.495
Palau	6	50.000	1.449	4	41.176	1.260
Panama	9	77.276	0.648	3	80.147	0.244
Papua New Guinea	6	45.644	1.648	4	60.000	0.741
Paraguay	6	48.634	1.510	2	88.409	0.084
Peru	5	79.770	0.385	3	88.839	0.130
Philippines	44	29.540	13.387	6	82.919	0.358
Poland	4	97.628	0.033	3	90.696	0.108
Portugal	2	98.995	0.007	2	92.254	0.055
Puerto Rico	4	51.326	0.964	3	64.829	0.472
Qatar	2	59.677	0.322	2	95.009	0.035
Reunion	7	61.386	1.120	2	88.235	0.085
Romania	14	90.679	0.279	3	86.841	0.156
Russia	36	86.592	0.617	5	72.356	0.560
Rwanda	2	93.591	0.045	4	64.987	0.625
St Kitts and Nevis	1	100.000	0.000	3	38.462	0.966
St Lucia	2	79.310	0.154	2	79.054	0.156
St Vincent and the Grenadines	2	99.107	0.006	4	41.964	1.236
Samoa	3	52.071	0.693	5	26.036	2.288
San Marino	1	100.000	0.000	2	88.462	0.083
São Tomé and Principe	3	86.131	0.165	2	89.781	0.073
Saudi Arabia	2	95.018	0.035	3	95.440	0.051
Senegal	10	45.795	2.484	3	92.021	0.092
Seychelles	6	40.113	1.924	2	88.462	0.083
Sierra Leone	13	45.764	3.019	3	60.000	0.552
Singapore	5	56.262	1.022	7	53.866	1.454
Slovakia	9	85.696	0.369	4	60.370	0.732
Slovenia	4	87.877	0.183	2	82.653	0.128
Solomon Islands	5	84.010	0.294	4	41.849	1.239
Somalia	2	98.253	0.012	2	99.853	0.001

Country or region	Language			Religion		
	NUM	POP	DIVERSITY	NUM	POP	DIVERSITY
South Africa	13	22.408	6.317	30	29.709	9.921
Spain	5	74.415	0.509	3	66.734	0.441
Sri Lanka	8	60.398	1.278	5	69.320	0.638
Sudan, The	11	49.371	2.367	4	72.998	0.454
Suriname	3	40.476	0.923	5	27.358	2.219
Swaziland	3	90.291	0.113	2	66.990	0.257
Sweden	13	89.541	0.308	2	86.456	0.098
Switzerland	5	63.624	0.796	3	46.067	0.809
Syria	3	90.007	0.116	5	73.968	0.520
Taiwan	13	66.713	1.349	13	47.734	2.821
Tajikistan	4	62.149	0.690	4	80.000	0.320
Tanzania	20	47.063	3.883	3	34.997	1.042
Thailand	10	52.566	1.981	4	94.802	0.075
Togo	35	19.802	16.311	5	58.774	0.942
Tonga	2	98.020	0.014	3	43.564	0.859
Trinidad and Tobago	4	93.495	0.094	6	29.389	2.544
Tunisia	6	69.881	0.715	2	99.458	0.004
Turkey	4	87.579	0.188	2	99.764	0.002
Turkmenistan	10	70.357	0.979	2	93.166	0.049
Tuvalu	2	92.632	0.052	2	85.437	0.106
Uganda	30	24.056	12.237	5	38.835	1.676
Ukraine	8	64.647	1.086	8	30.733	3.222
United Arab Emirates	2	58.140	0.337	3	80.156	0.244
United Kingdom	4	97.284	0.038	10	43.483	2.674
United States	50	86.176	0.717	15	50.503	2.821
Uruguay	2	95.611	0.031	2	78.616	0.160
Uzbekistan	13	71.284	1.089	3	87.997	0.141
Vanuatu	4	56.604	0.825	4	35.795	1.435
Venezuela	5	96.882	0.051	3	87.445	0.148
Vietnam	23	86.811	0.512	5	66.667	0.710
Virgin Islands (US)	4	80.612	0.308	3	44.330	0.843
West Bank	2	92.179	0.056	3	82.123	0.217
Western Sahara	1	100.000	0.000	1	100.000	0.000
Yemen	2	98.182	0.013	2	99.879	0.001
Yugoslavia	9	75.259	0.722	4	62.559	0.680
Zambia	31	20.218	14.482	4	33.262	1.522
Zimbabwe	6	49.282	1.481	5	40.543	1.604

Notes: NUM = number of linguistic (religious) groups; POP = ratio of population of the largest linguistic (religious) groups.

Source: calculation by the author based on Equation (5.2) and *Britannica Book of the Year 1996*.

Appendix 3 Cultural Similarity Matrices of Selected Countries

A3.1 Linguistic similarity matrix

Country	Brazil	China	Congo, DR	France	India	Japan	Saudi Arabia	United States
Afghanistan	0.000	0.000	0.000	0.003	0.000	0.000	0.000	0.000
Albania	0.000	0.000	0.000	0.000	0.000	0.000	0.000	0.002
Algeria	0.000	0.000	0.034	0.331	0.000	0.000	0.597	0.009
American Samoa	0.000	0.000	0.000	0.001	0.036	0.000	0.000	0.496
Andorra	0.109	0.000	0.034	0.095	0.016	0.000	0.000	0.093
Angola	0.259	0.000	0.000	0.011	0.000	0.000	0.000	0.002
Antigua and Barbuda	0.000	0.000	0.000	0.001	0.036	0.000	0.000	0.875
Argentina	0.004	0.000	0.000	0.008	0.000	0.000	0.000	0.073
Armenia	0.000	0.000	0.000	0.000	0.000	0.000	0.000	0.001
Aruba	0.000	0.000	0.000	0.005	0.036	0.000	0.000	0.164
Australia	0.010	0.017	0.002	0.024	0.036	0.002	0.008	0.873
Austria	0.006	0.000	0.000	0.004	0.000	0.000	0.000	0.010
Azerbaijan	0.000	0.000	0.000	0.000	0.000	0.000	0.000	0.002
Bahamas, The	0.000	0.000	0.034	0.105	0.036	0.000	0.000	0.883
Bahrain	0.000	0.000	0.000	0.025	0.000	0.000	0.683	0.001
Bangladesh	0.000	0.000	0.000	0.001	0.026	0.000	0.000	0.026
Barbados	0.000	0.000	0.000	0.001	0.036	0.000	0.000	0.875
Belarus	0.000	0.000	0.000	0.001	0.000	0.000	0.000	0.004
Belgium	0.010	0.000	0.034	0.354	0.000	0.000	0.016	0.026
Belize	0.006	0.000	0.000	0.005	0.036	0.000	0.000	0.588
Benin	0.000	0.000	0.034	0.133	0.000	0.000	0.000	0.007
Bermuda	0.000	0.000	0.000	0.001	0.036	0.000	0.000	0.875
Bhutan	0.000	0.000	0.000	0.000	0.000	0.000	0.000	0.000
Bolivia	0.000	0.000	0.000	0.004	0.000	0.000	0.000	0.068
Bosnia and Herzegovina	0.000	0.000	0.000	0.000	0.000	0.000	0.000	0.000
Botswana	0.000	0.000	0.000	0.001	0.036	0.000	0.000	0.286
Brazil	–	0.000	0.000	0.016	0.000	0.000	0.000	0.013
Brunei	0.000	0.095	0.000	0.001	0.033	0.002	0.000	0.038
Bulgaria	0.000	0.000	0.027	0.030	0.000	0.000	0.000	0.008
Burkina Faso	0.000	0.000	0.034	0.056	0.000	0.000	0.000	0.007
Burundi	0.000	0.000	0.034	0.085	0.000	0.000	0.000	0.007
Cambodia	0.000	0.031	0.000	0.000	0.000	0.002	0.000	0.007

Country	Brazil	China	Congo, DR	France	India	Japan	Saudi Arabia	United States
Cameroon	0.000	0.000	0.034	0.121	0.036	0.000	0.007	0.157
Canada	0.016	0.011	0.034	0.258	0.036	0.002	0.002	0.649
Cape Verde	0.975	0.000	0.000	0.011	0.000	0.000	0.000	0.002
Central African Republic	0.000	0.000	0.034	0.057	0.000	0.000	0.000	0.007
Chad	0.000	0.000	0.034	0.141	0.000	0.000	0.232	0.009
Chile	0.000	0.000	0.000	0.004	0.000	0.000	0.000	0.068
China	0.000	–	0.000	0.000	0.000	0.003	0.000	0.007
Colombia	0.000	0.000	0.000	0.005	0.001	0.000	0.000	0.069
Comoros	0.000	0.000	0.034	0.048	0.000	0.000	0.000	0.007
Congo, Dem. Rep. of the	0.000	0.000	–	0.034	0.000	0.000	0.000	0.007
Congo, Rep. of the	0.000	0.000	0.034	0.155	0.000	0.000	0.000	0.007
Costa Rica	0.000	0.002	0.000	0.005	0.020	0.002	0.000	0.090
Côte d'Ivoire	0.000	0.000	0.034	0.258	0.000	0.000	0.000	0.007
Croatia	0.000	0.000	0.000	0.000	0.000	0.000	0.000	0.000
Cuba	0.000	0.000	0.000	0.004	0.000	0.000	0.000	0.068
Cyprus	0.000	0.000	0.000	0.003	0.000	0.000	0.000	0.002
Czech Republic	0.005	0.000	0.000	0.001	0.000	0.000	0.000	0.010
Denmark	0.005	0.000	0.000	0.009	0.005	0.000	0.005	0.012
Djibouti	0.000	0.000	0.034	0.100	0.000	0.000	0.104	0.009
Dominica	0.000	0.000	0.034	0.477	0.036	0.000	0.000	0.532
Dominican Republic	0.000	0.000	0.000	0.005	0.020	0.000	0.000	0.088
Ecuador	0.000	0.000	0.000	0.004	0.000	0.000	0.000	0.068
Egypt	0.000	0.000	0.004	0.030	0.000	0.000	0.950	0.006
El Salvador	0.000	0.000	0.000	0.004	0.000	0.000	0.000	0.068
Equatorial Guinea	0.000	0.000	0.000	0.000	0.000	0.000	0.000	0.000
Eritrea	0.000	0.000	0.000	0.003	0.000	0.000	0.003	0.001
Estonia	0.000	0.000	0.000	0.000	0.000	0.000	0.000	0.002
Ethiopia	0.000	0.000	0.000	0.000	0.000	0.000	0.000	0.000
Faroe Islands	0.000	0.000	0.000	0.000	0.000	0.000	0.000	0.000
Fiji	0.000	0.000	0.000	0.001	0.397	0.000	0.000	0.172
Finland	0.000	0.000	0.000	0.000	0.000	0.000	0.000	0.001
France	0.016	0.000	0.034	–	0.001	0.000	0.025	0.021
French Guiana	0.000	0.000	0.034	0.937	0.000	0.000	0.000	0.007
French Polynesia	0.000	0.029	0.034	0.409	0.000	0.002	0.000	0.012
Gabon	0.000	0.000	0.034	0.252	0.000	0.000	0.000	0.007
Gambia, The	0.000	0.000	0.000	0.000	0.000	0.000	0.000	0.000
Gaza Strip	0.000	0.000	0.000	0.025	0.000	0.000	0.950	0.002
Georgia	0.000	0.000	0.000	0.000	0.000	0.000	0.000	0.002
Germany	0.010	0.000	0.000	0.009	0.000	0.000	0.000	0.016
Ghana	0.000	0.000	0.000	0.000	0.000	0.000	0.000	0.000
Gibraltar	0.000	0.000	0.000	0.027	0.036	0.000	0.074	0.877
Greece	0.000	0.000	0.000	0.003	0.000	0.000	0.000	0.002
Greenland	0.000	0.000	0.000	0.000	0.000	0.000	0.000	0.000
Grenada	0.000	0.000	0.000	0.001	0.036	0.000	0.000	0.875
Guadeloupe	0.000	0.000	0.034	0.937	0.000	0.000	0.000	0.007
Guam	0.004	0.015	0.000	0.001	0.036	0.007	0.000	0.620
Guatemala	0.000	0.000	0.000	0.004	0.000	0.000	0.000	0.068
Guernsey	0.000	0.000	0.000	0.001	0.036	0.000	0.000	0.875
Guinea	0.000	0.000	0.034	0.077	0.000	0.000	0.000	0.007
Guinea-Bissau	0.145	0.000	0.000	0.011	0.000	0.000	0.000	0.002

Country	Brazil	China	Congo, DR	France	India	Japan	Saudi Arabia	United States
Guyana	0.000	0.000	0.000	0.001	0.036	0.000	0.000	0.875
Haiti	0.000	0.000	0.034	0.937	0.000	0.000	0.000	0.007
Honduras	0.000	0.000	0.000	0.005	0.002	0.000	0.000	0.070
Hong Kong	0.001	0.766	0.000	0.001	0.036	0.002	0.000	0.212
Hungary	0.004	0.000	0.000	0.000	0.000	0.000	0.000	0.006
Iceland	0.000	0.000	0.000	0.000	0.000	0.000	0.000	0.000
India	0.000	0.000	0.000	0.001	–	0.000	0.000	0.037
Indonesia	0.000	0.000	0.000	0.000	0.000	0.000	0.000	0.000
Iran	0.000	0.000	0.000	0.015	0.000	0.000	0.012	0.002
Iraq	0.000	0.000	0.000	0.025	0.000	0.000	0.771	0.001
Ireland	0.000	0.000	0.000	0.001	0.036	0.000	0.000	0.741
Isle of Man	0.000	0.000	0.000	0.001	0.036	0.000	0.000	0.875
Israel	0.000	0.000	0.000	0.025	0.000	0.000	0.180	0.003
Italy	0.009	0.000	0.005	0.010	0.000	0.000	0.000	0.016
Jamaica	0.000	0.000	0.000	0.001	0.056	0.000	0.000	0.877
Japan	0.004	0.003	0.000	0.001	0.001	–	0.000	0.006
Jersey	0.000	0.000	0.000	0.001	0.036	0.000	0.000	0.875
Jordan	0.000	0.000	0.000	0.025	0.000	0.000	0.950	0.002
Kazakstan	0.006	0.009	0.000	0.000	0.000	0.005	0.000	0.010
Kenya	0.000	0.000	0.000	0.003	0.036	0.000	0.001	0.045
Kiribati	0.000	0.000	0.000	0.000	0.000	0.000	0.000	0.000
Korea, North	0.000	0.003	0.000	0.000	0.000	0.007	0.000	0.004
Korea, South	0.000	0.003	0.000	0.000	0.000	0.006	0.000	0.004
Kuwait	0.000	0.000	0.000	0.025	0.000	0.000	0.781	0.001
Kyrgyzstan	0.006	0.001	0.000	0.000	0.000	0.000	0.000	0.007
Lao PDR	0.000	0.000	0.000	0.000	0.000	0.000	0.000	0.000
Latvia	0.000	0.000	0.000	0.001	0.000	0.000	0.000	0.004
Lebanon	0.000	0.000	0.034	0.219	0.000	0.000	0.749	0.009
Lesotho	0.000	0.000	0.000	0.001	0.036	0.000	0.000	0.166
Liberia	0.000	0.000	0.000	0.001	0.036	0.000	0.000	0.520
Libya	0.000	0.000	0.000	0.025	0.000	0.000	0.950	0.001
Liechtenstein	0.010	0.000	0.000	0.008	0.000	0.000	0.000	0.011
Lithuania	0.000	0.000	0.000	0.001	0.000	0.000	0.000	0.004
Luxembourg	0.131	0.000	0.034	0.057	0.012	0.000	0.000	0.042
Macau	0.024	0.921	0.000	0.013	0.005	0.002	0.000	0.012
Macedonia (FYR of)	0.000	0.000	0.000	0.003	0.000	0.000	0.000	0.001
Madagascar	0.000	0.000	0.034	0.091	0.000	0.000	0.000	0.007
Malawi	0.000	0.006	0.000	0.001	0.036	0.000	0.000	0.048
Malaysia	0.000	0.070	0.000	0.001	0.036	0.002	0.000	0.251
Maldives	0.000	0.000	0.000	0.000	0.000	0.000	0.000	0.000
Mali	0.000	0.000	0.034	0.051	0.000	0.000	0.009	0.009
Malta	0.000	0.000	0.000	0.001	0.021	0.000	0.000	0.021
Marshall Islands	0.000	0.000	0.000	0.001	0.036	0.000	0.000	0.500
Martinique	0.000	0.000	0.034	0.937	0.000	0.000	0.000	0.007
Mauritania	0.000	0.000	0.034	0.055	0.000	0.000	0.000	0.007
Mauritius	0.000	0.004	0.034	0.742	0.014	0.002	0.000	0.014
Mayotte	0.000	0.000	0.034	0.203	0.000	0.000	0.000	0.007
Mexico	0.000	0.000	0.000	0.004	0.000	0.000	0.000	0.068
Micronesia	0.000	0.000	0.000	0.001	0.005	0.000	0.000	0.005
Moldova	0.000	0.000	0.000	0.000	0.000	0.000	0.000	0.002

Country	Brazil	China	Congo, DR	France	India	Japan	Saudi Arabia	United States
Monaco	0.004	0.000	0.034	0.425	0.036	0.000	0.000	0.077
Mongolia	0.000	0.005	0.000	0.000	0.000	0.000	0.000	0.000
Morocco	0.000	0.000	0.000	0.025	0.000	0.000	0.650	0.001
Mozambique	0.012	0.006	0.000	0.011	0.000	0.000	0.000	0.002
Myanmar	0.000	0.000	0.000	0.000	0.000	0.000	0.000	0.000
Namibia	0.006	0.000	0.000	0.001	0.036	0.000	0.000	0.084
Nauru	0.000	0.044	0.000	0.001	0.036	0.000	0.000	0.523
Nepal	0.000	0.000	0.000	0.000	0.029	0.000	0.000	0.001
Netherlands, The	0.000	0.000	0.000	0.013	0.000	0.000	0.009	0.002
Netherlands Antilles	0.000	0.000	0.000	0.001	0.036	0.000	0.000	0.079
New Caledonia	0.000	0.000	0.034	0.343	0.000	0.000	0.000	0.009
New Zealand	0.000	0.000	0.000	0.001	0.036	0.000	0.000	0.875
Nicaragua	0.000	0.000	0.000	0.001	0.009	0.000	0.000	0.009
Niger	0.000	0.000	0.034	0.131	0.000	0.000	0.000	0.007
Nigeria	0.000	0.000	0.000	0.003	0.036	0.000	0.001	0.256
Northern Mariana	0.004	0.039	0.000	0.001	0.036	0.007	0.000	0.484
Norway	0.000	0.000	0.000	0.001	0.005	0.000	0.000	0.006
Oman	0.000	0.000	0.000	0.025	0.000	0.000	0.767	0.001
Pakistan	0.000	0.000	0.000	0.001	0.036	0.000	0.000	0.105
Palau	0.000	0.009	0.000	0.001	0.036	0.002	0.000	0.505
Panama	0.000	0.003	0.000	0.005	0.036	0.002	0.000	0.212
Papua New Guinea	0.000	0.000	0.000	0.001	0.009	0.000	0.000	0.009
Paraguay	0.037	0.000	0.000	0.015	0.000	0.000	0.000	0.073
Peru	0.000	0.000	0.000	0.004	0.000	0.000	0.000	0.068
Philippines	0.000	0.001	0.000	0.001	0.036	0.001	0.000	0.343
Poland	0.006	0.000	0.000	0.001	0.000	0.000	0.000	0.009
Portugal	0.975	0.000	0.000	0.011	0.000	0.000	0.000	0.002
Puerto Rico	0.000	0.000	0.000	0.005	0.005	0.000	0.000	0.073
Qatar	0.000	0.000	0.000	0.025	0.000	0.000	0.403	0.001
Reunion	0.000	0.020	0.034	0.812	0.000	0.002	0.000	0.012
Romania	0.004	0.000	0.000	0.001	0.000	0.000	0.000	0.008
Russia	0.002	0.001	0.000	0.000	0.000	0.000	0.000	0.005
Rwanda	0.000	0.000	0.034	0.064	0.000	0.000	0.000	0.007
St Kitts and Nevis	0.000	0.000	0.000	0.001	0.036	0.000	0.000	0.875
St Lucia	0.000	0.000	0.000	0.001	0.036	0.000	0.000	0.207
St Vincent and the Grenadines	0.000	0.000	0.000	0.001	0.036	0.000	0.000	0.875
Samoa	0.000	0.000	0.000	0.001	0.006	0.000	0.000	0.006
San Marino	0.000	0.000	0.000	0.000	0.000	0.000	0.000	0.000
São Tomé and Principe	0.861	0.000	0.007	0.019	0.000	0.000	0.000	0.009
Saudi Arabia	0.000	0.000	0.000	0.025	0.000	0.000	–	0.001
Senegal	0.000	0.000	0.034	0.048	0.000	0.000	0.000	0.007
Seychelles	0.000	0.000	0.034	0.812	0.036	0.000	0.000	0.180
Sierra Leone	0.000	0.000	0.000	0.001	0.036	0.000	0.000	0.458
Singapore	0.000	0.563	0.000	0.001	0.036	0.002	0.000	0.277
Slovakia	0.001	0.000	0.000	0.001	0.000	0.000	0.000	0.003
Slovenia	0.000	0.000	0.000	0.000	0.000	0.000	0.000	0.001
Solomon Islands	0.000	0.000	0.000	0.001	0.019	0.000	0.000	0.019
Somalia	0.000	0.000	0.000	0.000	0.000	0.000	0.000	0.000
South Africa	0.000	0.000	0.000	0.001	0.036	0.000	0.000	0.091

Country	Brazil	China	Congo, DR	France	India	Japan	Saudi Arabia	United States
Spain	0.000	0.000	0.000	0.004	0.000	0.000	0.000	0.068
Sri Lanka	0.000	0.000	0.000	0.001	0.036	0.000	0.000	0.103
Sudan, The	0.000	0.000	0.000	0.025	0.000	0.000	0.494	0.001
Suriname	0.000	0.000	0.000	0.000	0.000	0.000	0.000	0.000
Swaziland	0.000	0.000	0.000	0.000	0.000	0.000	0.000	0.000
Sweden	0.005	0.000	0.000	0.017	0.004	0.000	0.008	0.020
Switzerland	0.010	0.000	0.034	0.197	0.000	0.000	0.000	0.019
Syria	0.000	0.000	0.000	0.025	0.000	0.000	0.900	0.001
Taiwan	0.000	0.921	0.000	0.000	0.000	0.002	0.000	0.005
Tajikistan	0.000	0.000	0.000	0.000	0.000	0.000	0.000	0.001
Tanzania	0.000	0.002	0.000	0.001	0.016	0.000	0.000	0.016
Thailand	0.000	0.121	0.000	0.000	0.000	0.002	0.000	0.006
Togo	0.000	0.000	0.034	0.146	0.000	0.000	0.000	0.007
Tonga	0.000	0.000	0.000	0.000	0.000	0.000	0.000	0.000
Trinidad and Tobago	0.000	0.000	0.000	0.001	0.063	0.000	0.000	0.030
Tunisia	0.000	0.000	0.000	0.025	0.000	0.000	0.950	0.001
Turkey	0.000	0.000	0.000	0.017	0.000	0.000	0.014	0.002
Turkmenistan	0.000	0.001	0.000	0.000	0.000	0.000	0.000	0.002
Tuvalu	0.000	0.000	0.000	0.000	0.000	0.000	0.000	0.000
Uganda	0.000	0.000	0.000	0.001	0.053	0.000	0.000	0.071
Ukraine	0.000	0.000	0.000	0.001	0.000	0.000	0.000	0.003
United Arab Emirates	0.000	0.000	0.000	0.025	0.000	0.000	0.419	0.001
United Kingdom	0.000	0.000	0.000	0.001	0.036	0.000	0.000	0.875
United States	0.013	0.008	0.034	0.021	0.037	0.005	0.001	–
Uruguay	0.000	0.000	0.000	0.004	0.000	0.000	0.000	0.068
Uzbekistan	0.000	0.003	0.000	0.003	0.000	0.005	0.000	0.004
Vanuatu	0.000	0.000	0.034	0.143	0.036	0.000	0.000	0.856
Venezuela	0.000	0.000	0.000	0.004	0.000	0.000	0.000	0.068
Vietnam	0.000	0.023	0.005	0.005	0.000	0.002	0.000	0.012
Virgin Islands (US)	0.000	0.000	0.031	0.036	0.036	0.000	0.000	0.881
West Bank	0.000	0.000	0.000	0.025	0.000	0.000	0.922	0.002
Western Sahara	0.000	0.000	0.000	0.025	0.000	0.000	0.950	0.001
Yemen	0.000	0.000	0.000	0.025	0.000	0.000	0.950	0.001
Yugoslavia	0.000	0.000	0.000	0.000	0.000	0.000	0.000	0.002
Zambia	0.000	0.000	0.000	0.001	0.036	0.000	0.000	0.132
Zimbabwe	0.000	0.000	0.000	0.001	0.036	0.000	0.000	0.322

Note: Languages included in the calculation are Amharic, Arabic, Armenian, Bengali, Chinese, Czech, Danish, Dutch, English, Finnish, French, Greek, Hebrew, Hindi, Hungarian, Italian, Japanese, Kazak, Korean, Kyrgyz, Miao, Mongol, Norwegian, Polish, Portuguese, Punjabi, Romanian, Samoan, Serbo-Croatian, Slovak, Spanish, Swedish, Tai, Tajik, Thai, Turkish, Uighur, Ukrainian, Vietnamese, Yao and Yiddish.

Source: Calculated based on Equation (7.3) and *Britannica Book of the Year 1996*.

A3.2 Religious similarity matrix

Country	Brazil	China	Congo, DR	France	India	Japan	Saudi Arabia	United States
Afghanistan	0.000	0.015	0.014	0.055	0.111	0.000	0.988	0.016
Albania	0.052	0.066	0.066	0.107	0.146	0.007	0.702	0.091
Algeria	0.000	0.015	0.014	0.055	0.111	0.000	0.988	0.016
Andorra	0.922	0.059	0.860	0.781	0.035	0.007	0.000	0.812
Angola	0.698	0.059	0.698	0.698	0.035	0.007	0.000	0.698
Antigua and Barbuda	0.846	0.059	0.846	0.781	0.035	0.007	0.000	0.812
Argentina	0.952	0.074	0.874	0.803	0.050	0.007	0.015	0.834
Armenia	0.000	0.000	0.000	0.000	0.000	0.000	0.000	0.024
Australia	0.703	0.059	0.703	0.703	0.035	0.007	0.000	0.727
Austria	0.828	0.059	0.828	0.781	0.035	0.007	0.000	0.812
Azerbaijan	0.000	0.015	0.014	0.055	0.111	0.000	0.933	0.037
Bahamas	0.941	0.059	0.860	0.781	0.035	0.007	0.000	0.812
Bahrain	0.000	0.015	0.014	0.055	0.111	0.000	0.823	0.016
Bangladesh	0.000	0.015	0.014	0.055	0.216	0.000	0.883	0.019
Barbados	0.672	0.059	0.672	0.672	0.035	0.007	0.000	0.672
Belarus	0.178	0.059	0.178	0.178	0.035	0.007	0.000	0.201
Belgium	0.879	0.059	0.860	0.781	0.035	0.007	0.000	0.812
Belize	0.921	0.059	0.860	0.781	0.035	0.007	0.000	0.812
Benin	0.210	0.074	0.224	0.265	0.146	0.007	0.120	0.226
Bhutan	0.000	0.085	0.000	0.000	0.260	0.409	0.000	0.011
Bolivia	0.955	0.059	0.860	0.781	0.035	0.007	0.000	0.812
Bosnia and Herzegovina	0.135	0.074	0.149	0.190	0.146	0.007	0.401	0.174
Botswana	0.440	0.059	0.440	0.440	0.035	0.007	0.000	0.440
Brazil	–	0.059	0.860	0.781	0.035	0.007	0.000	0.812
Brunei Darussalam	0.000	0.015	0.014	0.055	0.111	0.000	0.672	0.016
Bulgaria	0.000	0.015	0.014	0.055	0.111	0.000	0.131	0.039
Burkina Faso	0.100	0.074	0.114	0.155	0.146	0.007	0.500	0.116
Burundi	0.813	0.059	0.813	0.781	0.035	0.007	0.000	0.812
Cambodia	0.000	0.099	0.014	0.021	0.028	0.409	0.021	0.024
Cameroon	0.524	0.074	0.538	0.579	0.146	0.007	0.217	0.540
Canada	0.816	0.075	0.825	0.800	0.062	0.013	0.009	0.857
Cape Verde	0.955	0.059	0.860	0.781	0.035	0.007	0.000	0.812
Central African Rep.	0.426	0.074	0.440	0.481	0.146	0.007	0.150	0.442
Chad	0.348	0.074	0.362	0.403	0.146	0.007	0.540	0.364
Chile	0.892	0.059	0.860	0.781	0.035	0.007	0.000	0.812
China	0.059	–	0.073	0.074	0.057	0.092	0.015	0.082
Colombia	0.919	0.059	0.860	0.781	0.035	0.007	0.000	0.812
Comoros	0.007	0.021	0.021	0.062	0.117	0.007	0.988	0.023
Congo, Dem. Rep. of the	0.860	0.073	–	0.795	0.049	0.007	0.014	0.826
Congo, Rep. of the	0.653	0.074	0.666	0.672	0.054	0.007	0.019	0.668
Costa Rica	0.813	0.059	0.813	0.781	0.035	0.007	0.000	0.812
Côte d'Ivoire	0.260	0.074	0.274	0.315	0.146	0.007	0.387	0.276
Croatia	0.727	0.072	0.740	0.740	0.048	0.007	0.013	0.764
Cuba	0.000	0.015	0.014	0.055	0.111	0.000	0.395	0.016
Cyprus	0.035	0.050	0.049	0.090	0.145	0.007	0.233	0.074
Czech Republic	0.430	0.059	0.430	0.430	0.035	0.007	0.000	0.432
Denmark	0.871	0.059	0.860	0.781	0.035	0.007	0.000	0.812
Djibouti	0.027	0.042	0.041	0.082	0.138	0.007	0.973	0.043
Dominica	0.865	0.059	0.860	0.781	0.035	0.007	0.000	0.812

Country	Brazil	China	Congo, DR	France	India	Japan	Saudi Arabia	United States
Dominican Republic	0.882	0.059	0.860	0.781	0.035	0.007	0.000	0.812
Ecuador	0.925	0.059	0.860	0.781	0.035	0.007	0.000	0.812
Egypt	0.010	0.025	0.024	0.065	0.121	0.007	0.890	0.049
El Salvador	0.853	0.059	0.853	0.781	0.035	0.007	0.000	0.812
Equatorial Guinea	0.932	0.059	0.860	0.781	0.035	0.007	0.000	0.812
Eritrea	0.000	0.015	0.014	0.055	0.111	0.000	0.694	0.039
Estonia	0.137	0.059	0.137	0.137	0.035	0.007	0.000	0.161
Ethiopia	0.083	0.074	0.097	0.138	0.146	0.007	0.301	0.122
Fiji	0.530	0.074	0.543	0.584	0.495	0.007	0.078	0.549
Finland	0.858	0.059	0.858	0.781	0.035	0.007	0.000	0.812
France	0.781	0.074	0.795	–	0.090	0.007	0.055	0.807
French Guiana	0.546	0.059	0.546	0.546	0.035	0.007	0.000	0.546
French Polynesia	0.899	0.059	0.860	0.781	0.035	0.007	0.000	0.812
Gabon	0.681	0.059	0.681	0.681	0.035	0.007	0.000	0.681
Gambia	0.000	0.015	0.014	0.055	0.111	0.000	0.952	0.016
Georgia	0.000	0.015	0.014	0.055	0.110	0.000	0.110	0.039
Germany	0.767	0.074	0.781	0.789	0.056	0.007	0.021	0.783
Ghana	0.641	0.074	0.655	0.696	0.146	0.007	0.144	0.657
Greece	0.000	0.013	0.013	0.013	0.013	0.000	0.013	0.037
Grenada	0.673	0.059	0.673	0.673	0.035	0.007	0.000	0.673
Guadeloupe	0.814	0.059	0.814	0.781	0.035	0.007	0.000	0.812
Guatemala	0.955	0.059	0.860	0.781	0.035	0.007	0.000	0.812
Guinea	0.043	0.058	0.057	0.098	0.146	0.007	0.868	0.059
Guinea-Bissau	0.051	0.066	0.065	0.106	0.146	0.007	0.297	0.067
Guyana	0.389	0.074	0.403	0.444	0.466	0.007	0.091	0.409
Haiti	0.914	0.059	0.860	0.781	0.035	0.007	0.000	0.812
Honduras	0.955	0.059	0.860	0.781	0.035	0.007	0.000	0.812
Hong Kong	0.085	0.144	0.085	0.085	0.042	0.416	0.000	0.093
Hungary	0.886	0.059	0.860	0.781	0.035	0.007	0.000	0.812
Iceland	0.904	0.059	0.860	0.781	0.035	0.007	0.000	0.812
India	0.035	0.057	0.049	0.090	–	0.014	0.111	0.062
Indonesia	0.000	0.025	0.014	0.055	0.136	0.010	0.872	0.051
Iran, Islamic Rep. of	0.000	0.015	0.014	0.055	0.111	0.000	0.988	0.016
Iraq	0.030	0.045	0.044	0.085	0.141	0.007	0.970	0.046
Ireland	0.918	0.059	0.860	0.781	0.035	0.007	0.000	0.812
Israel	0.000	0.015	0.014	0.065	0.111	0.000	0.148	0.039
Italy	0.817	0.072	0.830	0.793	0.047	0.007	0.012	0.825
Jamaica	0.528	0.059	0.528	0.528	0.035	0.007	0.000	0.528
Japan	0.007	0.092	0.007	0.007	0.014	–	0.000	0.015
Jordan	0.035	0.050	0.049	0.090	0.146	0.007	0.965	0.051
Kazakstan	0.021	0.036	0.035	0.076	0.132	0.007	0.470	0.061
Kenya	0.601	0.074	0.615	0.656	0.094	0.007	0.059	0.617
Kiribati	0.537	0.059	0.537	0.537	0.035	0.007	0.000	0.537
Korea, DPR.	0.000	0.000	0.000	0.000	0.000	0.000	0.000	0.000
Korea, Republic	0.241	0.144	0.241	0.241	0.042	0.250	0.000	0.248
Kuwait	0.000	0.015	0.014	0.055	0.111	0.000	0.850	0.016
Kyrgyzstan	0.000	0.015	0.014	0.055	0.111	0.000	0.700	0.039
Lao PDR	0.000	0.085	0.000	0.000	0.007	0.409	0.000	0.008
Latvia	0.295	0.059	0.295	0.295	0.035	0.007	0.000	0.319
Lebanon	0.236	0.074	0.250	0.291	0.146	0.007	0.552	0.275
Lesotho	0.700	0.059	0.700	0.700	0.035	0.007	0.000	0.700

Country	Brazil	China	Congo, DR	France	India	Japan	Saudi Arabia	United States
Liberia	0.677	0.074	0.691	0.732	0.146	0.007	0.138	0.693
Libya	0.000	0.015	0.014	0.055	0.111	0.000	0.970	0.016
Lithuania	0.720	0.059	0.720	0.720	0.035	0.007	0.000	0.743
Luxembourg	0.952	0.059	0.860	0.781	0.035	0.007	0.000	0.812
Macau	0.000	0.085	0.000	0.000	0.007	0.169	0.000	0.008
Macedonia, FYR of	0.000	0.015	0.014	0.055	0.111	0.000	0.302	0.039
Madagascar	0.410	0.074	0.424	0.465	0.105	0.007	0.070	0.426
Malawi	0.484	0.074	0.498	0.539	0.146	0.007	0.200	0.500
Malaysia	0.064	0.159	0.078	0.119	0.223	0.180	0.529	0.091
Maldives	0.000	0.015	0.014	0.055	0.111	0.000	0.988	0.016
Mali	0.010	0.025	0.024	0.065	0.121	0.007	0.899	0.026
Malta	0.933	0.059	0.860	0.781	0.035	0.007	0.000	0.812
Martinique	0.875	0.059	0.860	0.781	0.035	0.007	0.000	0.812
Mauritania	0.000	0.015	0.014	0.055	0.111	0.000	0.988	0.016
Mauritius	0.272	0.074	0.286	0.327	0.654	0.007	0.167	0.291
Mexico	0.955	0.059	0.860	0.781	0.035	0.007	0.000	0.812
Moldova	0.000	0.000	0.000	0.000	0.000	0.000	0.000	0.024
Monaco	0.813	0.059	0.813	0.781	0.035	0.007	0.000	0.812
Mongolia	0.000	0.099	0.014	0.038	0.045	0.409	0.038	0.024
Morocco	0.000	0.015	0.014	0.055	0.111	0.000	0.988	0.016
Mozambique	0.248	0.074	0.262	0.303	0.146	0.007	0.130	0.264
Myanmar	0.049	0.149	0.063	0.087	0.086	0.416	0.038	0.076
Namibia	0.809	0.059	0.809	0.781	0.035	0.007	0.000	0.809
Nepal	0.000	0.093	0.014	0.035	0.845	0.078	0.035	0.027
Netherlands	0.540	0.074	0.738	0.581	0.076	0.007	0.041	0.556
Netherlands Antilles	0.738	0.059	0.554	0.738	0.035	0.007	0.000	0.738
New Caledonia	0.756	0.059	0.756	0.756	0.035	0.007	0.000	0.756
New Zealand	0.616	0.059	0.616	0.616	0.035	0.007	0.000	0.616
Nicaragua	0.918	0.059	0.860	0.781	0.035	0.007	0.000	0.812
Niger	0.000	0.015	0.014	0.055	0.111	0.000	0.870	0.016
Nigeria	0.348	0.074	0.362	0.403	0.146	0.007	0.430	0.364
Norway	0.882	0.059	0.860	0.781	0.035	0.007	0.000	0.812
Oman	0.040	0.054	0.054	0.095	0.221	0.007	0.876	0.059
Pakistan	0.020	0.035	0.034	0.075	0.148	0.007	0.950	0.039
Palau	0.647	0.059	0.647	0.647	0.035	0.007	0.000	0.647
Panama	0.945	0.059	0.860	0.781	0.035	0.007	0.000	0.812
Papua New Guinea	0.922	0.059	0.860	0.781	0.035	0.007	0.000	0.812
Paraguay	0.955	0.059	0.860	0.781	0.035	0.007	0.000	0.812
Peru	0.955	0.059	0.860	0.781	0.035	0.007	0.000	0.812
Philippines	0.907	0.074	0.874	0.826	0.081	0.007	0.046	0.828
Poland	0.907	0.059	0.860	0.781	0.035	0.007	0.000	0.827
Portugal	0.923	0.059	0.860	0.781	0.035	0.007	0.000	0.812
Puerto Rico	0.932	0.059	0.860	0.781	0.035	0.007	0.000	0.812
Qatar	0.000	0.015	0.014	0.055	0.111	0.000	0.950	0.016
Reunion	0.882	0.074	0.874	0.836	0.146	0.007	0.118	0.828
Romania	0.050	0.050	0.050	0.050	0.035	0.007	0.000	0.074
Russian Federation	0.009	0.024	0.023	0.068	0.109	0.007	0.100	0.053
Rwanda	0.740	0.070	0.751	0.751	0.045	0.007	0.010	0.751
Samoa	0.846	0.059	0.846	0.781	0.035	0.007	0.000	0.812
San Marino	0.885	0.059	0.860	0.781	0.035	0.007	0.000	0.812
São Tomé and Principe	0.955	0.059	0.860	0.781	0.035	0.007	0.000	0.812

Country	Brazil	China	Congo, DR	France	India	Japan	Saudi Arabia	United States
Saudi Arabia	0.000	0.015	0.014	0.055	0.111	0.000	–	0.016
Senegal	0.020	0.035	0.034	0.075	0.131	0.007	0.920	0.036
Seychelles	0.885	0.059	0.860	0.781	0.035	0.007	0.000	0.812
Sierra Leone	0.100	0.074	0.114	0.155	0.146	0.007	0.600	0.116
Singapore	0.129	0.159	0.143	0.184	0.186	0.416	0.149	0.156
Slovakia	0.667	0.059	0.667	0.667	0.035	0.007	0.000	0.667
Slovenia	0.827	0.059	0.827	0.781	0.035	0.007	0.000	0.812
Solomon Islands	0.949	0.059	0.860	0.781	0.035	0.007	0.000	0.812
Somalia	0.000	0.015	0.014	0.055	0.111	0.000	0.988	0.016
South Africa	0.943	0.074	0.874	0.809	0.085	0.007	0.024	0.838
Spain	0.667	0.071	0.679	0.679	0.047	0.007	0.011	0.679
Sri Lanka	0.069	0.159	0.083	0.124	0.273	0.416	0.076	0.096
St Kitts and Nevis	0.333	0.059	0.333	0.333	0.035	0.007	0.000	0.333
St Lucia	0.791	0.059	0.791	0.781	0.035	0.007	0.000	0.791
St Vincent and the Grenadines	0.741	0.059	0.741	0.741	0.035	0.007	0.000	0.741
Sudan	0.091	0.074	0.105	0.146	0.146	0.007	0.730	0.107
Suriname	0.373	0.074	0.387	0.428	0.419	0.007	0.196	0.392
Swaziland	0.670	0.059	0.670	0.670	0.035	0.007	0.000	0.670
Sweden	0.865	0.059	0.860	0.781	0.035	0.007	0.000	0.812
Switzerland	0.861	0.059	0.860	0.781	0.035	0.007	0.000	0.812
Syrian Arab Republic	0.055	0.070	0.069	0.110	0.146	0.007	0.860	0.071
Taiwan	0.034	0.121	0.037	0.037	0.044	0.235	0.002	0.045
Tajikistan	0.000	0.015	0.014	0.055	0.111	0.000	0.850	0.031
Tanzania	0.300	0.074	0.314	0.355	0.146	0.007	0.350	0.316
Thailand	0.005	0.105	0.019	0.046	0.053	0.414	0.040	0.029
Togo	0.283	0.074	0.297	0.338	0.146	0.007	0.121	0.299
Tonga	0.158	0.059	0.158	0.158	0.035	0.007	0.000	0.158
Trinidad and Tobago	0.591	0.074	0.605	0.646	0.331	0.007	0.059	0.610
Tunisia	0.000	0.015	0.014	0.055	0.111	0.000	0.988	0.016
Turkey	0.000	0.015	0.014	0.055	0.111	0.000	0.988	0.016
Turkmenistan	0.000	0.015	0.014	0.055	0.111	0.000	0.870	0.039
Uganda	0.612	0.074	0.626	0.667	0.101	0.007	0.066	0.627
Ukraine	0.117	0.059	0.117	0.126	0.035	0.007	0.000	0.150
United Arab Emirates	0.000	0.015	0.014	0.055	0.111	0.000	0.961	0.016
United Kingdom	0.643	0.074	0.657	0.663	0.061	0.007	0.014	0.677
United States of America	0.812	0.082	0.874	0.807	0.062	0.015	0.016	–
Uruguay	0.786	0.059	0.786	0.781	0.035	0.007	0.000	0.786
Uzbekistan	0.000	0.015	0.014	0.055	0.111	0.000	0.880	0.026
Vanuatu	0.500	0.059	0.500	0.500	0.035	0.007	0.000	0.524
Venezuela	0.922	0.059	0.860	0.781	0.035	0.007	0.000	0.812
Vietnam	0.087	0.144	0.087	0.087	0.042	0.416	0.000	0.095
Yemen	0.000	0.015	0.014	0.055	0.111	0.000	0.988	0.016
Yugoslavia	0.058	0.073	0.072	0.113	0.169	0.007	0.248	0.098
Zambia	0.398	0.059	0.398	0.398	0.035	0.007	0.000	0.398
Zimbabwe	0.417	0.059	0.417	0.417	0.035	0.007	0.000	0.417

Note: Religions included in the calculation are Christian, Eastern Orthodox, Jewish, Muslim, Buddhist, Chinese folk-religion (a mixture of Confucianism and Taoism), Hindu, Sikh and Bahai.

Source: Calculated based on Equation (7.3) and *Britannica Book of the Year 1996*.

Notes

Introduction

1. As a matter of fact, all the theories that have been established are based on a number of unrealistic assumptions. The art of successfully setting up a theory lies in introducing simplifying assumptions only when it is unavoidable and the final results are not compromised.
2. Cited from Lian and Oneal (1997, p. 61).

1. Concepts and Facts

1. Cited from Bodley (1994).
2. Cited from Cateora and Graham (1998, p. 112).
3. Based on Hu and Zhang (1982, p. 69), which also gives other references.
4. *The Economist*, 15 June 2002. Cited from Caselli and Coleman (2002).
5. Based on *Britannica Book of the Year* (1996) and other sources. Note that not all scholars agree in the genetic classification of languages. For example, sometimes Korean is also classified as a member of the Ural-Altaic phylum.
6. Calculated by the author based on *Britannica Book of the Year* (2001). Notice that according to these statistics several other languages (such as Phoenician, Akkadian, Moabite and Ugaritic of the Semitic family and Kott, Assan and Arin of the Paleo-Siberian phylum) have already become extinct.
7. According to Huntington (1996, p. 60), the share of English-speakers in the world population was 9.8 per cent in 1958, declining gradually to 9.1 per cent in 1970, 8.8 per cent in 1980 and 7.6 per cent in 1992.
8. Unless stated otherwise, 'Western Christianity' includes 'Roman Catholic', 'Protestant' and 'Anglican'.
9. In what follows, the terms 'Orthodox Christianity' and 'Eastern Orthodox' will be used interchangeably.
10. For an earlier study of the economic ethics of Confucianism, Hinduism, Buddhism and ancient Judaism, see Weber (1904); a more recent study of Jewish, Christian and Muslim economic ethics is Wilson (1997).
11. Horowitz (1985, p. 2) cited from Caselli and Coleman (2002, p. 8).

2. Culture as a Tool for Economic Analysis

1. Specifically, the World Bank (1996, p. 394) uses 'Sub-Saharan Africa' for East and Southern Africa, 'Asia' for 'East Asia and Pacific', and 'Europe and Central Asia' for Eastern Europe, Central Asia and the rest of Europe.
2. Calculated by the author based on *World Atlas* (1994). Figures within parentheses are number of countries involved.
3. Cited from www.answers.com/topic/authoritarianism.
4. The World Bank (1996, pp. 394–5) defined low-income economies, lower-middle-income economies, upper-middle-income economies and high-income

economies with the per capita GNPs of US$725 or less, US$726–2895, US$2896–8955 and US$8956 or more, respectively.

5. If X, Y and Z are used to denote the numbers of ethnic, linguistic and religious groups, respectively, the largest number of cultures (N) that encompass different kinds of the ethnic, linguistic and religious groups can be expressed by $N = X \cdot Y \cdot Z$.
6. Cited from Brown (2005).
7. The earliest literature would include Bacon (1946), Kroeber (1947), Naroll (1950) and Patai (1951), among others.
8. The terms 'civilization' and 'culture' can be used interchangeably.
9. Other authors who advanced similar arguments include Lind (1990, 1992, 1994), Buzan (1991), Gilpin (1993), Rostovanyi (1993), Vlahos (1991), Puchala (1994), Elmandjra (1994) and *The Economist* (1994, pp. 21–3).
10. For example, Northwest India belongs to the Islamic culture; and the Muslims and Tibetans in Northwest and Southwest China have nothing to do with the Han Chinese culture.
11. For example, Dutch, French and then English settlers created a multi-fragmented European culture in South Africa.
12. In what follows in this section, unless stated otherwise, all data cited are based on Figure 2.1.
13. *The Economist*, 27 November 1993, p. 33; 17 July 1993, p. 61.
14. It is noticeable that most of the non-religionists come from China, North Korea and Vietnam, which have adopted communist ideology.
15. It seems likely that as a result of the abandoning of communist ideology in some nations in this area, some non-religionists will transfer gradually to religious (mainly Orthodox) groupings.
16. On the role of fragments of European civilization creating new societies in North America, Latin America, South Africa and Australia, see Hartz (1964).

3. Multicultural Economic Comparisons and Differences

1. In 1998 the Technical Assistance in Statistics Team of the World Bank Development Economics Data Group conducted a survey to assess the quality of statistics in a number of transition countries. The findings suggest that in many countries the basic data are well below satisfactory level, with a strong correlation between average data quality and per capita dollar GDP in these countries. More details in this regard may be found in Belkindas et al. (1999).
2. There are alternative options for the PPP approach, which are usually based on either binary or multilateral comparisons. With regards to the latter, the Geary-Khamis approach (which was initiated by R.S. Geary in 1958 and developed by S.H. Khamis in 1970) is preferred by, among others, Maddison (1996, 2001 and 2003) whose estimates on the cross-national data of GDP will be employed in my multicultural comparison of the world economy from 1950 to 2000 later in this chapter.
3. This approach, which treats goods as providing a collection of characteristics – here speed, memory and so on – each with an implicit price, is called hedonic pricing ('hedonic' means pleasure in Greek) (Blanchard, 1997, p. 25).
4. All the per capita GDP data are measured in 1990 US dollars. Calculated by the author based on Maddison (2001), IMF (1997a, p. 1) and UN (2001).
5. Calculated by the author based on United Nations (2001) and World Bank (2001).

6. Based on data released from WRI (1999, pp. 236–7).
7. The reasons for using these data are that: (1) they are properly reconstructed according to internationally comparable measures (that is, Geary-Khamis dollars, or G-K$); and (2) they are all in 1990s constant prices.
8. Calculated by the author based on World Bank (1999) and United Nations (1996).
9. Note that the gender difference in life expectancy depends not only on living standards but also on many other factors.
10. Sources: World Bank (1983, pp. 218–19) and Statistical Division of the United Nations Secretariat. All data used here are measured in nominal values.
11. UNDP (1999, p. 3).
12. For an introduction to the empirical tests of the 'inverted-U' hypothesis, see Anand and Kanbur (1993a).
13. Calculated by the author based on Maddison (2001) for years 1950–98 and the linear regression for 1999 to 2000. Fifty-six economies are included in the calculation: Argentina, Australia, Austria, Bangladesh, Belgium, Brazil, Bulgaria, Canada, Chile, China, Colombia, Côte d'Ivoire, the Czech Republic and Slovakia, Democratic Republic of Congo, Denmark, Egypt, Ethiopia, Finland, the former USSR, France, Germany, Ghana, Greece, Hungary, India, Indonesia, Ireland, Italy, Japan, Kenya, Mexico, Morocco, Myanmar, Netherlands, New Zealand, Nigeria, Norway, Pakistan, Peru, Philippines, Poland, Portugal, Romania, South Africa, South Korea, Spain, Sweden, Switzerland, Taiwan, Tanzania, Thailand, Turkey, United Kingdom, United States, Venezuela and Yugoslavia.
14. For details about the Theil index as well as its decomposition, see, for example, Shorrocks (1983 and 1984) and Anand and Kanbur (1993a and b). Examples of its applications can be found in Mookherjee and Shorrocks (1982) and Jenkins (1995) for the UK, Tsakloglou (1993) for Greece, Tsui (1993) and Riskin et al. (2001) for China.

4. Causes for Intercultural Economic Differences

1. The critical role of scarce natural resources as retardant of growth has been discussed in, for example, Meadows (1972), Kassiola (1990) and Neurath (1994).
2. The earliest literature on neoclassical theory includes Solow (1956), Swan (1956), and Cass (1965) and Koopmans (1965).
3. Barro (1991) uses throughout the values of GDP expressed in terms of prices for the base year, 1980. The results using chain-weighted values of GDP, however, are not very different.
4. As will be discussed later in sections 4.2 and 4.3, education and technological innovation, the other two factors that contribute to economic development, are also poorly attained by these two culture areas.
5. For example, in 1870 the years of education per person aged 15–64 were only 3.92 for the USA, 4.44 for the UK and 1.50 for Japan; while they rose sharply to 18.04 for the USA, 14.09 for the UK and 14.87 for Japan in 1992 (Maddison, 1996, p. 37).
6. For example, while many countries consider primary school age to be 6–11 years, others do not.
7. For some countries with universal primary education, the gross enrolment ratios may exceed 100 per cent because some pupils are below or above the country's standard primary school age.

8. For example, the mean values of education of many coastal provinces such as Fujian (4.94 years), Zhejiang (5.59 years), Shandong (5.70 years) and Tianjin (6.34 years) were lower than that of Gansu (7.05 years) in western China in 1988 (Griffin and Zhao, 1993, pp. 292–3). Both the GDP growth rate and per capita GDP of Gansu province were, however, much lower than those of all the coastal provinces (Guo, 1999, p. 77).
9. For example, people throughout most of the world can now immediately get access to the latest information about technological progress and download electronic products from the Internet. This contrasts with the intercontinental spread of technological invention in ancient times, which was both costly and time-consuming and could take decades or even centuries.
10. See Box 3.1 for the interregional variations in economic growth from AD 1000 to 2000. See North and Thomas (1973), North (1981 and 1990) and Abramovitz (1986) for the varieties of European experience on the importance of institutions or differential social capability.
11. See, for example, Holesovsky (1977), Hwang (1993), Carson (1996), Kohler (1996), Schnitzer (1997), Gregory and Stuart (1998), McMahon and Square (2003) and Rodrik (2003).
12. Calculated by the author based on Maddison (2003) and IMF (2001, *Direction of Trade Statistics*).
13. International trade can also importantly benefit economic development as: (1) trade can lead to the full utilization of otherwise underemployed domestic resources; (2) trade makes possible division of labour and economies of scale by expanding the size of the market; (3) international trade develops managerial and other skills; (4) trade also stimulates and facilitates the international flow of capital from developed to developing nations; (5) in several large developing nations, the importation of new manufactured products has stimulated domestic demand until efficient domestic production of these goods became feasible. Finally, international trade is an excellent anti-monopoly weapon (when allowed to operate) because it stimulates greater efficiency by domestic producers to meet foreign competition (cited from Haberler, 1964, pp. 130–49).
14. Calculated by the author based on IMF (various issues).
15. A complete review of the theoretical and empirical analyses of cultural influences on international economic activities will be conducted in chapters 6 and 7, respectively.
16. For more analyses of the developmental dilemmas in India, see, for example, Behari (1992), Byres (1998) and Kapila (1999) and in some African economies, see, for example, Anunobi (1994), Ronald and Hope (1996) and Lewis (1998).
17. See Maddison (1996, p. 55). For a detailed account of the Indian economy during the colonial period, see Roy (1999).
18. Here the reader might need to pay attention to Max Weber and his work (see Box 4.1).
19. See Maddison (1992) for an analysis of twentieth-century constraints on performance in Brazil and Mexico, and Maddison (1995) for a much longer-term assessment of Mexico's institutional heritage.
20. For the recent literature on the comparisons between the transition economies in the former USSR and Eastern Europe and the market and other former centrally planned economies, see Desai (1997), Hardt and Kaufman (1995), Kaminski (1996), Lavigne (1999), Rumer (1996), Stephan (1999) and Woo et al. (1996).
21. More detailed and quantitative analyses on this topic will be presented in Section 5.5 of Chapter 5.

22. One notable point lies in the fact that Shinto has coexisted with Buddhism and Confucianism in Japan, and a Japanese can embrace both of them. But despite this tolerance of diverse religious traditions, Western religions have never taken hold in Japan (Rapoport, 1989, p. 18).

5. A Contribution to Economic Growth in Culturally Diverse Nations

1. Calculated by the author based on *Encyclopedia Britannica* (2001).
2. For example, an economic shock that may feel like only a ripple to an enormous economy like the United States, or even to a large developing economy like China, is a tidal wave for an economy the size of Ghana or Bangladesh.
3. However, others suggest that a multi-party system may lead to moderation and political flexibility by allowing centrist factions to intervene as neutral arbiters. See, for example, Horowitz (1971) for detailed analysis.
4. Similarly, Eckstein (1966) and Schattschneider (1960) propose that a two-party system is less stable than systems with more parties because decisions may appear to be zero-sum, straining the unity and peace of the society.
5. Comparatively recent surveys of the theories on the effects of income inequality on economic growth include Benabou (1996), Aghion et al. (1999) and Barro (2000).
6. See Perotti (1993), Alesina and Rodrik (1994), Persson and Tabellini (1994) and Benabou (1996), among others, for detailed analyses.
7. This effect arises if the economy is partly closed, so that domestic investment depends, to some extent, on desired national saving (Barro, 2000, p. 8).
8. There is an indication in Barro's (2000) study that growth tends to fall with greater inequality when per capita GDP is below around $2000 (1985 US dollars) and to rise with inequality when per capita GDP is above $2000.
9. Cited from Alesina and Ferrara (2005).
10. An early version of this section was presented at the UNU-WIDER Jubilee Conference 'WIDER Thinking Ahead: the Future of Development Economics' (Helsinki, 17–18 June 2005).
11. Since 1999 is the latest year in which we have been able to assemble the panel data on all the variables employed, we have to reduce the starting year to 1980 in order to equalize the two periods (the Cold War and the post-Cold War) in length.
12. The estimation is by three-stage least squares. Instruments are the actual values of the schooling and terms-of-trade variables, lagged values of the other variables aside from inflation and dummy variables for prior colonial status. Since some explanatory variables employed by Barro (such as a subjective index of the maintenance of the rule of law, a subjective for democracy, the ratio of inflation, the log of total fertility rate and the growth rate of the terms of trade) could either be influenced by cultural diversity or their data are not available, we ignore their effects on growth rates when calculating the data.
13. Note that the only difference between the two panel data is that five nations (Mali, Nicaragua, Singapore, Yemen and Zambia) are missing in the 1990s' sample.
14. We have also tested other forms of regressions (including those that include the interactive terms of GINI and lnGDPPC), none of which has yielded statistically meaningful results.

15. After deriving the first-order differential of the dependent variable with respect to RELIGION and letting it be zero, we can obtain a break-point value (that is, GINI* = (5.508–0.282lnGDPPC)/7.904) for each nation's income inequality.
16. For more discussions on the relation between cultural similarity and international trade, see chapters 6 and 7. There are also two empirical papers (Guo, 2004 and 2006).
17. Notice that in Barro's (2000) regressions, which are based on data for three periods (1965 to 1975, 1975 to 1985 and 1985 to 1995), higher inequality tends to retard growth in poor countries and to encourage growth in richer places.
18. The value is derived by letting the first-order differential of dependent variable with respect to GINI be zero: that is, DIVERSITY* = –11.338/(–7.904) ≈ 1.434.
19. Barro and McCleary (2003) find that economic growth responds positively to the extent of religious beliefs.

6. Cultural Influences on International Economic Analysis (I)

1. In an estimation of international trade, Frankel and Romer (1996, table 1) find that, for every 1 per cent increase in land area, trade falls by about 0.2 per cent.
2. Based on data from 93 countries, Guo (1996, pp. 85–6) finds that, for every increment of about 132.56 million ha of land area, a new metal will appear in a country.
3. Linnemann (1966) and Frankel et al. (1997) have estimated the effects of both GDP and GNP on trade, but no significant difference is found.
4. Frankel et al.'s (1997, p. 66) estimated coefficients on 'adjacency' range between 0.5 and 0.7. Because trade is specified in natural logarithmic form in their estimates, the way to interpret the coefficients on adjacency is to take the exponent: that is to say, two countries that share a common border will, *ceteris paribus*, increase their trade by about 65–101 per cent compared with two other countries.
5. For example, Linnemann (1966) puts the estimated coefficient as –0.77, Brada and Mendez (1983) and Oguledo and MacPhee (1994) as 0.76, Bikker (1987) as –0.90 to –1.1, Mansfield and Bronson (1997) as –0.51 to –0.69 (for 1950–90) and Rauch (1999) as –0.62 to –0.70 (1970–90).
6. In fact, as witnessed in Guo (2004, 2006) and as will be discussed in detail in Chapter 7, the exclusion of one or more cultural variables that have played a much more important role in international economic activities in the post-Cold War era than the Cold War era could have artificially magnified the effects of distance on trade, especially for the post-Cold War era.
7. See, for example, Leontief (1956), Kravis (1956a and 1956b), Keesing (1966), Kenen (1965), Baldwin (1971), Branson and Monoyios (1977), Leamer (1980, 1984, 1993), Stern and Maskus (1981), Bowen et al. (1987) and Salvatore and Barazesh (1990).
8. Frankel et al. (1997, p. 58). Of the many relevant works, some of the more important are Grossman and Helpman (1989, 1991), Rivera-Batiz and Romer (1991) and, for further references on the connections between trade and growth, Frankel et al. (1995).
9. Selected literature on the intra-industry trade includes Grubel and Lloyd (1975), Krugman (1980), Lancaster (1980), Greenaway and Milner (1986), Vona (1990) and Leamer (1993).

10. Details about these policy instruments as well as their impacts on trade can be found in most college textbooks on international economics and therefore are not presented here.
11. Notice that the values of LANGUAGE and RELIGION are less than '1' since in East Asia no economies have exactly the same languages and religions.
12. We define 'intercultural trade' as 'trade between countries or regions differing in one or more cultural elements'. To this end, 'intercultural trade' and 'international trade' are no longer different from each other since there are no countries that are same in all cultural elements.
13. IMF (various issues).
14. When manufactured goods are considered alone and the individual major languages are estimated independently, Frankel et al. (1994, table 5) found that the language coefficients lose all statistical significance.
15. It is worth noting that Boisso and Ferrantino (1997) constructed a measure of linguistic distance that is a continuous scalar, which has clearly improved the measurement of linguistic links.
16. More detailed description of the model construction can be found in Chapter 7 (especially in Equations (7.2) and (7.3)).
17. The measurement of a cultural similarity index will be illustrated in detail in Section 7.2 of Chapter 7.
18. A negative coefficient on per capita GDP may sometimes be found in gravity models on trade for homogeneous products if they are more agricultural and rich countries tend to have managed trade in agricultural products.

7. Cultural Influences on International Economic Analysis (II)

1. See, for example, Havrylyshyn and Pritchett (1991), Foroutan and Pritchett (1993), Frankel and Wei (1995), Frankel et al. (1997) and Rauch and Trindade (2002).
2. There is an exception in which Boisso and Ferrantino (1997) constructed a measure of linguistic distance that is a continuous scalar. Guo (2004, 2006) and Noland (2005) have also used a continuous measure for cultural variables.
3. The application of the gravity model in regional science and economic geography can be traced back as far as the 1940s (see, for example, Zipf, 1946; Stewart, 1948; and Isard, 1990 [1949]).
4. Note that if there are a significant number of zero values in the pair-wise trade, then Tobit regressions techniques should be used. However, in this research, the number of country-pairs identified by 'TRADE = 0' (that is, there is no trade for a country pair) is quite small.
5. In fact, there are no economies that have no economic ties in the age of globalization. It is almost certain that some 'illegal' (or unofficial) trade exists even for those economies that are officially reporting no bilateral trade flows.
6. For example, Frankel et al. (1997, p. 56) use Chicago for the major city of the United States rather than Washington, DC and Shanghai for China rather than Beijing.
7. The reader might note that it is possible to rewrite Equations (7.1) and (7.2), replacing the product of GNPs with the product of populations. As a result the coefficients on the products of GNPPCs in Equations (7.1) and (7.2) would equal $\alpha_1 + \alpha_2$ and $\beta_1 + \beta_2$, respectively.
8. This formula has been used in Guo (2004, 2006) and Noland (2005).
9. Boisso and Ferrantino (1997), for example, use $\sum x_i y_i$ as the formula of measurement.

10. Technically, the data of more years should be considered to represent each period. But this would increase the difficulties in the collection and calculation of cultural data.
11. Since the largest number of economies on which we have been able to assemble data on the variables employed in this research is 196, the number of country (region) pairs now becomes $196 \times (196 - 1) \div 2 = 19110$. It would seem impossible for us to collect the data of the thousands of linguistic and religious groups of all countries.
12. In the *Britannica Book of the Year* (1996), atheism and non-religion were each treated as a 'religious affiliation' in USA and China, but in other countries such as Austria, the Czech Republic, North Korea and so on, they were grouped as a single religious group.
13. These include the mountains of Altai (with Russia and Mongolia), Tian-shan (with Kazakhstan and Kyrgyzstan) and the Himalayas (with Bhutan, India and Nepal).
14. The break-point value is obtained by letting the first-order differential of the dependent variable (ln(TRADE*ij*+1)) with respect to RELIGION be zero.
15. It is noticeable that the case study of US and Chinese foreign trade (Guo, 2004), in which the panel data of 1987 and 1997 are used, show similar results to those of this chapter.

8. Location, Size and Political Economy of Cultures

1. In what follows, all information about the Three Kingdoms (Paekche, Shilla and Koguryo) is based on www.asianinfo.org/asianinfo/korea/history/three_kingdoms.htm.
2. Hwang (1993, p. 9). In what follows, all information about the tenth to twelfth-century history is based on Hwang (1993, pp. 9–13), which also gives other references.
3. Notice that from 1897 to 1910 the Chosen dynasty was renamed Taehan (great Korea).
4. Cited from Hwang (1993, p. 1).
5. Cited from www.answers.com/topic/authoritarianism.
6. Similar arguments are made by Alesina and Spolaore (1997, p. 1029) for an independent state.
7. There are six forms of cultural integration. (i) Configurational or thematic integration. It refers to an identity of meaning within a diversity of cultural items: their conformity to a common pattern, their embodiment of a common theme. (ii) Connective integration. It concerns the extent to which the diverse parts of culture are directly connected with one another. (iii) Logical integration. It concerns the extent to which cultural items tend to contradict one another. This perspective defines integration not as identity or as interlocking diversity but in terms of logical consistency – a criterion that primarily affects existential beliefs and systems of norms. (iv) Adaptive or functional integration. (v) Stylistic integration. It emerges from the mutual adaptation of parts of experience felt so intensively that their contrasts and organization produce an emotionally gratifying whole. Its locus is those characteristic modes of behaviour and manners of expression we term styles. (vi) Regulative integration. (See Levine (1972, pp. 375–8), which also gives other references.)
8. Source: www.asianinfo.org/asianinfo/korea/history/three_kingdoms.htm.

9. More detailed evidence can be found in *chosen yichao shilu* [Records of the Chosen Yi Dynasty], vol. 1.
10. This can be witnessed by the Yi's introduction of Confucian social norms and moral values which were to govern Korea for the next five centuries. The most productive period of the Yi dynasty came under its fourth king, Sejong (r. 1418–50), who was noted for his mastery of Confucian learning.
11. By the year 2000, North Korea had a land area of 123,000 square kilometres and a population of 27 million; South Korea had a land area of 99,000 square kilometres and a population of 47 million.
12. Examples of literature on the theoretical and empirical studies of the unification and break-up of nations would include Friedman (1977), Bolton and Spolaore (1996), Bolton and Roland (1997) and Alesina and Spolaore (1997).
13. Cited from www.answers.com/topic/authoritarianism.
14. See, for example, Oi (1992, pp. 99–129), Wong (1992), Shirk (1993) and Jin et al. (2001).
15. See, for example, Shen and Dai (1990, pp. 1–13) and Li (1993, pp. 23–36).
16. More detailed evidence may be found in Sun (1993, pp. 95–104), Feng (1993, pp. 87–94) and Goodman (1994, p. 1–20).
17. See *Beijing Youth*, 2 December 2002 (available at www.sina.com.cn).
18. There is a case study of interprovincial border disputes in Guo (2005, pp. 197–225).
19. Frankel et al. (1997, pp. 267–8), which also gives other references.

9. Globalization, Conflict Management and Culture

1. UNDP (1999, p. 25) and www.undp.org/hdro/report.html.
2. Cited from Huntington (1996, table 10.1).
3. Notice that there are some slight differences between the geographical scopes of the relevant culture areas defined in tables 9.1 and 9.2a and b.
4. From the perspective of economics, 'differentiation of production' implies 'comparative advantages', while the latter influences to some extent the potential benefit of trade and cooperation between the culture areas concerned. The term 'cultural monopolization of trade' is used here to denote that, since there are usually some culturally unique – both traditional and modern – commodities (see Box 9.1) in each culture area, intercultural exporters of these products can, at least in theory, realize a monopolized profit for each of their own. As a result, one culture area's gross benefit of exporting its products to the other culture area grows with greater cultural dissimilarity.
5. This is not, of course, to say that statistical analyses are unhelpful. On the contrary, they have brought out some intriguing features. Consider, for example, Hensel's findings in his fine study of patterns in territorial disputes in the Western hemisphere between 1816 and 1992 (Hensel, 2001).
6. Much has been written about the artificial birth of the Hutu-Tutsi split as part of the divide-and-conquer strategy of Belgium, the colonial power. For us, what is notable is the rich anecdotal evidence that physical attributes play a critical role in the conflict. On average, 'Tutsis' are taller and more slender than 'Hutus'; they have somewhat lighter skin and thinner noses.
7. Based on Grunfeld (1997).
8. Based on Ramdas (2005).

Epilogue

1. 'Culture change' is defined as 'the conceptual formulation that refers to the many ways in which societies change their patterns of culture' (Vogt, 1972, p. 554).
2. For example, internal factors played an important role in the culture change of North America before the fifteenth century, while external factors played an important role in the culture change after the 'discovery' of the New World.
3. An interesting fact suggests that certain languages might be related in that they have evolved from a common ancestral language. For a detailed description of linguistic evolution, see Spair ([1916] 1949).
4. For example, paper was introduced in China in the second century AD, came to Japan in the seventh century and was diffused westward to Central Asia in the eighth century, North Africa in the tenth, Spain in the twelfth and northern Europe in the thirteenth. Printing was invented in China in the eighth century AD and movable type in the eleventh century, but this technology only reached Europe in the fifteenth century. Another Chinese invention, gunpowder, made in the ninth century, disseminated to the Arabs after a few hundred years and reached Europe in the fourteenth century (see Braudel, 1981, p. 14).

Appendix 1

1. Practically, the best way to build a spatial model is to use the two-dimension figure. But this would result in extra mathematical loads in the expression and computation of the integral calculus.
2. Similar arguments are made by Alesina and Spolaore (1997, p. 1029) for an independent state.
3. Obviously, there exists an adverse correlation between α and β. For example, if α is maximized, then β is minimized, and vice versa.

Bibliography

Abramovitz, M. (1986), 'Catching up, Forging Ahead, and Falling Behind', *Journal of Economic History*, 56 (June), 23–34.

Abu-Taleb, F.M. (1994), 'Environmental Management in Jordan: Problems and Recommendations', *Environmental Conservation*, 21, 35–40.

Adelman, I. and C.T. Morris (1967), *Society, Politics, and Economic Development*, Baltimore: Johns Hopkins University Press.

Ager, D. (2001), *Motivation in Language Planning and Language Policy*, Clevedon: Multilingual Matters Ltd.

Aghion, P., E. Caroli and C. Garcia-Penalosa (1999), 'Inequality and Economic Growth: the Perspective of the New Growth Theories', *Journal of Economic Literature*, 37 (4), 1615–60.

Ahluwalia, M.S. (1976), 'Inequality, Poverty and Development', *Journal of Development Economics*, 3 (December), 1803–15.

Alesina, A. and D. Rodrik (1994), 'Distribution Politics and Economic Growth', *Quarterly Journal of Economics*, 109, 465–490.

Alesina, A. and E. Spolaore (1997), 'On the Number and Size of Nations', *Quarterly Journal of Economics*, 112 (November), 1027–56.

Alesina, A. and E.A. Ferrara (2005), 'Ethnic Diversity and Economic Performance', *Journal of Economic Literature*, 43 (3), 762–800.

Alesina, A. and R. Perotti (1996), 'Income Distribution, Political Instability and Investment', *European Economic Review*, 81, 1170–89.

Alesina, A., A. Devleeschauwer, R. Wacziarg and W. Easterly (2002), 'Fractionalization', unpublished draft, Stanford University, Stanford, CA.

Alesina, A., A. Devleeschauwer, W. Easterly, S. Kurlat and R. Wacziarg (2003), 'Fractionalization', *Journal of Economic Growth*, 8 (2), 155–94.

American Heritage Dictionary of the English Language (2000), 4th edn, updated in 2003, New York: Houghton Mifflin Company.

Anand, S. and S.M. Kanbur (1993a), 'The Kuznets Process and the Inequality and Development Relationship', *Journal of Development Economics*, 40, 25–52.

Anand, S. and S.M. Kanbur (1993b), 'Inequality and Development: a Critique', *Journal of Development Economics*, 41, 19–43.

Anunobi, F.O. (1994), *International Dimensions of African Political Economy: Trends, Challenges, and Realities*, Washington, DC: University Press of America.

Aono, T. (1979), *New Geography* (B) (in Japanese), Tokyo: Nigong Shiyoten.

Appleyard, D.R. and A.J. Field Jr (1998), *International Economics*, 3rd edn, Beijing: McGraw-Hill and China Machine Press.

Bacon, E. (1946), 'A Preliminary Attempt to Determine the Culture Areas of Asia', *Southwestern Journal of Anthropology*, 2, 117–32.

Bagby, P. (1958), *Culture and History: Prolegomena to the Comparative Study of Civilizations*, London: Longmans, Green.

Baldwin, R.E. (1971), 'Determinants of the Commodity Structure of US Trade', *American Economic Review*, 61 (March), 126–46.

Baldwin, R.E. (1989), 'The Political Economy of Trade Policy', *Journal of Economic Perspectives*, 3 (4), 119–37.

Banks, A.S. (1979), 'Cross-national Time-series Data Archive', Center for Social Analysis, State University of New York at Binghamton, September.

Banks, A.S. and R.B. Textor (1963), *A Cross-polity Survey*, Cambridge, MA: The MIT Press.

Barro, R.J. (1991), 'Economic Growth in a Cross-section of Nations', *Quarterly Journal of Economics*, 106 (May), 407–43.

Barro, R.J. (2000), 'Inequality and Growth in a Panel of Countries', *Journal of Economic Growth*, 5, 5–32.

Barro, R.J. and R.M. McCleary (2003), 'Religion and Economic Growth', mimeo, Harvard University, 8 April.

Barro, R.J. and X. Sala-i-Martin (1995), *Economic Growth*, New York: McGraw-Hill.

Barudel, F. (1994), *History of Civilizations*, New York: Allen Lane-Penguin Press.

Bates, R.H., A. Greif, M. Levi, J.-L. Rosenthal and B.R. Weingast (1998), *Analytic Narratives*, Princeton, NJ: Princeton University Press.

Bateson, G. (1958 [1936]), *Naven: a Survey of the Problems Suggested by a Composite Picture of the Culture of a New Guinea Tribe Drawn from Three Points of View*, 2nd edn, Stanford: Stanford University Press.

Behari, B. (1992), *Mismanagement of Indian Economy*, New Delhi: South Asia Books.

Belkindas, M., M. Dinc and O. Ivanova (1999), 'Statistical Systems Need Overhaul in Transition Economies', *Transition*, 10 (4), 22–4.

Benabou, R. (1996), 'Inequality and Growth', *NBER Macroeconomics Annual*, 11–73.

Bernhardt, R. (ed.) (1990), *Encyclopedia of Public International Law*, 12, Amsterdam: North Holland

Bhagwati, J.H. (ed.) (1969), *International Trade: Selected Readings*, Baltimore: Penguin.

Bhagwati, J.N. (ed.) (1981), *International Trade: Selected Readings*, Cambridge, MA: The MIT Press.

Bikker, J. (1987), 'An International Trade Flow Model with Substitution: an Extension of the Gravity Model', *Kyklos*, 40, 315–37.

Blanchard, O. (1997), *Macroeconomics*, Beijing: Tsinghua University Press and Prentice-Hall International, Inc.

Bluedorn, J.C. (2001), 'Can Democracy Help? Growth and Ethnic Divisions', *Economic Letters*, 70, 121–6.

Bodley, J.H. (1994), *Cultural Anthropology: Tribes, States, and the Global System*, available at www.wsu.edu:8001/vcwsu/commons/topics/culture/culture-definitions/bodley-text.html.

Boisso, D. and M. Ferrantino (1997), 'Economic Distance, Cultural Distance and Openness in International Trade: Empirical Puzzles', *Journal of Economic Integration*, 12, 456–84.

Bollen, Kenneth, A. and Robert Jackman (1985), 'Economic and Noneconomic Determinants of Political Democracy in the 1960s', in R.G. Braungart (ed.), *Research in Political Sociology*, Greenwich, CT: JAI, pp. 123–43.

Bolton, P. and E. Spolaore (1996), 'Economic Theories of Integration and Break-up of Nations', *European Economic Review*, 81, 697–705.

Bolton, P. and G. Roland (1997), 'The Breakup of Nations: a Political Economy Analysis', *Quarterly Journal of Economics*, 112, 1057–89.

Bond, M.H., K. Leung and K.C. Wan (1982), 'How Does Cultural Collectivism Operate?' *Journal of Cross-Cultural Psychology*, 13, 186–200.

Bowen, H.P., E.E. Leamer and L. Sveikauskas (1987), 'Multicountry, Multifactor Tests of the Factor Abundance Theory', *American Economic Review*, 77 (December), 791–809.

Brada, J. and J. Mendez (1983), 'Regional Economic Integration and the Volume of Intra-regional Trade: a Comparison of Developed and Developing Country Experience', *Kyklos*, 36, 589–603.

Branson, W.H. and N. Monoyios (1977), 'Factor Inputs in US Trade', *Journal of International Economics*, 20, 111–31.

Braudel, F. (1981), *The Structures of Everyday Life: Civilization and Capitalism: 15th–18th Century, vol 1*, New York: Harper and Row.

Braudel, F. (1994), *History of Civilizations*, New York: Allen Lane-Penguin Press.

Braungart, R.G. (ed.) (1985), *Research in Political Sociology*, Greenwich, CT: JAI.

Bräutigam, D. (1998), *Chinese Aid and African Development: Exporting Green Revolution*, London: Macmillan Press.

Britannica Book of the Year (various issues), Chicago: Encyclopedia Britannica, Inc.

Brown, N. (2005), 'Friedrich Ratzel, Clark Wissler, and Carl Sauer: Culture Area Research and Mapping', available at www.csiss.org/classics/content/15.

Buzan, B. (1991), 'New Patterns of Global Security in the Twenty-first Century', *International Affairs*, 67, 441–9.

Byres, T.J. (ed.) (1998, *The Indian Economy: Major Debates since Independence*, Oxford: Oxford University Press.

Carson, R.L. (1996), *Comparative Economic Systems: Market and State in Economic Systems*, 2nd edn, New York: M.E. Sharpe.

Caselli, F. and W.J. Coleman II (2002), 'On the Theory of Ethnic Conflict', unpublished draft, Harvard University, MA.

Cass, D. (1965), 'Optimum Growth in a Aggregative Model of Capital Accumulation', *Review of Economics and Statistics*, 32, 233–40.

Cateora, P.R. and J.L. Graham (1998), *International Marketing*, 7th edn, Burr Ridge, IL: Richard D. Irwin.

Cecchini, P. (1988), *The European Challenge: 1992*, Aldershot, UK: Wildwood House.

Chenery, H.B. and M. Syrquin (1975), *Pattern of Development, 1950–70*, New York: Oxford University Press.

Choucri, N. and R.C. North (1975), *Nations in Conflict*, San Francisco, CA: W.H. Freeman and Company.

Choucri, N. and R.C. North (1989), 'Lateral Pressure in International Relations: Concept and Theory', in M.I. Midlarsky (ed.), *Handbook of War Studies*, Ann Arbor: University of Michigan Press.

Choy, B.-Y. (1984), 'A History of the Korean Unification Movement: its Issues and Prospects', Bradley University, Ill, draft paper, cited from Hwang (1993).

Chua, E.G. and W.B. Gudykunst (1987), 'Conflict Resolution Styles in Low- and High-context Cultures', *Communication Research Reports*, 4, 32–7.

Cline, W. (1975), 'Distribution and Development: a Survey of the Literature', *Journal of Development Economics*, 2, 31–56.

Condon, J.C. (1985), *Good Neighbors: Communicating with the Mexicans*, Yarmouth, ME: Intercultural Press.

Cooley, J.K. (1984), 'The War over Water', *Foreign Policy*, 54, 3–26.

Copaken, S.N. (1996), 'The Perception of Water as Part of Territory in Israeli and Arab Ideologies between 1964 and 1993: Toward a Further Understanding of the Arab-Jewish Conflict', Working Paper No. 8, University of Haifa, Haifa, Israel, May.

Critchley, W.H. and T. Terriff (1993), 'Environment and Security', in R. Shultz, R. Godson and T. Greenwood (eds), *Security Studies for the 1990s*, Washington, DC: Brasseys, pp. 312–48.

Cullen, R. (1993), 'Human Rights Quandary', *Foreign Affairs*, 71 (Winter), 79–88.

Dahl, R. and E. Tufle (1973), *Size and Democracy*, Stanford, CA: Stanford University Press.
David, B.B. (ed.) (1982), *World Christian Encyclopedia: a Comparative Study of Churches and Religions in the Modern World 1900–2000*, Oxford: Oxford University Press.
Deardorff, A. (1998), 'Determinants of Bilateral Trade: Does Gravity Work in a Classical World?' in J.A. Frankel (ed.), *The Regionalization of the World Economy*, Chicago: University of Chicago, Press, pp. 213–43.
Deininger, K. and L. Squire (1998), 'New Ways of Looking at Old Issues: Inequality and Growth', *Journal of Development Economics*, 57, 259–87
Desai, P. (ed.) (1997), *Going Global: Transition from Plan to Market in the World Economy*, Cambridge, MA: The MIT Press.
Diehl, P.F. and N.P. Gleditsch (eds) (2001), *Environmental Conflict*, Boulder, CO: Westview.
Dodsworth, J. and D. Mihaljek (1997), 'Hong Kong, China: Growth, Structural Change, and Economic Stability during the Transition', International Monetary Fund Occasional Paper No. 152, Washington, DC: IMF.
Driver, H. (1962), *The Contribution of A.L. Kroeber to Culture Area Theory and Practice*, Indians University Publications in Anthropology and Linguistics, No. 18, Baltimore, MD: Waverly Press.
Duetsch, K.W. (1953), *Nationalism and Social Communication: an Inquiry into the Foundations of Nationality*, New York: Technology Press of the MIT.
Easterly, W. and R. Levine (1997), 'Africa's Growth Tragedy: Policies and Ethnic Division', *Quarterly Journal of Economics*, 112, 1203–50.
Eckstein, H. (1966), *Division and Cohesion in Democracy: a Study of Norway*, Princeton, NJ: Princeton University Press.
The Economist (1994), 'The New World Order: Back to the Future', January, 21–3.
The Economist, 23 July 1994, 31–2.
Eichengreen, B. and D. Irwin (1995), 'Trade Blocs, Currency Blocs and the Reorientation of Trade in the 1930s', *Journal of International Economics*, 38 (2), 89–106.
Eichengreen, B., F. Frieden and J. von Hagen (eds) (1995), *Monetary and Fiscal Policy in an Integrated Europe*, New York: Springer-Verlag.
Eichera, T.S. and C. Garcia-Penalosab (2001), 'Inequality and Growth: the Dual Role of Human Capital in Development', *Journal of Development Economics*, 66, 173–97
Ellis, H.S. and L.M. Metzler (eds) (1950), *Readings in the Theory of International Trade*, Homewood, Ill: Irwin.
Elmandjra, M. (1994), 'Cultural Diversity: Key to Survival in the Future', paper presented to the First Mexican Congress on Future Studies, Mexico City, September.
Esman, M.J. (1990), 'Economic Performance and Ethnic Conflict', in J.V. Montville and H. Binnendijk (eds), *Conflict and Peacemaking in Multiethnic Societies*, Lexington, MA: Lexington Books, pp. 41–76.
Esteban, J.-M. and D. Ray (1994), 'On the Measurement of Polarization', *Econometrica*, 62 (4), 819–51.
Farrand, L. (1904), *Basis of American History, 1500–1900*, New York: Ungar.
Fearon, J.D. (2003), 'Ethnic and Cultural Diversity by Country', *Journal of Economic Growth*, 8 (2), 195–222.
Fearon, J.D. and D.D. Laitin (2003), 'Ethnicity Insurgency and Civil War', *American Political Science Review*, 97 (1), 75–90.
Feng, L. (1993), 'On the "Wars" over the Purchase of Farm and Subsidiary Products', *Chinese Economic Studies*, 26 (5), 87–94.

Fields, G.S. (1991), 'Growth and Income Distribution', in G. Psachropoulos (ed.), *Essays on Poverty, Equity and Growth*, Oxford: Pergamon, pp. 41–5.

Forbes, K. (1997), 'A Reassessment of the Relationship between Inequality and Growth', unpublished paper, MIT.

Foroutan, F. and L. Pritchett (1993), 'Intra-Sub-Saharan African Trade: is it too Little?' *Journal of African Economics*, 2 (May), 74–105.

Fox, J. (1997), 'The Salience of Religious Issues in Ethnic Conflicts: a Large-N Study', *Nationalism and Ethnic Politics*, 3 (3), 807–21.

Frankel, J.A. (ed.) (1998), *The Regionalization of the World Economy*, Chicago: University of Chicago Press.

Frankel, J.A. and D. Romer (1996), 'Trade and Growth', NBER Working Paper No. 5476, Cambridge, MA: National Bureau of Economic Research.

Frankel, J.A. and S.-J. Wei (1995), 'European Integration and the Regionalization of World Trade and Currencies: the Economics and the Politics', in B. Eichengreen, F. Frieden, and J. von Hagen (eds), *Monetary and Fiscal Policy in an Integrated Europe*, New York: Springer-Verlag, pp. 89–123.

Frankel, J.A., D. Romer and T. Cyrus (1995), 'Trade and Growth in East Asian Countries: Cause and Effect?' Pacific Basin Working Paper Series No. 95–03, San Francisco: Federal Reserve Bank of San Francisco.

Frankel, J.A., E. Stein and S.-J. Wei (1994), 'Trading Blocs: the Natural, the Unnatural, and the Super-natural', Center for International and Development Economics Research (CIDER) Working Paper No. C94–034, University of California, Berkeley, April.

Frankel, J.A., E. Stein and S.-J. Wei (1997), *Regional Trading Blocs in the World Economic System*, Washington, DC: Institute for International Economics.

Frey, F. (1993), 'The Polical Context of Conflicts and Cooperation over International River Basins', *Water International*, 18, 504–68.

Friedman, D. (1977), 'A Theory of the Size and Shape of Nations', *Journal of Political Economy*, 85 (1), 59–77.

Gabrielides, C., W.G. Stephan, O. Ybarra, V.M.S. Pearson and L. Villareal (1997), 'Cultural Variables and Preferred Styles of Conflict Resolution: Mexico and the United States', *Journal of Cross-cultural Psychology*, 28, 661–7.

Galtung, J. (1992), 'The Emerging Conflict Formations', in K. Tehranian and M. Tehranian (eds), *Restructuring for World Peace: on the Threshold of the Twenty-first century*, Cresskill, NJ: Hampton Press, pp. 20–39

Gambari, I.A. (1999), 'Genocide in Rwanda: Shame on the World', mimeo.

Gastil, R.D. (1987), *Freedom in the World*, Westport, CT: Greenwood Press.

Gilpin, R. (1993), 'The Cycle of Great Powers: Has It Finally Been Broken?' Princeton, NJ: Princeton University, May.

Gleditsch, N.P. (2001), 'Armed Conflict and the Environment', in P.F. Diehl and N.P. Gleditsch (eds), *Environmental Conflict*, Boulder, CO: Westview, pp. 240–69.

Goodman, D.S.G. (1994), 'The Politics of Regionalism: Economic Development Conflicts and Negotiation', in D.S.G. Goodman and G. Segal (eds), *China Deconstructs: Politics, Trade, and Regionalism*, London and New York: Routledge, pp. 1–20.

Gottmann, J. (1973), *The Significance of Territory*, Charlottesville: University of Virginia Press.

Gould, D.M. and B.J. Ruffin (1993), 'What Determines Economic Growth?' *Economic Review*, 2nd Quarter, 25–40.

Goulet, D. (1995 [1980]), *Development Ethics: a Guide to Theory and Practice*, New York: Apex Press.

Graham, J.L. (1983), 'Brazilian, Japanese, and American Business Negotiations', *Journal of International Business Studies*, 14, 47–61.

Graham, J.L. (1985), 'The Influence of Culture on Business Negotiations', *Journal of International Business Studies*, 16, 81–96.

Graham, J.L. and J.D. Andrews (1987), 'A Holistic Analysis of Japanese and American Business Negotiations', *Journal of Business Communications*, 24, 63–77.

Green Cross (2000), *National Sovereignty and International Water Courses*, Hague: Green Cross International.

Greenaway, D. and C.R. Milner (1986), *The Economics of Intra-industry Trade*, Oxford: Basil Blackwell.

Greenstein, M. and T.M. Feinman (2000), *Electronic Commerce: Security, Risk Management*, Beijing: McGraw-Hill and China Machine Press.

Greertz, C. (1963), 'The Integrative Revolution: Primordial Sentiments and Civil Politics in the New States', in C. Greertz (ed.), *Old Societies and New States*, Chicago: Free Press of Glencoe, pp. 21–56.

Gregory, P.R. and R.C. Stuart (1998), *Comparative Economic Systems*, 6th edn, New York: Houghton Mifflin College.

Griffin, K. and R. Zhao (eds) (1993), *The Household Income Distribution in China*, New York: St Martin's Press.

Griliches, Z. (1979), 'Issues in Assessing the Contributions of Research and Development to Productivity Growth', *Bell Journal of Economics*, 10 (Spring), 92–116

Grossman, G. and E. Helpman (1989), 'Product Development and International Trade', *Journal of Political Economy*, 97 (December), 1261–83.

Grossman, G. and E. Helpman (1991), *Innovation and Growth in the World Economy*, Cambridge, MA: The MIT Press.

Grossman, G. and E. Helpman (1994), 'Endogenous Innovation in the Theory of Growth', *Journal of Economic Perspectives*, 8, 23–44.

Grubel, H.G. and P.J. Lloyd (1975), *Intra-industry Trade: the Theory and Measurement of International Trade in Differentiated Products*, London: Macmillan Press.

Grunfeld, L. (1997), 'Jordan River Dispute', ICE Case Studies, No. 6, available at www.american.edu/projects/mandala/TED/ice/JORDAN.HTM.

Guo, R. (1993), *Economic Analysis of Border-Regions: Theory and Practice of China* (in Chinese), Beijing: China Ocean Press.

Guo, R. (1996), *Border-regional Economics*, Berlin: Springer.

Guo, R. (1999), *How the Chinese Economy Works: a Multiregional Overview*, London: Macmillan Press.

Guo, R. (2003), 'Review of Culture and Economy', *Journal of Evolutionary Economics*, 13 (3), 155–7.

Guo, R. (2004), 'How Culture Influences Foreign Trade: Evidence from the US and China', *Journal of Socio-economics*, 33 (6), 785–812.

Guo, R. (2005), *Cross-border Resource Management: Theory and Practice*, Amsterdam: Elsevier.

Guo, R. (2006), 'Linguistic and Religious Influences on Foreign Trade: Evidence from East Asia', mimeo, forthcoming in *Asian Economic Journal*.

Gupta, A. and J. Ferguson (1997), *Culture, Power, Place: Explorations in Critical Anthropology*, Durham, NC: Duke University Press.

Gupta, D. (1990), *The Economics of Political Violence*, New York: Praeger.

Haberler, G. (1964), 'Comparative Advantage, Agricultural Production and International Trade', *International Journal of Agrarian Affairs*, May, 130–49.

Hagen, E.E. (1986), *The Economics of Development*, Homewood, Ill: Irwin.

Hannan, M.T. and G.R. Carroll (1981), 'Dynamics of Formal Political Structure: an Event-history Analysis', *American Sociological Review*, 46 (February), 567–98.
Hardt, J.P. and R.F. Kaufman (eds) (1995), *East-Central European Economies in Transition*, New York: M.E. Sharpe.
Harris, P.R., R.T. Moran and S. Moran (2004), *Managing Cultural Differences: Global Leadership Strategies for the 21st Century*, Amsterdam: Butterworth-Heinemann.
Harrison, L.E. (1993), *Who Prospers? How Cultural Values Shape Economic and Political Success*, New York: Basic Books.
Harrison, L.E. (2000), *Underdevelopment is a State of Mind*, 2nd edn, New York: Madison Books.
Harrison, L.E. and S.P. Huntington (eds) (2001), *Culture Matters: How Values Shape Human Progress*, New York: Basic Books.
Harrison, L.E. (2006), *The Central Liberal Truth: How Politics can Change a Culture and Save it as Itself*, New York: Oxford University Press.
Hartz, L. (1964), *The Founding of New Societies: Studies in the History of the United States, Latin America, South Africa, Canada, and Australia*, New York: Harcourt, Brace and World.
Haug, M.R. (1967), 'Social and Cultural Pluralism as a Concept in Social System Analysis', *American Journal of Sociology*, 73 (November), 294–304.
Havrylyshyn, O. and L. Pritchett (1991), 'European Trade Patterns after the Transition', Policy, Research and External Affairs Working Paper Series No. 74, Washington, DC: World Bank.
Heckscher, E.F. (1919), 'The Effect of Foreign Trade on the Distribution of Income', *Ekonomisk Tidskirift*, 497–512. Reprinted in H.S. Ellis and L.M. Metzler (eds), *Readings in the Theory of International Trade*, Homewood, III: Irwin, pp. 272–300.
Helpman, E. (1987), 'Imperfect Competition and International Trade: Evidence from Fourteen Industrial Countries', *Journal of the Japanese and International Economies*, 1 (March), 62–81.
Hensel, P.R. (2001), 'Contentious Issues and World Politics: the Management of Territorial Claims in the Americas, 1816–1992', *International Studies Quarterly*, 45 (1) (March), 81–109.
Hensel, P.R., S.M. Mitchell and T.E. Sowers II (2004), 'Conflict Management of Riparian Disputes: a Regional Comparison of Dispute Resolution', paper presented at the 2004 International Studies Association Meeting, Montreal, Quebec.
Hibbs, D. (1973), *Mass Political Violence: a Cross-sectional Analysis*, New York: Wiley.
Hill, H. and A. Weidemann (1989), 'Regional Development in Indonesia: Patterns and Issues', in H. Hill (ed.), *Unity and Diversity: Regional Economic Development in Indonesia since 1970*, Singapore: Oxford University Press, pp. 1–7.
Hillman, A.L. (1989), *The Political Economy of Protection*, Chur, Switzerland: Harwood Academic Publishers.
Hoebel, A. (1960), *Man, Culture and Society*, New York: Oxford University Press.
Hofstede, G. (2003 [1980]), *Culture's Consequences: Comparing Values, Behaviors, Institutions, and Organizations across Nations*, Newbury Park, CA: Sage.
Holesovsky, V. (1977), *Economic Systems: Analysis and Comparison*, New York: McGraw-Hill.
Holms, W. (1903), 'Classification and Arrangement of the Exhibits of an Anthropological Museum', Washington DC: Government Printing Office.
Homer-Dixon, T.F. (1999) *Environment, Scarcity, and Violence*, Princeton, NJ: Princeton University Press.
Hong, L. and S.E. Page (1998), 'Diversity and Optimality', Santa Fe Institute, Working Paper 98-08-077.

Horowitz, D.L. (1971), 'Three Dimensions of Ethnic Politics', *World Politics*, 23 (January), 232–44.

Horowitz, D.L. (1985), *Ethnic Groups in Conflict*, Berkeley, CA: University of California Press.

Horwitz, J. (1998), 'All Life is Connected: the Shaman's Journey', available at www.users.dircon.co.uk/~snail/scss/Articles/All%20Life.htm.

Hu, H. and S. Zhang (1982), *World Population Geography*, Shanghai: East China Normal University Press.

Huntington, S.P. (1993), 'The Clash of Civilizations?' *Foreign Affairs*, 71 (Summer), 2–32.

Huntington, S.P. (1996), *The Clash of Civilizations and the Remaking of World Order*, New York: Simon & Schuster.

Hwang, E.-G. (1993), *The Korean Economies: a Comparison of North and South*, Oxford: Clarendon Press.

Inglehart, R. and W.E. Baker (2000), 'Modernization, Cultural Change, and the Persistence of Traditional Values', *American Sociological Review*, 65 (February), 19–51.

International Encyclopedia of the Social Sciences (1972), vol. 3, by David L. Sills, New York: The Macmillan Company and The Free Press; and London: Collier-Macmillan Publishers.

International Monetary Fund (1997a), *World Economic Outlook*, May, Washington DC: IMF.

International Monetary Fund (1997b), *International Financial Statistics Yearbook*, Washington DC: IMF.

International Monetary Fund (various years), *Direction of Trade Statistics*, Washington DC: IMF.

Isard, W. (1990 [1949]), 'Gravity, Potential, and Spatial Interaction Models', in C. Smith (ed.), *Practical Methods of Regional Science and Empirical Applications: Selected Papers of Walter Isard*, vol. 2, New York: New York University Press, pp. 1–23.

Israel-PLO (1995), 'Agreement on Establishing the Palestinian Self-rule in Most of the West Bank', signed by the Government of Israel and the Palestinian Liberation Organization (PLO), Washington DC, 28 September.

Jenkins, S. (1995), 'Accounting for Inequality Trends: Decomposition Analysis for the UK, 1971–86', *Economica*, 62, 29–63.

Jha, S. (1996), 'The Kuznets Curve: a Reassessment', *World Development*, 24, 773–80.

Jin, H., Y. Qian and B. Weingast (2001), 'Regional Decentralization and Fiscal Incentives: Federalism, Chinese Style', mimeo, Stanford University, Stanford, CA.

Johnson, H.G. (ed.) (1968), *Readings in International Economics*, Homewood, Ill: Irwin.

Kaminski, B. (ed.) (1996), *Economic Transition in Russia and the New States of Eurasia*, The International Politics of Eurasia, 8, New York: M.E. Sharpe.

Kapila, U. (1999), *Indian Economy since Independence*, New Delhi: South Asia Books.

Kassiola, J.J. (1990), *The Death of Industrial Civilization: the Limits to Economic Growth and the Repoliticization of Advanced Industrial Society*, New York: State University of New York Press.

Keesing, D.B. (1966), 'Labor Skills and Comparative Advantage', *American Economic Review*, 56 (May), 249–58.

Kendall, H.M. (1976), *Introduction to Cultural Geography*, London: Arnold.

Kenen, P. (1965), 'Nature, Capital and Trade', *Journal of Political Economy*, 73 (October), 437–60.

Kim, Y. and W. Gudykunst (eds) (1988), *Theories in Intercultural Communication*, Newbury Park, CA: Sage.
Kirmani, S. (1990), 'Water, Peace and Conflict Management: the Experience of the Indus and the Mekong River Basins', *Water International*, 15 (1), 200–5.
Knight, C., S. Kagan and S. Martinez-Romero (1982), 'Culture and Development of Conflict Resolution Style', *Journal of Cross-cultural Psychology*, 13, 43–59.
Kockel, U. (ed.) (2002), *Culture and Economy: Contemporary Perspectives*, Aldershot, UK: Ashgate.
Kohler, H. (1996), *Economic Systems and Human Welfare: a Global Survey*, Cincinnati, Ohio: South-Western College Publishing Co.
Koopmans, T.C. (1965), 'On the Concept of Optimal Economic Growth', in *The Econometric Approach to Development Planning*, Amsterdam: North-Holland.
Kravis, I.B. (1956a), 'Wages and Foreign Trade', *Review of Economics and Statistics*, 38 (February), 14–30.
Kravis, I.B. (1956b), 'Availability and Other Influences on the Commodity Composition of Trade', *Journal of Political Economy*, 73 (April), 143–55.
Kroeber, A.L. (1939), *Cultural and Natural Areas of Native North America*, Berkeley, CA: University of California Press.
Kroeber, A.L. (1947), 'Culture Groupings in Asia', *Southwestern Journal of Anthropology*, 3, 322–30.
Krugman, P.R. (1980), 'Scale Economies, Product Differentiation, and the Pattern of Trade', *American Economic Review*, 70 (December), 950–9.
Krugman, P.R. (1995), 'Growing World Trade: Causes and Consequences', *Brookings Papers on Economic Activity*, 1, 327–62.
Kuznets, S. (1955), 'Economic Growth and Income Inequality', *American Economic Review*, 45 (March), 1–8.
La Porta, R., F. Lopez de Vilanes, A. Shleifer and R.W. Vishni (1999), 'The Quality of Government', *Journal of Law, Economics and Organization*, 15 (1), 222–79.
Lancaster, K. (1980), 'Intra-industry Trade under Perfect Monopolistic Competition', *Journal of International Economics*, 23, 151–75.
Landes, D.S. (1999), *The Wealth and Poverty of Nations: Why Some Are so Rich and Some so Poor*, New York: Norton.
Laudy, M. (2004), 'The Vatican Mediation of the Beagle Channel Dispute: Crisis Intervention and Forum Building', available at http://wwics.si.edu/subsites/ccpdc/pubs/words/11.pdf.
Lavigne, M. (1999), *The Economics of Transition: from Socialist Economy to Market Economy*, 2nd edn, London: Macmillan Press.
Leamer, E.E. (1980), 'The Leontief Paradox Reconsidered', *Journal of Political Economy*, 88 (June), 495–503.
Leamer, E.E. (1984), *Sources for International Comparative Advantage*, Cambridge, MA: The MIT Press.
Leamer, E.E. (1993), 'Factor-supply Differences as a Source of Comparative Advantage', *American Economic Review*, 83 (May), 436–44.
Lee, R. and J. Wills (eds) (1997), *Geographies of Economies*, London: Arnold.
Lee, S.-W. (2002), 'Preventive Diplomacy and UN Peacekeeping in Conflict Regions: Lessons from the Rwanda Genocide', *Korea Review of International Studies*, 5 (1), 71–91.
Lemco, J. (1991), *Political Stability in Federal Governments*, New York: Praeger.
Leontief, W. (1954), 'Domestic Production and Foreign Trade: the American Capital Position Re-examined', *Economia Internationale*, February, 2–32.

Leontief, W. (1956), 'Factor Proportions and the Structure of American Trade: Further Theoretical and Empirical Analysis', *Review of Economics and Statistics*, 38 (November), 386–407.

Leung, K. (1987), 'Some Determinants of Reactions to Procedural Models for Conflict Resolution: a Cross-national Study', *Journal of Personality and Social Psychology*, 53, 898–908.

Levine, D.N. (1972), 'Cultural Integration', in D.L. Sillis (ed.), *International Encyclopedia of the Social Sciences*, vol. 3, New York,: The Macmillan Company & The Free Press, pp. 372–80.

Lewis, P. (ed.) (1998), *Africa: Dilemmas of Development*, Boulder, CO: Westview Press.

Li, H. and H. Zou (1998), 'Income Inequality is not Harmful for Growth: Theory and Evidence', *Review of Development Economics*, 2, 318–34.

Li, Z. (1993), 'In-depth Exploration of the Question of Regional Blockades', *Chinese Economic Studies*, 26 (5), 23–36.

Lian, B. and J.R. Oneal (1997), 'Cultural Diversity and Economic Development: a Cross-national Study of 98 Countries, 1960–1985', *Economic Development and Cultural Change*, 46 (1), 61–77.

Lijphart, A. (1977), *Democracies in Plural Societies: a Comparative Exploration*, New Haven, CT: Yale University Press.

Lijphart, A. (1990), 'The Power-sharing Approach', in J.V. Montville and H. Binnendijk (eds), *Conflict and Peacemaking in Multiethnic Societies*, Lexington, MA: Lexington Books, pp. 13–34.

Lin, J.Y. (2001), 'Development Strategy, Viability, and Economic Convergence', The Inaugural D. Gale Johnson Lecture, University of Chicago, 14 May.

Lind, M. (1990), 'American as an Ordinary Country', *American Enterprise*, 1, 19–23.

Lind, W.S. (1992), 'North-South Relations: Returning to a World of Cultures in Conflict', *Current World Leaders*, 35, 1075–80.

Lind, W.S. (1994), 'Defending Western Culture', *Foreign Policy*, 84, 40–50.

Linder, S.B. (1961), *An Essay on Trade and Transformation*, New York: John Wiley and Sons.

Linnemann, H. (1966), *An Econometric Study of International Trade Theory*, Amsterdam: North-Holland.

Londregan, J.B. and K.T. Poole (1989), 'Coups d'Etat and the Military Business Cycle', working paper No. 36-88-89, Carnegie Mellon University, March.

Lucas, R.E., Jr (1988), 'On the Mechanics of Development Planning', *Journal of Monetary Economics*, 22, 3–42.

Luqmani, M., Z.A. Quraeshi and L. Deline (1980), 'Marketing in Islamic Countries', *MSU Business Topics*, Summer.

Maddison, A. (1992), 'A Long-run Perspective on Saving', *Scandinavian Journal of Economics*, June, 181–203.

Maddison, A. (1995), *Explaining the Economic Performance of Nations: Essays in Time and Space*, Cheltenham, UK and Northampton, MA, USA: Edward Elgar.

Maddison, A. (1996), *A Retrospect for the 200 Years of the World Economy, 1820–1992*, Paris: OECD Development Center.

Maddison, A. (2001), *The World Economy: a Millennial Perspective*, Paris: OECD Development Centre.

Maddison, A (2003),*The World Economy: Historical Statistics*, Paris: OECD Development Centre.

Malthus, T.R. (1798), *An Essay on the Principle of Population*, London: W. Pickering. Reprinted in 1986.

Mandelbaum, D. (ed.) (1949), *Edward Spair, Selected Writings in Language, Culture and Personality*, Berkeley, CA: University of California Press.
Mansfield, E. and R. Bronson (1997), 'The Political Economy of Major-power Trade Flows', in E. Mansfield and H. Milner (eds), *The Political Economy of Regionalism*, New York: Columbia University Press, pp. 213–56.
Markusen, J. (1986), 'Explaining the Volume of Trade: an Eclectic Approach', *American Economic Review*, 76 (December), 1002–11.
Maslichenko, S. (2004), 'Institutional Determinants of Economic Development', mimeo, University of Oxford, Oxford.
Mauro, P. (1995), 'Corruption and Growth', *Quarterly Journal of Economics*, 110, 681–712.
McMahon, G. and L. Square (eds) (2003), *Explaining Growth*, London: Palgrave Macmillan.
McNeil, W.H. (1963), *The Rise of the West: a History of the Human Community*, Chicago: University of Chicago Press.
Meadows, D.H. (1972), *Limits to Growth: a Report of the Club of Rome's Project on the Predicament of Mankind*, Rome: the Club of Rome.
Melko, M. (1969), *The Nature of Civilizations*, Boston: Porter Sargent.
Mishra, G.P. (ed.) (1985), *Regional Structure of Development and Growth in India*, New Delhi: Ashish Publishing House.
Molinar, J. (1991), 'Counting the Number of Parties: an Alternative Index', *American Political Science Review*, 85, 1383–91.
Montalvo, J.G. and M. Reynal-Querol (2002), 'Why Ethnic Fractionalization? Polarization, Ethnic Conflict and Growth', unpublished, Universitat Pompeu Fabra.
Montalvo, J.G. and M. Reynal-Querol (2003), 'Ethnic Polarization, Potential Conflict, and Civil Wars', University of Pompeu Fabra, Economic Working Papers No. 770, available at http://ideas.repec.org/p/upf/upfgen/770.html.
Montalvo, J.G. and M. Reynal-Querol (2005), 'Ethnic Diversity and Economic Development', *Journal of Development Economics*, 76, 293–323.
Montville, J.V. and H. Binnendijk (eds) (1990), *Conflict and Peacemaking in Multiethnic Societies*, Lexington, MA: Lexington Books.
Mookherjee, D. and A.F. Shorrocks (1982), 'A Decomposition of the Trend in UK Income Inequality', *Economic Journal*, 92, 886–902.
Naff, W. E. (1986), 'Reflections on the Question of "East and West" from the Point of Japan', *Comparative Civilizations Review*, 14, 224–36.
Nair, K.R.G. (1985), 'Inter-state Income Differentials in India, 1970–71 to 1979–80', in G.P. Mishra (ed.), *Regional Structure of Development and Growth in India*, New Delhi: Ashish Publishing House, pp. 132–59.
Naroll, R.S. (1950), 'A Draft Map of the Culture Areas of Asia', *Southwestern Journal of Anthropology*, 6, 183–7.
Nelson, R. and E.S. Phelps (1966), 'Investment in Humans, Technological Diffusion, and Economic Growth', *American Economic Review*, 56, 69–75.
Neurath, P. (1994), *From Malthus to the Club of Rome and Back: Problems of Limits to Growth, Population Control, and Migrations*, Columbia University Seminars, New York: M.E. Sharpe.
The New Columbia Encyclopedia, 4th edn (1975), New York: Columbia University Press.
New Palgrave: a Dictionary of Economics (2001), 4 vols, eds John Eatwell, Murray Milgate and Peter Newman, Basingstoke: Palgrave Macmillan.
Noland, M. (2005), 'Affinity and International Trade', Institute for International Economics, Washington DC, Working Paper Series No. WP 05–3, June.

Nordlinger, E.A. (1972), *Conflict Regulation in Divided Societies*, Cambridge, MA: Harvard University Center for International Affairs.
North, D.C. (1981), *Structure and Change in Economic History*, New York: Norton.
North, D.C. (1990), *Institutions, Institutional Change and Economic Performance*, Cambridge: Cambridge University Press.
North, D.C. (1991), 'Institutions', *Journal of Economic Perspectives*, 5 (1), 97–112.
North, D.C. and R.P. Thomas (1973), *The Rise of the Western World*, Cambridge: Cambridge University Press.
Ofosu-Amaah, G. (1990), 'Niger River Regime', in R. Bernhardt (ed.), *Encyclopedia of Public International Law*, vol. 12, Amsterdam: New Holland, pp. 246–8.
Oguledo, V. and C. MacPhee (1994), 'Gravity Models: a Reformulation and an Application to Discriminatory Trade Arrangement', *Applied Economics*, 26, 107–20.
Ohlin, B. (1933), *Interregional and International Trade*, Cambridge, MA: Harvard University Press.
Oi, J. (1992), 'Fiscal Reform and the Economic Foundations of Local State Corporatism in China', *World Politics*, 45 (October), 99–129.
OMVS (1988), 'The Senegal River Basin Development Authority', UN Natural Resources Water Series (UN Conference on River and Lake Basin Development, Addis Ababa, 10–15 October), No. 2, 276–94.
The Oxford English Dictionary, 2nd edn (1989), Oxford: Clarendon Press.
Pack, H. (1994), 'Endogenous Growth Theory: Intellectual Appeal and Empirical Shortcomings', *Journal of Economic Perspectives*, 8, 55–72.
Patai, R. (1951), 'Nomadism: Middle Eastern and Central Asian', *Southwestern Journal of Anthropology*, 7, 401–14.
Paukert, F. (1973), 'Income Distribution at Different Levels of Development: a Survey of Evidence', *International Labor Review*, August–September, 32–45.
Pearson, L. (1955), *Democracy in World Politics*, Princeton, NJ: Princeton University Press.
Pearson, V.M.S. and W.G. Stephan (1999), 'Preferences for Styles of Negotiation: a Comparison of Brazil and the US', *International Journal of Intercultural Relations*, 22, 67–83.
Perotti, R. (1993), 'Political Equilibrium, Income Distribution and Growth', *Review of Economic Studies*, 60, 755–76.
Perotti, R. (1996), 'Growth, Income Distribution, and Democracy: What the Data Say', *Journal of Economic Growth*, 1, 149–87.
Persson, T. and G. Tabellini (1994), 'Is Inequality Harmful for Growth? Theory and Evidence', *American Economic Review*, 84, 600–21.
Pinker, S. (1994), *The Language Instinct*, London: Penguin Books.
Posner, D.N. (2004), 'Measuring Ethnic Fractionalization in Africa', *American Journal of Political Science*, 48 (4), 849–63.
Pöyhönen, P. (1963), 'A Tentative Model for the Volume of Trade between Countries', *Weltwirtschaftliches Archiv*, 90 (1), 93–9.
Psachropoulos, G. (ed.) (1991), *Essays on Poverty, Equity and Growth*, Oxford: Pergamon
Puchala, D.J. (1994), 'The History of the Future of International Relations', *Ethics and International Affairs*, 8, 177–202.
Quigley, C. (1979), *The Evolution of Civilizations: an Introduction to Historical Analysis*, 2nd edn, Indianapolis: Liberty Press.
Rae, D.W. (1967), *The Political Consequences of Electoral Laws*, New Haven, CT: Yale University Press.

Ramdas, A.L. (2005), 'Kashmir, Nuclear Weapons and Peace', Institute of Energy and Environment Research, Takoma Park, Maryland, USA, 22 March, available at: www.ieer.org/latest/ramukashmir.html.

Rangeley, R., B. Thiam, R. Andersen and C. Lyle (1994), 'International River Basins in Sub-Saharan Africa', World Bank Technical Paper No. 250, Washington DC: the World Bank.

Rapoport, C. (1989), 'Understanding How Japan Works', *Fortune*, 120 (13), 17–19.

Rauch, J.E. (1999), 'Networks versus Markets in International Trade', *Journal of International Economics*, 48, 7–35.

Rauch, J.E. and V. Trindade (2002), 'Ethnic Chinese Networks in International Trade', *Review of Economics and Statistics*, 84 (1), 116–30.

Ravallion, M. (2001), 'Growth, Inequality and Poverty: Looking beyond Averages', *World Development*, 29, 173–97

Rebelo, S. (1991), 'Long Run Policy Analysis and Long Run Growth', *Journal of Political Economy*, 99 (3) (June), 500–21.

Reynolds, L.G. (1985), *Economic Growth in the Third World, 1850–1980*, New Haven, CT: Yale University Press.

Ricardo, D. (1817), *The Principles of Political Economy and Taxation*, London: J.M. Dent and Sons, reprinted in 1948.

Riskin, C., R. Zhao and S. Li (eds) (2001), *China's Retreat from Equality: Income Distribution and Economic Transition* (Asia and the Pacific/an East Gate Book), New York: M.E. Sharpe.

Rivera-Batiz, L. and P. Romer (1991), 'International Trade and Endogenous Growth', *Quarterly Journal of Economics*, 106 (May), 531–55.

Rodrik, D. (2003), 'Institutions, Integration, and Geography: in Search of the Deep Determinants of Economic Growth,' in D. Rodrik (ed.), *In Search of Prosperity: Analytic Narratives on Economic Growth*, Princeton, NJ: Princeton University Press, pp. 1–20.

Romer, P.M. (1986), 'Increasing Returns and Long-run Growth', *Journal of Political Economy*, 94 (5) (October), 1002–37.

Romer, P.M. (1990), 'Endogenous Technological Change', *Journal of Political Economy*, 98 (5) (October), S71–S102.

Ronald, K. and S. Hope (1996), *African Political Economy: Contemporary Issues in Development*, New York: M.E. Sharpe.

Rose, A. (2004), 'Do We Really Know that the WTO Increases Trade?' *American Economic Review*, 94, 98–114

Rostovanyi, Z. (1993), 'Clash of Civilizations and Cultures: Unity or Disunity of World Order', unpublished paper, March.

Roy, T. (1999), *Traditional Industry in the Economy of Colonial India*, Cambridge Studies in Indian History and Society, 5, Cambridge: Cambridge University Press.

Rumer, B. (ed.) (1996), *Central Asia in Transition: Dilemmas of Political and Economic Development*, New York: M.E. Sharpe.

Ruttan, W. (1991), 'What Happened to Political Development?' *Economic Development and Cultural Change*, 39 (January), 1–16.

Salman, M., A. Salman and K. Uprety (1999), 'Hydro Politics in South Asia: a Comparative Analysis of the Mahakali and Ganges', *Natural Resources Journal*, 39 (2), 295–344.

Salvatore, D. (1995), *International Economics*, 5th edn, New York: Prentice-Hall International, Inc.

Salvatore, D. and R. Barazesh (1990), 'The Factor Content of US Foreign Trade and the Heckscher-Ohlin Theory', *International Trade Journal*, 16 (winter), 149–81.

Samuelson, P.A. (1948), 'International Trade and the Equalization of Factor Prices', *Economic Journal*, 58 (June), 165–84.
Samuelson, P.A. (1949), 'International Factor-price Equalization Once Again', *Economic Journal*, 59 (June), 181–97.
Sapir, E. (1949), *Selected Writings in Language, Culture, and Personality*, ed. David G. Mandelbaum, Berkeley, CA: University of California Press.
Sapper, K. (1968), 'The Verapaz in the Sixteenth and Seventeenth Centuries: a Contribution to the Historical Geography and Ethnography of Northeastern Guatemala', Occasional Papers of the Institute of Archaeology, UCLA, Los Angeles, No. 13.
Savenije, H.G. and P. van der Zaag (2000), 'Conceptual Framework for the Management of Shared River Basins with Special Reference to the SADC and EU', *Water Policy*, 2, 9–45.
Saville, J. (2002), 'Language and Equity: a Development Perspective', in U. Kockel (ed.), *Culture and Economy: Contemporary Perspectives*, Aldershot, UK: Ashgate, pp. 196–220.
Sayer, A. (1997), 'The Dialect of Culture and Economy', in R. Lee and J. Wills (eds), *Geographies of Economies*, London: Arnold, pp. 16–26.
Schattschneider, E.E. (1960), *The Semisovereign People: a Realist's View of Democracy in America*, New York: Holt, Rinehart and Winston.
Schnitzer, M.C. (1997), *Comparative Economic Systems*, 7th edn, Cincinnati, Ohio: South-Western College Publishing Co.
Schulz, T.W. (1961), 'Investment in Human Capital', *American Economic Review*, 51 (March), 213–26.
Sen, A. (2000), 'Culture and Development', Global Development Conference, Tokyo, January.
Sen, A. (2004), 'Remarks at the Inaugural Meeting of the GDN Conference on Understanding Reform', Global Development Conference, New Delhi, January.
Shanker, R. (1996), 'Culture and Development', *Development Express*, no. 8, Hull, Québec: International Development Information Center.
Shen, L. and Y. Dai (1990), 'Chinese Federal Economy: Mechanisms, Impacts, and Sources', (in Chinese), *Jingji Yanjiu* [Economic Research Journal], no. 3, 1–13.
Shirk, S.L. (1993), *The Political Logic of Economic Reform in China*, Berkeley, CA: University of California Press.
Shorrocks, A.F. (1983), 'Ranking Income Distributions', *Economica*, 50, 3–17.
Shorrocks, A.F. (1984), 'Inequality Decomposition by Population Subgroup', *Econometrica*, 52, 1369–85.
Shultz, R., R. Godson and T. Greenwood (eds) (1993), *Security Studies for the 1990s*, Washington DC: Brassey's.
Sillis, D.L. (ed.) (1972), *International Encyclopedia of the Social Sciences*, 3, New York: The Macmillan Company & The Free Press.
Smith, A. (1776), *An Inquiry into the Nature and Causes of the Wealth of Nations*, Book IV, 1977 edn, London: J.M. Dent and Sons.
Smith, C. (ed.) (1990), *Practical Methods of Regional Science and Empirical Applications: Selected Papers of Walter Isard*, 2, New York: New York University Press.
Solow, R.M. (1956), 'A Contribution to the Theory of Economic Growth', *Quarterly Journal of Economics*, 71, 65–94.
Spair, E. (1949 [1916]), 'Time Perspective in Aboriginal American Culture: a Study in Method', in D. Mandelbaum (ed.), *Edward Spair, Selected Writings in Language, Culture and Personality*, Berkeley, CA: University of California Press, pp. 389–462.
Spengler, O. (1928), *Decline of the West*, New York: A. A. Knopf.

State Council (1981), 'Regulations of the P. R. China Concerning the Resolutions of the Disputes on Borders of the Administrative Divisions', Beijing: State Council.

State Council (1988), 'Regulations of the P. R. China Concerning the Resolutions of the Disputes on Borders of the Administrative Divisions', revised version, Beijing: State Council.

Stephan, J. (1999), *Economic Transition in Hungary and East Germany: Gradualism and Shock Therapy in Catch-up Development*, Studies in Economic Transition, New York: St Martin's Press.

Stern, R.M. and K.E. Maskus (1981), 'Determinants of the Structure of US Foreign Trade', *Journal of International Economics*, 24, 207–24.

Stewart, J.Q. (1948), 'Demographic Gravitation: Evidence and Applications', *Sociometry*, 2, 31–58.

Summers, R. and A. Heston (1988), 'A New Set of International Comparison of Real Product and Price Levels: Estimates for 130 Countries', *Review of Income and Wealth*, 34, 1–25.

Sumner, W.G. (1906), *Folkways: a Study of the Sociological Importance of Usage, Manners, Customs, Mores, and Morals*, New York: Dover. Reprinted in 1959.

Sun, Z. (1993), 'Causes of Trade Wars over Farm Products, their Effects, and Suggested Solutions', *Chinese Economic Studies*, 26 (5), 95–104.

Swan, T.W. (1956), 'Economic Growth and Capital Accumulation', *Economic Record*, 32 (November), 334–61.

Taagepera, R. and M.S. Shugart (1989), *Seats and Votes: the Effects and Determinants of Electoral Systems*, New Haven, CT: Yale University Press.

Tehranian, K. and M. Tehranian (eds) (1992), *Restructuring for World Peace: on the Threshold of the Twenty-first Century*, Cresskill, NJ: Hampton Press.

Tinbergen, J. (1962), 'An Analysis of World Trade Flows, the Linder Hypothesis, and Exchange Risk', in J. Tinbergen (ed.), *Shaping the World Economy*, New York: The Twentieth Century Fund, pp. 20–42.

Ting-Toomey, S. (1988), 'Intercultural Conflict Styles: a Face-Negotiation Theory', in Y. Kim and W. Gudykunst (eds), *Theories in Intercultural Communication*, Newbury Park, CA: Sage, pp. 213–35.

Tocqueville, A. (1873), *Democracy in America*, 5th edn, Boston: John Allyn.

Toynbee, A. (1961), *A Study of History*, London: Oxford University Press.

Trubisky, P., T. Toomey and L. Sung (1991), 'The Influence of Individualism, Collectivism and Self-monitoring on Conflict Styles', *International Journal of Intercultural Relations*, 15, 65–84.

Tsakloglou, K. (1993), 'Aspects of Inequality in Greece', *Journal of Development Economics*, 40, 53–74.

Tsui, K. (1993), 'Decomposing of China's Regional Inequalities', *Journal of Comparative Economics*, 17, 600–27.

Tylor, E.B. (1958 [1871]), *Primitive Culture: Researches into the Development of Mythology, Philosophy, Religion, Art and Custom*, vol. 1: 'Origins of Culture', Gloucester, MA: Smith.

UNESCO (1999), *UNESCO Statistical Yearbook 1999*, Paris: UNESCO, available at www.unesco.org.

United Nations (1986), *Annual Statistical Yearbook*, New York: United Nations.

United Nations (1996), *World Population Prospects, 1950–2050*, New York: United Nations.

United Nations (2001), *Annual Statistical Yearbook*, New York: United Nations.

United Nations Development Program (UNDP) (1999), *Human Development Report 1999*, available at www.undp.org/hdro/report.html.

Venieris, Y. and D. Gupta (1986), 'Income Distribution and Sociopolitical Instability as Determinants of Savings: a Cross-sectional Model', *Journal of Political Economy*, 94, 873–83.

Vlahos, M. (1991), Culture and Foreign Policy', *Foreign Policy*, 82, 59–78.

Vogt, E.E. (1972), 'Culture Change', in D.L. Sillis (ed.), *International Encyclopedia of the Social Sciences*, vol. 3, New York: The Macmillan Company & The Free Press, pp. 554–8.

Vona, S. (1990), 'Intra-industry Trade: a Statistical Prefect or a Real Phenomenon?' *Banca Naz. Lavoro Quarterly Review*, December, 487–97.

Wagner, R.E. (1983), *Public Finance*, Boston: Little Brown.

Weber, M. (1930 [1904]), *The Protestant Ethic and the Spirit of Capitalism*, London: Allen & Unwin.

Wheeler, L., H.T. Reis and M.H. Bond (1989), 'Collectivism-individualism in Everyday Social Life: the Middle Kingdom and the Melting Pot', *Journal of Personality and Social Psychology*, 57, 79–86.

Wiegersma, N. and J. Medley (2000), *US Economic Development Policies towards the Pacific Rim: Successes and Failures of US Aid*, London: Palgrave Macmillan.

Williamson, J.G. (1965), 'Regional Inequality and the Process of National Development: a Description of Patterns', *Economic Development and Cultural Change*, 13 (4), 165–204.

Wilson, E.A. (1980), *Sociobiology*, Cambridge, MA: Belknap.

Wilson, R. (1997), *Economics, Ethics and Religion: Jewish, Christian and Muslim Economic Thought*, New York: New York University Press.

Wissler, C. (1917), *The American Indian: an Introduction to the Anthropology of the New World*, 3rd edn, Gloucester, MA: Smith.

Wolf, A.T. (1998), 'Conflicts and Cooperation along International Waterways', *Water Policy*, 1, 251–65.

Wong, C. (1992), 'Fiscal Reform and Local Industrialization', *Modern China*, 18 (April), 23–42.

Woo, T.W., S. Parker and J. Sachs (eds) (1996), *Economies in Transition: Comparing Asia and Eastern Europe*, Cambridge, MA: The MIT Press.

World Atlas, Rand McNally & Company, 1994.

World Bank (1983), *World Development Report 1982–1983*, Washington DC: The World Bank.

World Bank (1986), *World Bank Atlas*, Washington DC: The World Bank.

World Bank (1988), *World Bank Atlas*, Washington DC: The World Bank.

World Bank (1992), *World Development Report 1991–1992*, Washington DC: The World Bank.

World Bank (1993), *World Development Report 1993*, New York: Oxford University Press.

World Bank (1996), *Social Indicators of Development*, Baltimore: Johns Hopkins University Press.

World Bank (1999), *World Development Indicators*, CD-ROM, Washington DC: the World Bank.

World Bank (2001), *World Development Indicators*, Washington DC: the World Bank.

World Commission on Culture and Development (WCCD) (1995), *Our Creative Diversity*, Paris: UNESCO.

World Resource Institute (1999), *World Resources 1998–99*, Washington DC: WRI.

Zhang, H. (1990), 'Importance of Adjusting the Transprovincial Borders in China' (in Chinese), *Journal of East China Normal University*, 1, 1–10.

Zhao, R. (2001), 'Increasing Income Inequality and its Causes in China', in C. Riskin, R. Zhao and S. Li (eds), *China's Retreat from Equality: Income Distribution and Economic Transition*, New York: M.E. Sharpe, pp. 25–43.
Zipf, G.K. (1946), 'The P^1P^2/D Hypothesis: on the Intercity Movement of Persons', *American Sociological Review*, 11 (6), 677–86.

Index